Presidential Speechwriting

NUMBER SEVEN
Presidential Rhetoric Series
Martin J. Medhurst, General Editor

Presidential Speechwriting

FROM THE NEW DEAL TO THE REAGAN REVOLUTION AND BEYOND

Edited by Kurt Ritter and Martin J. Medhurst

TEXAS A&M UNIVERSITY PRESS   COLLEGE STATION

Copyright © 2003 by the Program in Presidential Rhetoric
Manufactured in the United States of America

The paper used in this book meets the minimum requirements
of the American National Standard for Permanence
of Paper for Printed Library Materials, z39.48-1984.
Binding materials have been chosen for durability.

Library of Congress Cataloging-in-Publication Data

Presidential speechwriting : from the New Deal to the Reagan revolution
    and beyond / edited by Kurt Ritter and Martin J. Medhurst. —
    1st ed.
        p. cm. — (Presidential rhetoric series ; no. 7)
    Includes bibliographical references and index.
    ISBN 1–58544–225–9 (cloth : alk. paper)
        1. Presidents—United States—History—20th century.
2. Presidents—United States–Biography.   3. Rhetoric—Political
aspects—United States—History—20th century.   4. Political
oratory—United States—History—20th century.   5. Speechwriting—United States—History—20th century.   6. Speechwriters—United States—Biography.   7. United States—Politics
and government—1945–1989.   I. Ritter, Kurt W.   II. Medhurst,
Martin J.   III. Series.
    E176.1.P896   2002
    808.5'1'088351–dc21   2002012919

In Memory of

Paul D. Erickson

1954–1997

CONTENTS

ACKNOWLEDGMENTS

The chapters in this volume were first presented in a preliminary form at the Second Annual Conference on Presidential Rhetoric, held at Texas A&M University from March 1–3, 1996. These annual conferences are sponsored by the Program in Presidential Rhetoric, a joint venture of the Department of Speech Communication and the George Bush School of Government and Public Service at Texas A&M.

Many hands helped to make the conference a success. We are particularly grateful to the former presidential and vice presidential speechwriters who participated in the conference: Jim McGrath, Sandy Muir, Curt Smith, Craig R. Smith, and Gordon Stewart. Another former speechwriter, Paul Erickson, never made it to the White House, but wrote for several presidential candidates. Paul participated in the 1996 conference as an academic. A Harvard-trained Ph.D. in American Studies, Paul had discovered the field of speech communication and was teaching in the Communication Department at Emerson College until his untimely death, in 1997, at age forty-three. He will be missed.

Much has changed in the six years since these essays were originally presented. In 1996, the Program in Presidential Rhetoric was part of the Center for Presidential Studies, under the direction of Professor George C. Edwards III. Today, we remain a part of the newly renamed Center for Policy and Governance, now under the able direction of Professor Kenneth J. Meier. In 1996, the George Bush Presidential Library Foundation, under executive director Don Wilson, was a strong supporter of our program. Today, the Bush Foundation, under the leadership of former ambassador Roman Popadiuk, is the major funding source for our annual conferences. In 1996, the Bush Presidential Library had yet to open its doors. Its first director-in-waiting, David Alsobrook, was an enthusiastic participant in the activities of the Program in Presidential Rhetoric. Today, Bush Library director Douglas Menarchik is exploring ways in which to partner with the Program in Presidential Rhetoric to deliver even better public programming. In 1996, the Department of Speech Communication was guided by Linda Putnam. Today, it is under the direction of Richard L. Street, Jr. To all of these individuals, both past and present, we owe a debt of thanks.

But, of course, not everything has changed. In 1996, Linda and Herman Giesen of Dallas, Texas, became the first private donors to support the

Program in Presidential Rhetoric. Today, they are still supporting the Program—and we thank them. They have been joined by Clementine and Emil Ogden of College Station, Texas. We thank them, too. In 1996, Professor Ron Carpenter of the University of Florida conducted his speechwriting workshop called "Write Well, Right Now" as part of the conference. He has continued to offer the workshop over the intervening years, and we appreciate his continuing efforts.

We express our thanks to all of the faculty and graduate students in the Department of Speech Communication who helped to make these annual conferences a reality. We could not do it without them. We also thank all of the conference participants—those who chaired panels, responded to papers, facilitated discussion groups, or served on scholarly roundtables. Finally, we acknowledge the members of the Program in Presidential Rhetoric who put on the 1996 conference—Leroy Dorsey, Marty Medhurst, Tarla Rai Peterson, Rick Rigsby, Kurt Ritter, and Joe Shadler. And we welcome the members we have added since 1996, Jim Aune and Vanessa Beasley.

Presidential Speechwriting

Presidential Speechwriting

Ten Myths that Plague Modern Scholarship

MARTIN J. MEDHURST

I will live and lead by these principles: to advance my convictions with civility, to pursue the public interest with courage, to speak for greater justice and compassion, to call for responsibility and try to live it as well. In all these ways I will bring the values of our history to the care of our times.

What you do is as important as anything government does. I ask you to seek a common good beyond your comfort, to defend needed reforms against easy attacks, to serve your nation, beginning with your neighbor. I ask you to be citizens. Citizens, not spectators. Citizens, not subjects. Responsible citizens, building communities of service and a nation of character.
—*President George W. Bush, January 20, 2001*

For those who had observed Bush during his years as Texas governor or during the early stages of his primary campaign, the eloquence of the inaugural must have come as somewhat of a shock. How could a man who only months before had managed to mangle sentences, mispronounce words, and give a new meaning to Bush-speak,[1] now articulate his ideas with such force, conviction, and poetic rhythm? Certainly practice was one of the answers. Bush had become better with each passing month of the primary and on into the general election season. Both his nomination acceptance address and his three debate performances were better than most people expected. Comparison may also have played a role. After all, Bush was following William Jefferson Clinton to the inaugural podium. Clinton, whatever his other faults may have been, was clearly a superior communicator and Bush, it was widely believed, could only suffer by comparison. Yet Bush did well and far exceeded those expectations. Why?

One reason was the talent of Bush's chief speechwriter, Mike Gerson. Affectionately referred to as "the scribe" by Bush, Gerson had penned the major addresses of the campaign season, the acceptance address, and now the inaugural. Formerly a speechwriter for Senator Daniel Coats (R-IN) and before that a ghostwriter for Charles Colson, Gerson came out of the evangelical Christian community and reflected both the language and style of that community. George W. Bush, as a born-again Methodist, found a soulmate in Mike Gerson.[2] They were on the same page philosophically, emotionally, and intellectually. Yet, the role played by Gerson in the rhetorical transformation of George W. Bush is not unique.

Unfortunately, there is more than a little misunderstanding about presidential speechwriting and its role in the creation and shaping of presidential discourse. Much of this misunderstanding has come about as a result of misinformation and its circulation and recirculation in scholarly venues. One goal of this book is to correct some of those misunderstandings. Each chapter deals with a specific president, starting with Franklin D. Roosevelt and concluding with Ronald Reagan. But there are ten myths about presidential speechwriting that recur throughout the literature and across presidencies. It is important to address those myths first before turning to the specific administrations.

Myth #1: "In the good old days, presidents always wrote their own speeches."

The fact is that presidents have requested and received assistance with their speeches, messages, letters, bills, memoirs, and the like since the beginning of the Republic. George Washington had ready assistance close at hand in the persons of Alexander Hamilton, James Madison, and John Jay. Even Lincoln, the most rhetorically astute and accomplished presidential orator of the nineteenth century, occasionally turned to aides such as William Seward for help. Yet it is true that presidents from Washington through Woodrow Wilson were, for the most part, the authors of their own words. Assistance was truly occasional and there was no such thing as an Office of Speechwriting in the White House. Even so, such seminal documents as Washington's Farewell Address, Jackson's Bank Veto Message, and Lincoln's First Inaugural were all produced with the assistance of one or more speechwriters. So the view that speechwriting is somehow new or that it represents a radical change from the way things used to be done is simply not true.

Myth #2: "Franklin Roosevelt was the first modern president to use speechwriters on a regular basis."

Insofar as we know, the first president to hire a full-time speechwriter in the White House was Warren G. Harding. The man's name was Judson P. Welliver and his official title was literary executive secretary to the president. He continued to assist Calvin Coolidge after Harding's death. From that moment forward there has always been someone close to the president whose primary job was to assist with presidential discourse. Even Herbert Hoover, who tried to write most of his own major policy addresses, had the assistance of a man named French Strother. Given the quality of Hoover's speeches, perhaps he should have called on Strother more frequently.

With the election of Franklin D. Roosevelt in 1932, presidential discourse witnessed several profound changes. The most important concerned Roosevelt himself. Unlike Harding, Coolidge, and Hoover, Roosevelt was a natural born communicator. He enjoyed speaking and it showed. He was also blessed with a deep and resonant voice that was perfectly matched to the dominant medium of his day—radio. Since 1922–23, radio had become a truly mass medium of communication. While both Coolidge and Hoover had tried to use the new medium, neither possessed the voice or the rhetorical skills of Franklin D. Roosevelt. Roosevelt had been using radio as a political tool since 1928. By the time of his first inaugural address on March 4, 1933, he was one of the most accomplished radio speakers in the nation, though only people in the state of New York knew that at the time.

From the outset of his administration, Roosevelt recognized the need for expert advice on matters rhetorical. Even though he was, himself, a uniquely gifted communicator, and even though he could easily have written his own inaugural address with no assistance, he chose to involve others in its preparation, foremost among them Raymond Moley. The story of Moley's role in the preparation of Roosevelt's first inaugural address has already been told,[3] but it is instructive to realize that the modern use of speechwriters in the White House—Judson Welliver and French Strother notwithstanding—really began with the Roosevelt administration. For it was Roosevelt who hired not just a single assistant but a veritable phalanx of writers, editors, idea men, lawyers, and policy wonks who came to be known collectively as the "brains trust." At one time or another, virtually every member of the brains trust wrote for President Roosevelt. Some of the members of the trust—Moley, Rexford G. Tugwell, Thomas Corcoran, Benjamin Cohen, Samuel Rosenman, Robert Sherwood, and Archibald McLeish foremost among them—quickly found that writing presidential prose was to be one of their chief occupations.

Myth #3: "The people who write speeches for the president of the United States have always been called speechwriters."

Until the late 1960s, most people who wrote presidential speeches were not hired primarily as speechwriters. Often they did not carry the title of speechwriter or anything like it. They were administrative assistants to the president, each of whom had wide-ranging responsibilities that also included writing or editing speeches. Some of these people were talented writers; others were not. Some had close relationships with their principals; others did not. Some of the earlier speechwriters were also policy advisors and nearly all had direct access to policy-making sessions and discussions even if they were not, themselves, policy advisors. There was a clear recognition, even as late as the Nixon administration, that speechwriting could not easily be separated from knowledge of policy. Even more important, there was a clear recognition that the people who wrote for the president must have direct interaction with the president. That began to change in the mid-to-late 1960s; by the early 1970s there were people hired specifically as "speechwriters" and their access to the president was severely limited. No longer advisors who also wrote speeches, the speechwriting function was, in many cases, reduced to wordsmithing. The unspoken assumption behind this change was that ideas and policy were one thing, but words, language, and expression were something else. One could, it came to be held, develop the policy in one part of the White House, then ship it across the street to the Old Executive Office Building where the speechwriters could put some "language" in it. Hence speechwriting, in many instances, was reduced to wordsmithing—it was speechwriting without the act of rhetorical invention, for the ideas had already been constructed elsewhere.

Myth #4: "Presidential speechwriters—whatever title they might have—are always employed as members of the White House staff."

Today, it is generally true that those who write for the president are formal members of the White House staff. But it was not always so. Indeed, for much of the twentieth century presidential speechwriters were drawn from other "agencies" within the federal government, particularly the Bureau of the Budget. By allowing these individuals to remain on the payroll in some other bureau or agency, the White House could expand its rhetorical arsenal without drawing undue attention to the increase in staffing. Much the same thing could be accomplished by drawing on writers from outside of the government—academicians, journalists, even businesspeople, on occasion, have served as surrogate speechwriters for the president of the United States. In short, just because a small group of people—maybe five or six— has the official title of speechwriter does not mean that only five or six people are supplying speech ideas—or even entire speech drafts—to the White House. Presidents have often turned to people outside of the official structure for assistance with their speeches.

Myth #5: "Speechwriters merely reflect what the president's policies are. Their role is one of ornamentation and amplification, not invention."

Sometimes speechwriters do, in fact, ornament and amplify. Far more often, however, their roles are substantially greater. They invent ideas—sometimes in the traditional sense of coming up with original ideas on their own, what the ancients called rhetorical invention—but more often in the modern sense of taking ideas already generated by policy advisors, other speechwriters, or even the president himself and subjecting them to the rigors of the drafting process. This is a sort of processual invention whereby ideas become transformed in the process of working with them in a written text. In an earlier work, I called this process evolutionary invention and described it like this:

> What starts as a change of terminology in draft #2, becomes a change of verb form in draft #3, then a rearrangement of sentences in draft #4, then part of a new paragraph in draft #5, necessitating in draft #6 a new illustration which, itself, necessitates further stylistic changes until by the final draft the original sentiment may be eliminated entirely.

This is not, of course, invention in the traditional sense, yet it is precisely how ideas come about in a ghostwritten text. It is organic evolution at work in the world of art.[4]

And it is the speechwriters who are primarily responsible for these evolutionary changes in the text. The power of such access to the text should not be overlooked or underestimated. As Theodore Sorensen once noted, "Between speechwriting and phrasing and shading and policy making there's a very thin line indeed. The man who controls the pen has a great deal of influence over what ultimately becomes presidential policy."[5] Speechwriters may or may not be policy advisors in their own right, but once they start operating on a text, even the most junior "wordsmith" has the potential of becoming an important policy innovator.

Myth #6: "Speechwriting reduces presidents to marionettes who merely mouth the words that others write for them."

This is a charge usually made about presidents we do not like. It is somehow comforting to believe that the leader is such a dunce that he cannot even write his own speeches, doubtless because he has no ideas of his own to call on. Most recently, charges of this sort were leveled against Ronald Reagan, perhaps to try to undercut his image as "The Great Communicator" or perhaps because he had been a professional actor earlier in life. While it is true that different presidents have been involved to very different degrees in the speechwriting process, it has seldom been the case that a president simply mouthed the words penned for him by someone else. That such a charge has been seriously leveled against Reagan is particularly odd inasmuch as Reagan was far more involved in his presidential speeches than most of his twentieth-century predecessors. Unlike several of those predecessors and at least one of his successors, Reagan enjoyed speechwriting, believed it to be of central importance to his success, and spent considerable time and energy on all of his major addresses. There is considerable documentary evidence at the Reagan Library that Reagan did, in fact, draft substantial portions of many of his most famous speeches.[6] While presidents seldom do a first draft of their speeches, they are often highly involved in both the subsequent drafting and editing processes.

Eisenhower was such a close editor of his speechwriters' work that he often transformed the final product through his editing pen alone. Of course, Ike had the advantage of being the only president to have been a professional speechwriter before assuming the presidency. Even presidents such as Truman, Johnson, Ford, and Bush the elder, who were not especially gifted writers or editors, nevertheless spent many hours going over their speeches with their writers and advisors. At the presidential level, there is simply no truth to the charge that words are being put into the president's mouth. The presidents are too involved and the staffing process is too rigorous for anything like that to happen. The typical presidential speech—if there is such a thing as a typical speech—is vetted by anywhere from five to twenty people before it is finalized. Given such a process, it is hard for any one individual to dictate what the president will say.

Myth #7: "The most successful presidential speechwriters have displayed a passion for anonymity."

Until the Kennedy administration, many presidential speechwriters did strive to keep a low profile, in keeping with an admonition about "anonymity" first articulated in the Brownlow Report of 1937 on government reorganization. Indeed, with the exception of one or two Roosevelt writers who were public figures before starting to work for the White House, most people would be hard pressed to identify even one presidential speechwriter from 1920–61. That tradition began to change with the delivery of JFK's Inaugural Address. The speech made such an impact that reporters naturally inquired into its authorship and JFK made no secret of his reliance on Theodore Sorensen as his chief wordsmith and policy advisor. Words were important to Kennedy and Sorensen's abilities in the realm of speechwriting were on display for the whole world to see.[7] Because he was a policy advisor as well as the chief speechwriter (his actual title was special counsel to the president), Sorensen was involved in most of the crucial policy decisions in the JFK White House. His name would, from time to time, appear in the newspapers. He was not anonymous.

But the real breach in the "code" of anonymity happened in 1963 and the culprit was not Ted Sorensen but Emmet John Hughes. For nine months in 1953, Emmet Hughes had been the chief speechwriter for Dwight Eisenhower. In the years immediately following, he would be called on from time to time to write important speeches for the Eisenhower White House, including the Second Inaugural Address. But in the final years of Ike's administration Hughes fell out of favor. In 1963, he published a memoir of his years with Eisenhower *Ordeal of Power*.[8] It did not reflect well on Ike, John Foster Dulles, or American foreign policy. When JFK read the book, he was appalled that someone with such access could display such disloyalty to his principal. He ordered that no one on his staff was ever to produce such an expose once his administration left office. No one did. Instead, Sorensen became internationally known for his bestseller, *Kennedy.* The year was 1965.

From the days of Emmet John Hughes and Theodore Sorensen until the present, the role of presidential speechwriter has become increasingly more public. While LBJ's White House tried to enforce the code of anonymity, it was a losing proposition. Soon names like Bill Moyers (Johnson), Patrick Buchanan (Nixon), James Fallows (Carter), Peggy Noonan (Reagan), Tony Snow (Bush), and Michael Waldman (Clinton) started to appear in media accounts of the presidency. Today, feature stories on Mike Gerson, George W. Bush's chief speechwriter, are so common that we even know the nickname that the president has given to him. The day of the presidential assistant with a "passion for anonymity" is no more.

Myth #8: "Presidential discourse would be better if we could eliminate speechwriters and let the presidents write their own speeches."

This myth depends, of course, on what one means by "better." Certainly there is little or no evidence to suggest that presidents as a class are or have been more adept with language than their speechwriters. Even the most literate of presidents—a Wilson, or a Roosevelt, or a Kennedy—was not the equal of an Archibald McLeish or a Theodore Sorensen when it came to literary expression or rhetorical design. But what most people seem to mean by this claim is that the speeches would somehow be better ethically inasmuch as they would represent the true beliefs and attitudes of the president rather than those of the president's speechwriters and advisors. As appealing as this line of reasoning may be, it is, I believe, fundamentally mistaken—for several reasons.

First, presidents represent the nation, not merely themselves. They speak on behalf of the people and represent the views of the nation as refracted through the lenses of party, ideology, political and economic constraints, and situational variables. They do not—and cannot—simply state their own personal views. They need good advisors and speechwriters precisely for this reason—so that their discourse represents the best articulation of policy or position possible. The nation expects—and deserves—no less.

Second, some presidents have real difficulty putting their ideas into words. Would the nation or the world be better off by having a president reveal his lack of rhetorical talent? Not every president is a Jefferson, or a Lincoln, or a Wilson, all of whom had innate rhetorical abilities. Sometimes the nation is led by a Ford, not a Lincoln. Would we really be better off by depriving our leaders of the specific types of help that they need?

Finally, history has demonstrated the wisdom of having presidential speechwriters and advisors. One thinks, for example, of the mediating role played by Clark Clifford during the Truman administration. When President Truman penned a speech during the railroad strike of 1946 that suggested, among other outrageous ideas, that we "hang a few traitors" it was Clifford who stepped forward to scuttle the speech by providing a new and "improved" draft. In so doing, the speechwriter served not only his principal but the nation at large.[9]

All in all, presidential speechwriters have served the nation well. Presidents know that, which is why they continue to use them.

Myth #9: "The practice of speechwriting makes it impossible to judge what presidents really believe by examining their speeches because the words are not their own."

This criticism is also of the ethical variety inasmuch as it points to questions of character and the ability of the president to display his character through his speech. The criticism was first articulated in the 1960s by Professor Ernest Bormann, who wrote:

> Under the impetus of the ghostwriter, American public address moves more and more in the direction of the rhetoric of the Second Sophistic. It becomes a ritual, or an exhibition, produced at the expected time. As the public becomes more and more cynical about the authorship of speeches, the ethos of the speaker is undermined; the speech loses its hold upon the public as a vital force in public affairs. The level of rhetoric declines and its function as a fundamental tool for the winnowing of ideas in a democratic society is lost.[10]

Bormann's criticism is a fair one as far as it goes, but it does not go far enough because it seems to presume that presidential rhetoric exists in a vacuum—that the only thing one can examine is the words themselves. This is simply not true. Rhetoric cannot be separated from the exigencies and constraints which gave rise to the discourse, or from the actions of the person who delivers the discourse, or from the actions, statements, and values of those who labor at the pleasure of the president and under his direct authority—cabinet members, staff members, party operatives, and, yes, speechwriters themselves. Rhetoric cannot—and should not—be treated as an entity unto itself. It always exists in a dynamic relationship with people, policies, practices, and circumstances that give shape and substance to the discourse. Absent a full and comprehensive understanding of all of these factors, no rhetorical critique could hope to illumine presidential beliefs, values, or intentions. Certainly examining the discourse in isolation will not be very helpful.

Recent scholarship has shown the utility of treating rhetoric as a strategic response to a particular situation.[11] Rhetorical criticism that seeks to understand that situation, the people and forces operative in it, and the rhetorical adaptations that are made in an effort either to conform to or resist the situational exigencies, is necessarily criticism that goes beyond the confines of the text itself. Such scholarship sometimes focuses on the development of policy, or the trajectory of ideas, or the beliefs of the people who advised the president, or the ideologies at play, or the textual evolution of the speech, or other factors that give the final presidential discourse its tone, texture, and resonance. To understand any presidential utterance, one must be willing to go beyond or behind the words to discover their real significance and meaning.

Myth #10: "Speechwriting is a relatively minor part of the larger policy-making process and the further we can keep the speechwriters from the policy discussions the better off we will be."

The tenth and final myth is one shared more by policy advisors than by scholars, though sometimes that distinction becomes blurred as former White House advisors write books that then enter into the scholarly conversation. There are really two claims here, neither of which is warranted. The first claim—that speechwriting is a minor part of the policy-making process—can only be true if one hypothesizes a radical disjunction between form and substance, between ideational content and the expression of that content to an audience. In classical rhetorical theory no such disjunct is allowed. The speaker first finds his ideas, then he decides how best to present those ideas to an audience. It is one organic process. Over the past thirty years or so, however, presidential speechwriting has been the victim of just this sort of disjunctive logic—the belief that the people who come up with the ideas and the policies need have little or no relation to the people who are expected to put those policies into words. Policy advisors are one thing; speechwriters are another. Hence the reduction of speechwriting to mere wordsmithing.

Several things need to be said about this state of affairs. First, it was not always so. When Raymond Moley wrote FDR's first inaugural address, he was intimately involved in all the discussions concerning economic policy and the banking crisis. All of Truman's major writers—Clark Clifford, George Elsey, Charles Murphy—were also policy advisors. So, too, were C. D. Jackson and Bryce Harlow under Eisenhower, and Ted Sorensen under Kennedy. Under Johnson, Harry McPherson, Douglass Cater, and Richard Goodwin were heavily involved in policy discussions. Even under the pretorian guard that surrounded Nixon's Oval Office, Ray Price, Bill Safire, and Pat Buchanan had access both to the president and to policy sessions. If the quality of presidential discourse has declined since the 1960s, one reason may be the decision to separate speechwriting from policy making.

But it is also important to realize why such a claim is made in the first place. It has to do with power—who has it, who can hold it, and who will wield it inside the White House. All parties realize that words are the coin of the realm and he who controls the words controls the direction of the administration. Policy makers try to articulate policies that they believe will benefit the administration—and they do not like it when anyone messes with their policy. But, of course, the job of a speechwriter is precisely to mess with language—to try to improve it, sharpen it, clarify it. In so doing, speechwriters inevitably cross swords with various and sundry policy advisors who often believe that the speechwriters are trying to usurp the authority and prerogatives—to make policy—that is rightfully their own. Hence, one way to guard one's power is to banish the speechwriters to administrative hell—out of the White House and into the bowels of the Old Executive Office Building where they will be physically, as well as structurally and emotionally, removed from the mainstream of administrative life.

This leads to the second claim—that the further speechwriters can be kept from the policy-making process, the better. What is not specified, of course, is "better" for whom? It is not better for the president and, I will argue, not better for the nation to have presidential speechwriters separated physically, emotionally, and structurally from the policy-making process. Yet that is precisely what has happened between the late 1960s and today. By forming the White House Office of Communications and by deciding to make the Office of Speechwriting a subdivision of Communications that reports to the director of the office rather than to the chief of staff or directly to the president, speechwriters have often been cut out of the policy-making loop altogether. They have been asked to write presidential prose without having had the benefit, many times, of hearing the policy discussions or even getting the president's own thoughts on what he wants to say. For most of the later Nixon, Ford, Carter, Reagan, and Bush presidencies, speechwriters have been relegated to second-class citizens, with little or no access to their principal and no direct input into the policies about which they have been told to write. Indeed, it is not unheard of for a speechwriter to be asked to write a speech about a topic on which no policy has even been articulated, much less adopted by the president. To try to "invent" discourse under such conditions is not in the best interests of the president—or of the nation.

The situation of presidential speechwriters improved materially under the Clinton regime—mostly because Bill Clinton loved to speak and write, but also because two of his chief speechwriters, David Kusnet and Michael Waldman, had been policy advisors before taking on the speechwriting functions. Waldman, who wrote speeches for five of Clinton's eight years in office, had close relations with the domestic and economic policy advisors. Unlike his predecessors in the Bush speechwriting office, Waldman had good access to the president and to policy-making discussions.[12] One need not be a partisan Democrat or a defender of the Clinton administration to recognize the rhetorical artistry that characterized many of Clinton's major speeches. He was the best presidential orator since Ronald Reagan and John Kennedy, and it is not too far-fetched to hypothesize that his speechwriters had something to do with that.

The administration of George W. Bush is only eight months old as I write this—too soon to know what the ultimate relationship between the principal and his writers will be. But the early signs are encouraging. Both the inaugural address and the speech to a joint session of Congress were well received. More telling still—Michael Gerson has an office in the White House itself, not in the Old Executive Office Building. As any speechwriter will testify, access is everything. Much remains to be studied. And that is why the eight chapters in this book have been put together—to begin the process of understanding better the complex role of speechwriting in the modern presidency.

In chapter one, Halford Ryan argues that the "success of FDR's presidential rhetoric was his ability to invent a policy rhetorically for its eventual acceptance politically." Rhetoric, in other words, preceded policy and served as the vehicle by which policy positions were tested, refined, and ultimately accepted or rejected. Ryan holds that one key to FDR's presidential rhetoric, both its successes and its failures, is in understanding how Roosevelt used metaphor. He examines both failed metaphors—"quarantine," "nine-old-men," and "purge"—and more successful ones such as "politician-as-teacher," "money-changers," "war," and "garden hose." Ryan holds that "when Roosevelt marshaled metaphors that brought before the eyes action-oriented images that the American people perceived to be genuine and needed, he persuaded."

Diana B. Carlin examines the speechwriting operation of the Truman White House in chapter two. Unlike FDR, Truman's "public speaking did not always call attention to his leadership qualities." In part, this was because Truman's writers were more concerned with what they perceived to be substance as opposed to style. Truman was unconcerned with eloquence—and so, too, were his writers. Carlin argues that Truman's rhetorical skills were manifested most clearly in his political "whistlestop" addresses moreso than in his formal policy speeches. "Through Truman's candor and common touch on the campaign train," Carlin writes, "Americans were encouraged to view the man in the White House as one of them—as someone looking out for their interests."

In chapter three, Charles J. G. Griffin conducts a case study of speechwriting in the Eisenhower White House, using the 1954 State of the Union address as an exemplar. He analyzes how this one speech was created, focusing on "three compositional features of the message" and exploring "the extent to which these features proved broadly characteristic of speechwriting methodology in the Eisenhower White House." By examining the principles of flexible staffing, presidential involvement, and synthesis of speechwriting and policy making, Griffin demonstrates how Ike "employed a speechwriting regime which reflected as well as served his leadership style, lending credence to the view that behind the famous Eisenhower smile resided a shrewd and resourceful rhetorical strategist."

Theodore O. Windt, Jr., traces the process of speechwriting in the Kennedy administration in chapter four. Windt holds that "in the Kennedy White House there was not one process for producing speeches, but a variety of approaches that usually depended on the occasion, the topic, time constraints, and the purpose the speech was to serve." To illustrate this thesis, Windt surveys Kennedy's speeches on the 1961 Berlin crisis, the

American University address, and the speech of June 11, 1963, on civil rights, among others. Central to this survey is the role played by Theodore Sorensen. Windt analyzes the Kennedy-Sorensen "collaboration," concluding that "JFK and Sorensen wanted their speeches not only to be instrumental in gaining support for policies, but also to be enduring as linguistic monuments to the Kennedy administration."

In chapter five Moya Ann Ball investigates Lyndon Johnson's famous speech of March 31, 1968, in which he announced to a stunned world his intention not to seek re-election to the presidency. Ball does not, however, conduct a close reading of the speech text; rather, her focus is "less with the finished product (the speech) than with the mosaic of interactions involved in the eventual need for it." She argues that several external constraints played a role in LBJ's decision not to seek re-election and details how those constraints shaped the speechwriting process, starting as early as LBJ's "Let Us Continue" speech and continuing on through the Johns Hopkins University address of April, 1965, the San Antonio Formula speech of September, 1967, and, ultimately, the speech of March 31, 1968.

Chapter six, on speechwriting in the Nixon and Ford administrations, is written by Craig R. Smith who, along with his scholarly credentials, also brings to the task his experience as a White House writer for President Ford.[13] Smith explores the speechwriting function under Nixon and Ford in terms of the presidents' rhetorical education, their acceptance addresses and the influence that the preparation of those addresses had on subsequent speechwriting operations, the role played by credibility in the quest for access to and influence on the president, and the "importance of delivery as a dimension of speechwriting." Smith holds that to be most effective speechwriters "should do more than write in an oral style. They need to be delivery coaches." This is particularly important in a media age where "the presidential speech is not merely written; it is scripted, staged, and produced."

The Carter White House is the focus of chapter seven. John H. Patton traces the travails of the Carter speechwriters who worked for a president who basically distrusted language. As Patton notes, "The irony here is that Carter tried to do extensive editing on texts, yet texts were the very instruments he disdained most and trusted least." Carter, a man of deep moral and religious convictions nevertheless found it difficult to transform his beliefs into policy positions. So much so that, as Patton notes, "The tensions between Carter's creative impulses with language and his notion of language as artificial remained largely unresolved during his presidency."

Only in Carter's post-presidential poetry does Patton discover any consistent appreciation for rhetorical artistry.

In chapter eight, William K. Muir, Jr., examines the relationship of Ronald Reagan to his speechwriters—a subject he knows well, as one who served as a writer for Vice President Bush in the Reagan White House. Muir notes that "more than any other modern president, Ronald Reagan sought to exploit the moral possibilities of the rhetorical presidency. He used his 'bully pulpit' to try to convince the public that his values and ideas about personal responsibility and the good society were right." Consequently, speechwriting was important in the Reagan White House. The speechwriters saw themselves as keepers of the ideological torch—and they were.[14] As Muir notes, Reagan "inspired his speechwriters to do their best." By drawing on personal interviews with the Reagan writers, Muir shows precisely how they attempted to live up to the confidence that the president placed in them.

The book concludes with an afterword that features a brief discussion of four enduring issues faced by those studying presidential speechwriting in the twentieth century—access to the president, the relationship of speechwriting to policy making, internal and external constraints on the speechwriting process, and the relationship of speech making to presidential leadership. Each of these issues—and many others—are addressed in the chapters that follow. In the afterword, I attempt to step back and consider these enduring issues and their implications for the presidency in the twenty-first century.

Notes

Epigraph Source. George W. Bush, "Inaugural Address, January 20, 2001." Reprinted in "Bush Speech: 'I Will Work to Build a Single Nation of Justice and Opportunity,'" *New York Times,* Jan. 21, 2001 <http://www.nytimes.com/2001/01/21/politics/21BTEX.html>.

1. Bush-speak originally referred to the speech patterns and malapropisms of the nation's forty-first president, George Herbert Walker Bush. See *Bush-Isms* (New York: Workman Publishing Co., 1992). On the forty-third president's linguistic escapades see "Bush Pulls Big Guns in Verbal Arsenal," *Houston Chronicle,* April 1, 2001, 18A; Frank Bruni, "The President's Sense of Humor Has Also Been Misunderstood," *New York Times,* April 1, 2001 <http://www.nytimes.com/2001/04/01weekinreview/01WORD.html>; Frank Bruni, "At Night, Bush-Speak Goes into Overdrive," *New York Times,* Aug. 19, 2001 <wysiwyg://1/http://

www.nytimes.com/2001/08/19/national/19BUSH.html?todaysheadlines>. See also Mark Crispin Miller, *The Bush Dyslexicon: Observations on a National Disorder* (New York: W. W. Norton and Co., 2001).

2. Michael Gerson, interview by author, Washington D.C., May 16, 2001. See also David L. Greene, "Speechwriter Aims to Mix Moral Themes with Directness," *St. Louis Post-Dispatch,* Feb. 27, 2001.

3. The story has been told in several places, but nowhere better than in Davis W. Houck, *FDR and Fear Itself: The First Inaugural Address* (College Station: Texas A&M University Press, 2002).

4. Martin J. Medhurst, "Ghostwritten Speeches: Ethics Isn't the Only Lesson," *Communication Education* 36 (1987): 247.

5. Theodore Sorensen, interview with the author and Thomas W. Benson, New York City, March 16, 1984.

6. This conclusion is one I reached independently after examining the speechwriting files at the Ronald Reagan Presidential Library in Simi Valley, California. Other scholars reached the same conclusion at a much earlier date, particularly my colleague Kurt Ritter. See Kurt Ritter and David Henry, *Ronald Reagan: The Great Communicator* (Westport, Conn.: Greenwood Press, 1992). Reagan's own speechwriters have consistently credited him with being the foremost speechwriter in the White House. See for example, Martin J. Medhurst, "Writing Speeches for Ronald Reagan: An Interview with Tony Dolan," *Rhetoric & Public Affairs* 1 (1998): 245–56. On Reagan's skill in writing his pre-presidential radio addresses see Kiron K. Skinner, Annelise Anderson, and Martin Anderson, eds., *Reagan, In His Own Hand* (New York: Free Press, 2001).

7. On the collaboration between Kennedy and Sorensen as it manifested itself in the 1961 inaugural address see Ronald H. Carpenter, *Rhetorical Eloquence: John F. Kennedy's Inaugural Address* (College Station: Texas A&M University Press, forthcoming).

8. Emmet John Hughes, *Ordeal of Power: A Memoir of the Eisenhower Years* (New York: Atheneum, 1963).

9. For the complete story of this episode see Robert Underhill, *The Truman Persuasions* (Ames: Iowa State University Press, 1981), pp. 166–76.

10. Ernest G. Bormann, "Ghostwriting and the Rhetorical Critic," *Quarterly Journal of Speech* 41 (1960): 288.

11. See, for example, Martin J. Medhurst, "Rhetoric and Cold War: A Strategic Approach," and "Eisenhower's 'Atoms for Peace' Speech: A Case Study in the Strategic Use of Language," both in Medhurst et al., *Cold War Rhetoric: Strategy, Metaphor, and Ideology,* rev. ed. (East Lansing: Michigan State University Press, 1997), pp. 19–50. Also, Martin J. Medhurst, *Dwight D. Eisenhower: Strategic Communicator* (Westport, Conn.: Greenwood Press, 1993).

12. Michael Waldman, interview with author, College Station, Tex., Oct. 5, 2000. See also Michael Waldman, *POTUS Speaks: Finding the Words That Defined the Clinton Presidency* (New York: Simon and Schuster, 2000).

13. See Craig R. Smith, "Contemporary Political Speech Writing," *Southern Speech*

Communication Journal 42 (1976): 52–67; Smith, "Addendum to 'Contemporary Political Speech Writing,'" *Southern Speech Communication Journal* 42 (1977): 191–94.

14. See Peggy Noonan, *What I Saw at the Revolution* (New York: Random House, 1990); William Ker Muir, Jr., *The Bully Pulpit: The Presidential Leadership of Ronald Reagan* (San Francisco: ICS Press, 1992); Medhurst, "Writing Speeches for Ronald Reagan," pp. 250.

CHAPTER 1

Franklin Delano Roosevelt

Rhetorical Politics and Political Rhetorics

HALFORD RYAN

Scholars in this volume address the initial classical canon of rhetoric, which the Greeks termed heuristic and the Romans called *inventio,* as they investigate the creation of presidential persuasions. The critics also acknowledge a classical practice, begun by Antiphon, generally accepted as one of the first Athenian logographers, that political rhetoric can be ghostwritten. These ancient concepts of inventio and logography inhere in twentieth-century presidential speaking. As presidents since George Washington have used speechwriters, scholars ask whether, and to what extent, a presidential speechwriter creates a policy while inventing a speech.[1]

How these two foci converge is consequential, for their consolidation can revise the nexus of rhetorical politics and political rhetorics. The received construct is to regard rhetoric, the art of persuasive speaking, as the handmaiden of statecraft: A political president contrives a policy and, undergoing a metamorphosis, transforms himself into a rhetorical president to persuade the people and the Congress to acquiesce. With regard to Franklin Delano Roosevelt and his speechwriters, this construct can be turned on its head.

But first, let a Ciceronian *partitio* clarify my argument. I do not treat instances when a policy was made without public rhetoric, such as the undeclared, secret naval war with Nazi Germany in 1939–41; nor do I examine cases wherein a speechwriter made a policy that was not accompanied by a presidential address, such as Raymond Moley's major role in crafting and shepherding bills of the Hundred Days legislation. Neither am I vexed by the ethical implications of presidential speechwriters, of unmasking Lois Einhorn's ghosts, who, in FDR's case, were never masked.

Nor am I troubled by an expedient necessity: As a president requires assistance from unelected persons on political issues, such as Professors George Warren and Frank Pearson, the "Gold Dust Twins," whose theory FDR followed with regard to the government's ill-fated gold-buying scheme in 1933, so does a president require help from speechwriters, who served Roosevelt admirably well.[2]

Rather, I examine those significant cases when Roosevelt and a speechwriter and a presidential speech coalesced to make policy. The triad usually functioned persuasively, for FDR-the-rhetorical-president was antecedent to FDR-the-political-president. The success of FDR's presidential rhetoric was his ability to invent a policy rhetorically for its eventual acceptance politically. FDR's first inaugural address (1933) and his 1940 "Lend-Lease" press conference are situations where the triad—FDR, writers, policy—functioned first rhetorically and then politically. Governor Roosevelt's celebrated Commonwealth Club address in 1932, a precursor for New Deal policies, is a touchstone for the admixture of speech invention and rhetorical politics.

Occasionally, the triad malfunctioned. Such was the case with his 1937 speeches on packing the Supreme Court, his speech of the same year on the quarantine of Japan, and his 1938 speech seeking to purge conservative Democrats from the Congress. FDR's rhetorical handling of those addresses represents quintessential cases of policies gone awry by failures in his public persuasions. In those cases, the formulation of the policy preceded the inventional rhetoric, which was detrimental to the policy, to the address, to FDR. These situations resulted because he did not conceive his plans in persuasive language, to paraphrase Donald Bryant's famous chiasmus, that could adjust his policies to the people and the people to his policies. The triad's dysfunction was usually attributable directly to FDR, to his determination to forge ahead, despite contrary advice from his speechwriters. Thus, Carol Gelderman's finding is warranted: "As a rule, the more that contemporary presidents have avoided working closely with their speechwriters—even when, like Clinton, they do a lot of their own writing—the more they have tended to find themselves in various kinds of political trouble." Granted, FDR was occasionally ill advised by his speechwriters. Even so, the onus was on him, for Arthur Larson's dictum, although pertaining to President Dwight Eisenhower, applies as well to FDR: "the President's speech is the President's speech."[3]

FDR's principal writers took that position with respect to their collaboration with him. Raymond Moley composed the initial draft for Roosevelt's first inaugural. As Moley tossed his draft into the fireplace at Hyde Park, after FDR had finished copying in longhand Moley's draft, he said: "This is your speech now." Donald Richberg, a collaborator on FDR's second inaugural address, complained that FDR's famous statement, "I see one-third of a nation ill-housed, ill-clad, ill-nourished," misled with regard to the fraction: "I ventured to suggest that if one were going to pull a figure out of the sky it would at least be safer to say one-fourth rather than one-third. But F.D.R. had a certain feeling for numbers which had been commented on by other observers. He liked the one-third and he wasn't particularly bothered by using a fraction which, even if it could not be supported, could not be disproved." Samuel Rosenman addressed the question of whether speechwriters made policy. Of course they did, Rosenman replied in his oral history: "The point I want to make is that speech-writers do prepare policy—if no statement of policy is given to them before the speech or message is written. . . . Scores of times the President would tell us what policy he wanted put into his speech. In that event, we certainly didn't originate policy." For Rosenman, the president's speech was FDR's: "Very frequently we did literally make policy in putting down things which we had not previously touched on in discussion with him. But these were of course always submitted to him, because he went very carefully over every draft of a speech. And although we would make policy in the sense that we would suggest that this is something he might want to say, it was always up to him, of course, to cross it out—which he did very frequently."[4]

Deceit often lurks in the connection between president and speech staff. Although FDR was not at pains to hide his helpers, neither was he entirely candid. Kenneth Davis believed that FDR's copying Moley's initial draft of the first inaugural address was cunning, for the act "was done with de-liberate *intent* to deceive posterity [italics in original]." In the 1936 volume of his *Public Papers and Addresses,* FDR let readers infer that he composed his speeches. However, Earnest Brandenburg believed the veracity of FDR's version depended on the "definition of the word *write* [italics in original]." In the five persuasions under investigation here, the inventional process and who contributed what naturally varied from speech to speech; how-ever, a great deal of the ideas, the overall intention of the rhetoric, many of the emendations, and the policies were primarily FDR's inventions.[5]

Roosevelt's persuasions have been treated, to varying degrees, by many of the principal speechwriters and helpers in FDR's four terms. Samuel Rosenman, the equal-among-equals, Donald Richberg, Robert Sherwood, Raymond Moley, and Grace Tully, FDR's personal secretary, contributed books that illuminated the speechwriting process. Most recently, Kenneth Davis and Frank Freidel wrote histories that described FDR's rhetoric, not to mention myriad works published since 1933. Moreover, I explicated FDR's presidential rhetoric in a book-length study. In fine, to offer something new on the interplay between FDR and his speech staff is a daunting task, but one that can be discharged by relying on classical rhetoric.[6]

To describe how FDR deployed rhetoric, I concentrate on the classical canon of style or word choice, denoted by the Greek word *lexis* and the Roman term *elocutio,* and particularly on metaphor. When one thinks of FDR's great presidential persuasions, one encounters metaphors as the energizing, persuasive function. Metaphors furthered FDR's persuasive goals in the following representative speeches: the 1932 New Deal acceptance address, the Grilled Millionaire speech at Chapel Hill in 1938, the Hand That Held the Dagger commencement address at the University of Virginia in 1940, the 1941 Shoot on Sight speech, and the Fala address in the 1944 campaign. Metaphors also enervated the effects of Roosevelt's court-packing, quarantine, and purge speeches.

Aristotle helps us to understand how metaphors function rhetorically. The author of *On Rhetoric* held that metaphors should, among other things, bring-before-the-eyes an image, thus Aristotle stressed the visual efficacy of metaphors, and that metaphors should possess *energeia,* the Greek word for energy, action, motion. Hence, the graduates at Mr. Jefferson's University, as well as the newsreel audience and the reading public, readily visualized an active image of Mussolini's perfidiously stabbing France in the back with a stiletto. However, metaphors can militate against one, as Roosevelt ruefully realized.[7]

FDR's Failures with Metaphors
THE COURT-PACKING SCHEME

The man who vanquished Alf Landon in the 1936 election with metaphors—"I have just begun to fight," "economic royalists," "Tory press"—victimized himself, even as his political opponents skewered him, with metaphors at the inception of his second term.

The court-packing scheme is the quintessential exemplar of a policy that was not first conceived in rhetorical terms, of rhetorics that were not assisted by FDR's able writers until it was too late, and of FDR's political hubris. The failure of the judicial reorganization bill was attributable directly to Franklin D. Roosevelt's rhetoric.

Roosevelt faced a genuine exigency with the Supreme Court. The Court had overruled twelve New Deal laws and, with the Wagner Act and the Social Security Act before the Court, the president reasonably feared it would continue to void New Deal legislation. To counter the Court, Roosevelt conspired with Homer Cummings, the attorney general, to concoct legislation that would reorganize the federal judiciary by adding justices to the high bench. The Judicial Reorganization bill, announced in a press conference on February 5, 1937, allowed the president to appoint a new justice to the Court for every justice over seventy, as long as the reconfigured Court did not exceed fifteen justices. Given that six justices were over seventy, FDR could appoint six additional, liberal justices, thus ending the conservative's domination of the Court.

The reorganization message was connived by Cummings and the president the day before and after Christmas of 1936. Although both men realized the persuasive perils of attacking the Court, they chose the circuitous route, rather than a frontal attack. The direct argument was that a conservative Court had thwarted the expressed will of the people and their Congress and their president; therefore the Court needed to change its judicial stance, which would reasonably occur only if liberal justices were added. But the first speech draft, the authorship of which is unknown, stressed a sham exigence, which centered on the metaphor of tired, old men. Roosevelt and Cummings embraced this line of attack because of its political, rather than its rhetorical, appeal. FDR savored the irony that his plan was earlier proposed by then-attorney general James McReynolds in Woodrow Wilson's administration. (McReynolds, now a Supreme Court justice, was one of FDR's most conservative adversaries.) The other motivation pivoted on FDR's political hubris, on what Kenneth Davis depicted as FDR's "actual identification of himself with the power he wielded as God's chosen instrument."[8]

In early February, 1937, Stanley Reed, the solicitor general, and Donald Richberg, the administrator of the National Recovery Administration, which had been declared unconstitutional by the Court on May 27, 1935, joined Samuel Rosenman in the drafting process. They faced a first draft that comprised Cummings' ideas and FDR's dictated thoughts. These writers objected to the message's bent and flavor, which they tried to ameliorate in two successive drafts, but they were unable rhetorically to improve the message. For instance, the first draft portrayed old men metaphorically: "new facts becoming blurred through old glasses," "new blood must be added," and "younger judges . . . make headway against an unwieldy docket." On the second draft, which the speech team tried to soften, Roosevelt continued to stress metaphorically the old-age argument [FDR's additions are italicized and his deletions are bracketed]: "[Mental or] *Lessening mental or* physical [decrepitude] *vigor,*" and "a constant and systematic [infusion of new] *addition of younger blood.*" Despite their efforts, and at FDR's insistence, the message stressed old age and inefficiency, which was Cummings' contribution.[9]

To compress the political history, FDR's message backfired. Opponents quickly demonstrated that the Court was abreast of its work, and that age per se was a bogus issue, for two liberal judges, Louis Brandeis and Benjamin Cardozo, were over seventy. Even the president admitted his error: "I made one major mistake when I first presented the plan. I did not place enough emphasis on the real mischief—the kind of decisions which, as a studied and continued policy, had been coming down from the Supreme Court. I soon corrected that mistake—in the speeches which I later made about the plan."[10]

President Roosevelt's Victory Dinner address, March 4, 1937, is considered one of his best fighting speeches. As an aggressive defense, he eloquently took to the airwaves to justify his reorganization bill and to purify his motives. He corrected his earlier mistake and judiciously made a frontal assault—the kind that High, Richberg, and Rosenman had originally wanted—against the Court. But, FDR returned to his thematic old-age metaphor in his Fireside Chat on the Judiciary, March 9, 1937.

This chat, composed by Rosenman from FDR's dictated thoughts, reintroduced the age metaphor, which FDR had wisely eschewed in his Victory Dinner address. The president depicted a Court peopled by tired old men: "This plan will save our national Constitution from hardening of the judicial arteries"; "It seeks to maintain the Federal bench in full vigor"; "It is the clear intention of our public policy to provide for a constant flow of new and younger blood into the Judiciary"; and "a Court in which five justices will be over seventy-five years of age before next June and one over seventy."[11]

Two representative letters in the Franklin D. Roosevelt Library's public reaction files testify to the polarity of typical responses to his Court speeches. An unemployed steel worker from Canton, Ohio, supported FDR: "They can stay in the Supreme Court till 80 but we are kicked out at 45 making laws that does not help us but kick us out to Big Steel or die from worry"; but an anonymous writer opined: "I wonder if everyone who trusted you is in such a daze as I after the message regarding the Supreme Court . . . and this curious play of words doesn't enlighten anybody."[12]

The Court-packing scheme was a political and rhetorical failure. The Senate denied FDR his additional Supreme Court justices. Moreover, his rhetorics validated the very image his critics summoned against him. Owing to the ersatz argument in the reorganization message, then a new tack in the Victory Dinner address, then a lapse to the old-age argument in the Fireside Chat, Roosevelt authenticated the disingenuousness of his speeches. In fact, in his Fireside Chat, the president was at pains to counter the metaphor that his critics had marshaled so successfully against him, for Franklin claimed that he was not "packing the Court."[13]

The political failure emanated from a rhetorical deficiency. "This time," Kenneth Davis observed, "having directly consulted no one save Cummings while deciding the substance of his proposal, he asked none for advice as to the way in which the proposal should be presented or about the strategy to be employed in the legislative war for its enactment." And an original dissenter from Roosevelt's court-packing rhetoric, Samuel Rosenman pinpointed the persuasive dysfunction: "I repeat that I think he was beaten not because of the merits of the cause, but because of the way it was presented."[14]

THE QUARANTINE ADDRESS

FDR's famous speech, delivered in Chicago on October 5, 1937, was a metaphor without a fitting policy and a policy without a fitting metaphor. Critics were baffled by the speech's purpose. *Newsweek* noted then that "the President left his audience puzzled as to what form the 'quarantine' should take," and more recently Robert Divine opined that "Roosevelt's intentions in delivering his Chicago address remain mysterious today as they were to contemporary observers in 1937."[15]

The speech was a metaphor without a plan. Roosevelt raised expectations of a vigorous policy. As a metaphor, "quarantine" denotes action toward isolating a sick person for the community's benefit. In the rhetorical situation of 1937, the metaphor functioned connotatively to announce a new policy, albeit not a militaristic one, but surely a diplomatic initiative that the United States would lead to isolate Japan as the aggressor in China. FDR's diction and delivery certainly portrayed an action-oriented, bring-ing-before-the-eyes metaphor. He even ad-libbed a verbal preview so that the audience would not miss this important part of his speech (slashes delineate his vocal phrasing and italics his ad-libbed words): "It seems to be unfortunately true / that the epidemic of world lawlessness is spreading / *And mark this well* / When an epidemic of physical disease starts to spread / the community approves and joins in / a quarantine / of the patients / in order to protect the health of the community / against the spread of the disease/ [applause] It is my determination / to pursue a policy of peace."[16]

But the quarantine metaphor was the wrong prescription. The precise problem was that FDR's quarantine image satisfied too well Aristotle's conception of a persuasive metaphor. The audience could easily envision Doctor Roosevelt's posting a quarantine on Nippon's portal on behalf of the world community.

But President Roosevelt would not, because he could not, owing to the Neutrality Act of 1936, enact Doctor Roosevelt. The president advanced a chimerical policy that belied the quarantine metaphor. He apparently did not have a concrete policy in mind, certainly not one that he could sustain politically in terms of a quarantine of Japan. FDR admitted as much in a press conference the next day, October 6, for he allowed that his address was "an attitude, and it does not outline a program; but it says we are looking for a program." He misled metaphorically. He retreated from a "quarantine" to "looking for a program," from action to inaction.[17]

Indeed, his speech curiously reflected the start-stop, approach-avoidance feelings that Americans experienced at this time. A letter from Bangor, Maine, aptly stated the dilemma that Americans and their president faced: "The war should be stopped before we have another world war, but I don't think we should go to the extent to get into war ourselves."[18]

The quarantine address illustrates anew rhetorical failures, for it contains the elements that contributed to the political debacle. The idea of the quarantine was apparently FDR's. Rosenman recalled that Sumner Welles, under secretary of state, declared that Roosevelt spoke to him of a quarantine in the summer of 1937, although Harold Ickes, secretary of the interior, claimed credit for the word, which was not in the original draft that was prepared by Norman Davis of the State Department. Kenneth Davis, relying on Grace Tully, stated that FDR had the key words, "community," "contagious disease," and "quarantine" in his speech notes as FDR dictated the final draft to Tully.[19]

FDR maladroitly used the medical metaphor to encourage hopes beyond the political constraints of 1937. He gave little thought to how such a policy could be implemented: He threw sanctions "out of the window" in his press conference the next day. He should not have selected a bringing-before-the-eyes metaphor that connoted rhetoric that he could not enact politically.[20]

THE PURGE

In 1938, President Roosevelt embarked on a policy that was politically damaging. Evoking action-oriented images of Joseph Stalin's eliminating the Old Bolsheviks and Adolf Hitler's exterminating early Nazis, the "purge" was labeled by the press and FDR's political opponents, for the term so aptly characterized the president's figurative and literal actions. Marquis Childs, sympathetic to FDR's ends, nevertheless noted FDR's self-inflicted wound: "What has happened is a sufficient excuse to set the whole pack to baying again."[21]

The plot was hatched by James Roosevelt, the president's son, Harry Hopkins, Tom Corcoran, Harold Ickes, and FDR because they ostensibly wanted to elect in 1938 Democrats who were truly liberal, rather than closet conservatives, who had broken with the president over the Court battle and had sided with Republicans against FDR's wages and hours bill. Samuel Rosenman, Tom Corcoran, and Ben Cohen drafted the speech. Because FDR was unable to present a compelling rhetorical case against conservative Democrats, his ploy was quickly exposed for what it was: a vindictive response to his defeat on the Court battle.[22]

Roosevelt made two rhetorical-political mistakes in his Fireside Chat, "On the Purge," June 24, 1938. First, since he was unable to specify a political exigency, as his wages and hours bill, although watered down, had been passed reluctantly by Congress, FDR could not muster a rhetorical justification for his purge. True enough, he colorfully complained of "Copperheads" in his own party, but it was merely a sideswipe. Instead, he relied on vague characterizations of target Democrats, such as "general attitude," "inward desire," and a "yes, but" position on New Deal legislation. His general aspersions did not suffice, for FDR failed to specify a liberal litmus test on legislation, which would have enabled voters to assess a candidate's position. The lack of a political exigency hinted at a personal vendetta.

Franklin's second rhetorical-political mistake was a metaphorical distinction, too clever by half, as he relied on figurative language that betrayed his true intentions. "As president of the United States," Roosevelt averred, "I am not asking the voters of the country to vote for Democrats next November as opposed to Republicans or members of any other party," and immediately following, in another apophasis, the classical term for affirmation-by-denial, Roosevelt piously allowed, "Nor am I, as president, taking part in Democratic primaries." (Both pledges he would subsequently break.) Rather, Roosevelt would speak as "the head of the Democratic party" when he encountered "a clear-cut issue between candidates for a Democratic nomination involving these [liberal] principles, or involving a clear misuse of my own name."[23]

Lacking a clear political exigency and utilizing disingenuous rhetoric, Roosevelt inadvertently invited personal and political attacks that inexorably defeated him. Perhaps the best bringing-before-the-eyes counter metaphor was birthed by the *Atlanta Constitution,* normally a supporter of FDR's, as it defended Georgian Senator Walter George, a purgee, against the president, who, the newspaper editorialized, would "turn the United States Senate into a gathering of ninety-six Charlie McCarthys with himself as the sole Edgar Bergen to pull the strings and supply the vocalisms." As for the efficacy of Roosevelt's fine differentiation on his figurative titles, Raymond Moley, a former speechwriter now turned New Deal critic, pinpointed the president's persuasive problem: "This bit of mysticism, however, did not sit well with the country—largely, it seems, because such a conception of dualism not only affronted the logic of the intelligent, but strained the credulity of the ignorant."[24]

To summarize these case studies, FDR's political problems were concomitant rhetorical problems. He faced genuine political predicaments—the need to react to Japanese aggression, the exigency of a conservative Court, and the necessity for Democrats to be Democrats, albeit of the Rooseveltian genre. Although other political and rhetorical factors played their parts, Franklin Roosevelt's maladroitness with metaphor was a major factor in his defeats. The quarantine was an inappropriate, action-oriented metaphor when no policy was actually envisioned. The nine-old-men metaphor backfired and encouraged the packing image that torpedoed FDR's judicial reorganization of the Supreme Court. The purge was an image that Roosevelt invited but never voided because he validated the charge with dualistic, deceitful metaphors that the public repudiated.

FDR's Triumphs with Metaphors
1932: PROGRESSIVE GOVERNMENT

In contrast to FDR's occasional failures with metaphors, his famous campaign address on September 23, 1932, before the San Francisco Commonwealth Club illustrates a successful relationship between language and policy. That address is a prime example of speechwriters contouring policy while inventing rhetoric. Adolph Berle composed this speech and the Brains Trust revised it. Drafts are incomplete, and FDR made no emendations on extant drafts.[25]

The speech functioned metaphorically on several levels. Berle's title, "Progressive Government," evoked late nineteenth- and early twentieth-century progressivism as a reform philosophy. The title also implied FDR's new, action-oriented government, which, in reacting to the stagnation of the Depression and to Herbert Hoover's perceived inactivity, would advance the country. From another perspective, Wil Linkugel demonstrated how Berle cast Roosevelt in the figurative persona of a professor. Donning the teacher's mantle, Roosevelt lectured the audience on the implications of U.S. history to 1932.[26]

The focus here is on the famous extended metaphor in the Commonwealth Club address. The passage is Berle's portraiture of the politician-as-teacher: "Government includes the art of formulating a policy and using the political technique to attain so much of that policy as will receive general support; persuading, leading, sacrificing, teaching always, because the greatest duty of a statesman is to educate." In situating the nexus of politics and rhetoric, Berle and the Brains Trust believed that "formulating a policy" was antecedent to the "political technique" of gaining "general support" by "persuading" and "teaching always." Thus, they affirmed the traditional view of rhetoric as the handmaiden of politics. Or did they?[27]

If the "greatest duty"—note the conduct implied—of a statesman is "to educate," then rhetoric can be situated antecedent to politics. The Progressive Government speech functioned in that manner. Before expounding policies, Berle first had Roosevelt-the-professor detail a philosophy of government, which figuratively transferred the ethos of the educator to that of Roosevelt-the-politician. Roosevelt taught the lesson in politics rhetorically, for he used the persuasive technique of the disjunctive syllogism, or method of residues, first discussed by Aristotle. Berle framed the disjunct in a verbose chiasmus: "The issue of Government has always been whether individual men and women will have to serve some system of government or economics, or whether a system of government and economics exists to serve individual men and women." The audience reasonably inferred that President Herbert Hoover and the Republican Party favored the first disjunct whereas the governor and the Democratic Party championed the second course of action. In the body of the speech, FDR then argued,

using rhetorical examples, why the outmoded philosophy should be rejected. And only then did Roosevelt-the-rhetorical-educator metamorphose
into Roosevelt-the-rhetorical-policy-maker. For FDR communicated the
policy of progressive government as a veiled rhetorical threat: "Government may properly be asked to apply restraint" and "Government must be
swift to enter and protect the public interest."[28]

1933: FIRST INAUGURAL ADDRESS

Roosevelt's first investiture speech, invented by Raymond Moley, attended
by Louis Howe who added the famous fear statement, emended extensively by Governor Roosevelt, and delivered by the president, is the most
rhetorically robust of his four inaugurals and is one of the best inaugural
addresses ever delivered. The speech also endures as one of Roosevelt's most
persuasive addresses, for its rhetoric framed the president's New Deal as a
response to the Depression.

Although the address is remembered today for its famous fear statement, "the only thing we have to fear is fear itself," the fear statement was
not a metaphor but a maxim. Moreover, the maxim did not capture immediately the attention of the listening and reading audiences. Rather,
military metaphors energized the speech. The departure points for a study
of this speech are my "Franklin D. Roosevelt's First Inaugural: A Study of
Technique" and Suzanne Daughton's "Metaphorical Transcendence: Images of the Holy War in Franklin Roosevelt's First Inaugural." Both articles
affirm that Roosevelt deployed numerous military metaphors in his address of March 4, 1933.[29]

I advance beyond those studies to treat FDR's use of military metaphors from the perspective of power, which Theodore Windt declared is
the pith of presidential persuasions: "Presidential rhetoric is a study of
how Presidents gain, maintain, or lose support of the public. . . . It is a
study of power, of the fundamental power in a democracy: public opinion
and public support." (This study of Roosevelt's rhetoric has advised that
presidents need also to gain and maintain support of the Congress.)[30]

Roosevelt's first speech as president is a prototype, which he would emu-
late often and successfully in subsequent persuasions, of rhetoric's being
coexistent with, if not antecedent to, the creation of policy. On inauguration day, Moley had FDR seek acquiescence for the New Deal from the
public, the Congress, and most importantly from Wall Street. Specifically,
Moley had in mind the banking legislation that would follow. Yet, the

genesis of the New Deal in general and the banking legislation in particular cannot be separated from its first inaugural and rhetorical matrix.

The order in which FDR trained his rhetorical salvos is intriguing. With a Democratic Congress and the people assumedly his allies, the president first targeted the entrenched enemy. Using the rhetorical technique of *accumulatio,* FDR arrayed a bill of particulars against the patricians who caused the Depression, and then he cast them as the scapegoat: "Primarily, this is because the rulers of the exchange of mankind's goods have failed. . . . Practices of the unscrupulous money-changers stand indicted in the court of public opinion, rejected by the hearts and minds of men." FDR vanquished them with a bringing-before-the-eyes, action-oriented metaphor that equated Franklin Roosevelt with Jesus Christ: "Yes, the money-changers have fled from their high seats in the temple of our civilization. We may now restore that temple to the ancient truths," which was the first rhetoric that the audience applauded. After promising to put people to work with military images, such as "direct recruiting" and "emergency of war," FDR subtly situated victory as contingent on taking power from Wall Street. He claimed "we require two safeguards against a return of the evils of the old order." He actually listed three policies that shifted power from Wall Street to Washington and the White House. His strictures were a "strict supervision" of banking and investments, an "end to speculation," and a "sound currency." The audience applauded.[31]

But Roosevelt required additional power. Since he would not be a laissez-faire president, such as Herbert Hoover, Roosevelt wanted more than an electoral mandate to govern. He craved centralized, executive authority in the White House. In the latter part of his speech where he directly addressed the people, he arrayed his military imagery to recruit the citizenry. Alf Landon, Republican governor of Kansas, cabled FDR that he would "enlist for the duration of the war," but Landon concluded his stint was over in 1936 and ran against his commander in chief. If Americans enrolled in Roosevelt's army, they necessarily gave up some freedoms as one does in the armed forces. The net result was that patricians and plebeians' freedoms were curtailed and shifted to the executive. The audience did not applaud.[32]

Even though the Congress was overwhelmingly Democratic, FDR exacted from it unusual power in peacetime. Averring that he would prefer to work with the Congress (the carrot), Roosevelt menaced the Congress (the stick). Should the Congress "fail," FDR would not "evade the clear course of duty," for he would ask for "broad executive power to wage a war against the emergency, as great as the power that would be given to me if we were in fact invaded by a foreign foe." The audience applauded.

The court-packing, quarantine, and purge metaphors were vivid, action-oriented figures, and the military metaphors in the first inaugural address functioned similarly. Militaristic words, such as "retreat into advance," "victory," "mobilization," and "duty," dutifully portrayed a regimented nation that would defeat the Depression. These metaphors, posted individually throughout the speech and marshaled massively in certain sections, connoted action. The efficacy of these figures became clear and unified in the speech's conclusion. For in truth, these bringing before the eyes, action-oriented military metaphors fused with the speaker who spoke them. Nowhere is this clearer than in FDR's peroration where policy and president and persuasion were one: "The people of the United States have not failed. In their need they have registered a mandate that they want direct, vigorous action. They have asked for discipline and direction under leadership. They have made me the present instrument of their wishes. In the spirit of the gift, I take it." And the audience applauded.

1940: LEND-LEASE

With a third term secure, FDR turned to World War II. The British were in dire straits, as they needed ships to replace those sunk by Nazi U-boats. FDR responded with Lend-Lease, using the metaphor of neighborly lending to sell it to the Congress and country. To be sure, the metaphor was not FDR's alone. Harold Ickes had written FDR in August of 1940 about the possibility of leasing American vessels, and Ickes used the analogy that Americans were refusing to sell or lend their fire extinguishers to their neighbors. The figure ripened in Roosevelt's mind until December of 1940 when, on a cruise in the Caribbean, he launched Lend-Lease. (Could a case be made that FDR remembered the "good neighbor" policy in world affairs that he enunciated in his first inaugural address?)[33]

FDR commenced his rhetorical skirmish with the conservatives and isolationists in a press conference on December 17, 1940. In this press conference, he also laid the semantic foundation for his follow-up speeches, the "Arsenal of Democracy" Fireside Chat on December 29, 1940, and the "Four Freedoms" Annual Message (now termed the State of the Union Address) of January 6, 1941. Although these two speeches are remembered by their catchy titles, neither sobriquet brings-before-the-eyes an action-oriented metaphor as well as the one FDR used in his press conference.

To the assembled reporters, FDR propounded, and Rosenman claimed it was done so extemporaneously: "Suppose my neighbor's home catches fire, and I have a length of garden hose four or five hundred feet away. If he can take my garden hose and connect it up with his hydrant, I may help him to put out his fire. Now, what do I do? I don't say to him before that operation, "Neighbor, my garden hose cost me $15; you have to pay me $15 for it." What is the transaction that goes on? I don't want $15—I want my garden hose back after the fire is over." This press conference also demonstrated FDR's rhetorical acumen in not allowing himself to be drawn from the figurative level to the literal level. Reporters tried to pin him down. Roosevelt refused their ruse. "I can't go into details," he told them, and he continued in that vein with responses, such as "no use asking legal questions" and "Let us leave out the legal phase of it entirely," in order to maximize the ambiguity in the garden hose metaphor.[34]

Like the problematic metaphor of quarantining Japan, the metaphor of lending a garden hose was devious. Conservative Republican Senator Robert Taft countered with his own nauseating simile that "lending war equipment is a good deal like lending chewing gum. You don't want it back." Yet, FDR's metaphor successfully personalized America's relationship to England in its time of trouble. It was not repudiated but rather acclaimed as one of FDR's most successful subterfuges.[35]

Conclusion

When President Roosevelt fulfilled his "greatest duty . . . to educate," his rhetorical politics and his political rhetorics were successful. In Karl Wallace's conception that the substance of rhetoric is good reasons, Roosevelt schooled the American people with reasoned discourse. In particular, when Roosevelt marshaled metaphors that brought-before-the-eyes action-oriented images that the American people perceived to be genuine and needed, he persuaded. He did offer a New Deal to assuage the Depression. He did deploy military metaphors to array the plebeians against the patricians. He did grill millionaires in order to redistribute income. Mussolini did stab France in the back and Republicans did malign "my little dog Fala." And lending the garden hose seemed the neighborly thing to do.[36]

Roosevelt's rhetorics, and hence his policies, were unsuccessful when his speeches lacked good arguments. He chose not to, but he could have adduced genuine justifications for his enlargement of the Supreme Court. He chose not to, but he could have discussed why conservative Southern

Democrats, who impeded the South's economic growth, deserved to be attacked in the 1938 primaries. The want of good reasons in his rhetoric invited counter, subversive metaphors. The court-packing and purge metaphors, coined by his opponents, contributed handily to his defeats, for these images appeared to be warranted in each case. As for the quarantine metaphor, the problem was real enough, but FDR used a vivid metaphor that he would not sustain politically. He dashed the expectations of many who read the metaphor as a clarion call to battle the isolationists.

Metaphor played a major role in Franklin Roosevelt's rhetorical presidency. When coupled with good reasons, FDR's metaphors typically adjusted his policies to the people and the people to his policies. He usually mastered metaphors, but sometimes metaphors mastered him. On these occasions, FDR had failed to prove his case.

Mindful that FDR's successful persuasions far outweighed his failures, I end with an action-oriented, bringing-before-the-eyes metaphor that he adapted from Endicott Peabody, his headmaster at Groton, for use in the president's fourth inaugural address: "a line drawn through the middle of the peaks and valleys of the centuries always has an upward trend."[37]

Notes

1. See Richard Leo Enos, *Greek Rhetoric Before Aristotle* (Prospect Heights, Ill.: Waveland Press, 1993), p. 3.

2. Lois Einhorn, "The Ghosts Unmasked: A Review of Literature on Speechwriting," *Communication Quarterly* 30 (1981): 41–47; William E. Leuchtenburg, *Franklin D. Roosevelt and the New Deal* (New York: Harper and Row, 1963), pp. 78–80.

3. See Donald C. Bryant, "Rhetoric: Its Function and Its Scope," *Quarterly Journal of Speech* 39 (1953): 413; Carol Gelderman, "All the Presidents' Words," *The Wilson Quarterly* 19 (Spring, 1995): 72; Arthur Larson, *Eisenhower: The President Nobody Knew* (New York: Scribner's, 1968), p. 150.

4. Raymond Moley, *The First New Deal* (New York: Harcourt, Brace & World, 1966), p. 114; Donald Richberg, *My Hero* (New York: G. P. Putnam's Sons, 1954), pp. 281–82; Samuel I. Rosenman, "The Reminiscences of Samuel I. Rosenman" (1959), Oral History Collection of Columbia University, Franklin D. Roosevelt Library, Hyde Park, N.Y., pp. 137–38, 128. Hereafter materials in the Roosevelt Library are given as FDRL.

5. Kenneth S. Davis, "FDR as a Biographer's Problem," *American Scholar* 53 (1983–84): 102; *The Public Papers and Addresses of Franklin D. Roosevelt, 1936*, ed. Samuel I. Rosenman, 13 vols. (New York: Random House, 1938–50), pp. 391–92. [hereaf-

ter sources in these volumes will be given as *PPA* with the year]; Earnest
Brandenburg, "The Preparation of Franklin D. Roosevelt's Speeches," *Quarterly
Journal of Speech* 35 (1949): 214.

6. See (listed chronologically) Raymond Moley, *After Seven Years* (New York: Harper,
1939); Robert E. Sherwood, *Roosevelt and Hopkins: An Intimate History* (New
York: Harper and Brothers, 1948); Grace Tully, *F.D.R.: My Boss* (New York:
Charles Scribner's Sons, 1949); Samuel I. Rosenman, *Working with Roosevelt* (New
York: Harper Brothers, 1952); Donald Richberg, *My Hero;* Frank Freidel, *Franklin
D. Roosevelt: A Rendezvous with Destiny* (Boston: Little, Brown, and Company,
1990); Kenneth S. Davis, *FDR: The New Deal Years, 1933–1937* (New York: Ran-
dom House, 1986) and *FDR: Into the Storm, 1937–1940* (New York: Random
House, 1993). For studies from a rhetorical perspective, see (chronological): Waldo
W. Braden and Earnest Brandenburg, "Roosevelt's Fireside Chats," *Speech Monographs* 22 (1955): 290–302; G. Jack Gravlee, "Franklin D. Roosevelt's Speech
Preparation During his First National Campaign," *Speech Monographs* 31 (1964):
437–60; Hermann G. Stelzner, "'War Message,' December 8, 1941: An Approach
to Language," *Speech Monographs* 33 (1966): 419–37; Thomas W. Benson, "Inaugu-
rating Peace: Franklin D. Roosevelt's Last Speech," *Speech Monographs* 36 (1969):
138–47; Halford R. Ryan, "Roosevelt's First Inaugural: A Study of Technique,"
Quarterly Journal of Speech 65 (1979): 137–49; Halford R. Ryan, "Roosevelt's
Fourth Inaugural Address: A Study of its Composition," *Quarterly Journal of
Speech* 67 (1981): 157–66; Halford Ross Ryan, *Franklin D. Roosevelt's Rhetorical
Presidency* (Westport, Conn.: Greenwood Press, 1988); G. Jack Gravlee, *"President
Franklin D. Roosevelt and the 'Purge',"* in *Oratorical Encounters: Selected Studies and
Sources of Twentieth-Century Political Accusations and Apologies,* ed. Halford Ross
Ryan (Westport, Conn.: Greenwood Press, 1988), pp. 63–77; Suzanne M.
Daughton, "Metaphoric Transcendence: Images of the Holy War in Franklin
Roosevelt's First Inaugural," *Quarterly Journal of Speech* 79 (1993): 427–46;
Michael Weiler, "President Franklin D. Roosevelt's Second Inaugural Address,
1937" and "President Franklin D. Roosevelt's Third Inaugural Address, 1941," both
in *Inaugural Addresses of Twentieth-Century American Presidents,* ed. Halford Ryan
(Westport, Conn.: Praeger, 1993), pp. 105–15, 117–27; Halford Ryan, "Franklin D.
Roosevelt," in *U.S. Presidents as Orators,* ed. Halford Ryan (Westport, Conn.:
Greenwood Press, 1995), pp. 146–67; Carol Gelderman, *All the Presidents' Words:
The Bully Pulpit and the Creation of the Virtual Presidency* (New York: Walker,
1997), pp. 11–35; and Davis W. Houck, *Rhetoric as Currency: Hoover, Roosevelt, and
the Great Depression* (College Station: Texas A&M University Press, 2001).

7. Aristotle, *On Rhetoric,* trans. George A. Kennedy (New York: Oxford University
Press, 1991), pp. 248–49.

8. Davis, *FDR, 1937–1940,* p. 58.

9. Remarks, FDR Message to Congress on the Judiciary, Feb. 5, 1937, Draft 1, p. 7,
Draft 2, p. 8, Rosenman Papers, Box 20, FDRL.

10. *PPA, 1937,* p. lxv.

11. Ibid., pp. 123, 125, 126, 128–30.

12. Victory Dinner Speech, PPF 200-B, Box 70, Judiciary Reorganization Act of 1937, Box 1, FDRL.

13. *PPA, 1937*, p. 129.

14. Davis, *FDR, 1937–1940*, pp. 60–61; Rosenman, Oral History, p. 154, FDRL.

15. "America Condemns Japan as an Aggressor," *Newsweek*, Oct. 18, 1937, p. 10; Robert A. Divine, *The Illusion of Neutrality* (Chicago: University of Chicago Press, 1962), p. 212.

16. *PPA, 1937*, p. 410.

17. Ibid., p. 423.

18. FDR, Quarantine Address, Oct. 5, 1937, PPF 200-B, Box 82, FDRL.

19. Rosenman, *Working with Roosevelt*, pp. 164–65; Davis, *FDR, 1937–1940*, pp. 129–30.

20. *PPA, 1937*, p. 423.

21. Marquis W. Childs, "They Still Hate Roosevelt," *New Republic*, Sept. 14, 1938, p. 148.

22. Rosenman, *Working with Roosevelt*, p. 177. For a study of the purge from the perspective of political accusations and apologies, see Gravlee, *"President Franklin D. Roosevelt and the 'Purge',"* pp. 63–77.

23. *PPA, 1938*, p. 399.

24. Quoted in "Roosevelt Now Seeks to 'Pack' the Senate with 'Yes Men' Says Atlanta Constitution," *New York Times*, August, 1938, p. 1; Raymond Moley, "Why the Purge Petered Out," *Newsweek*, July 25, 1938, p. 40.

25. Ryan, *Franklin D. Roosevelt's Rhetorical Presidency*, p. 43. The "Brains Trust" was formed in March of 1932 and functioned through the presidential campaign. The quintet was Samuel Rosenman, Raymond Moley, Basil O'Connor, Rexford Tugwell, and Adolph Berle.

26. Berle Papers, Box 18, FDRL; Wil A. Linkugel, "FDR: Master Campaigner," Central States Speech Association, Cincinnati, 1986.

27. *PPA, 1928–32*, p. 756.

28. Aristotle, *On Rhetoric*, p. 196; *PPA, 1928–32*, pp. 743, 755.

29. See Ryan, "Roosevelt's First Inaugural," pp. 137–49; Daughton, "Metaphoric Transcendence," pp. 427–46. For non-generic qualities of the address, see Halford Ryan, "President Franklin D. Roosevelt's First Inaugural Address, 1933," *Inaugural Addresses of Twentieth-Century American Presidents*, ed. Halford Ryan (Westport, Conn.: Praeger, 1993), pp. 93–103. For a conception of the address as a political jeremiad, see Craig Allen Smith and Kathy B. Smith, *The White House Speaks: Presidential Leadership as Persuasion* (Westport, Conn.: Praeger, 1994), pp. 140–43.

30. Theodore Windt, *Presidential Rhetoric (1961 to the Present)*, 3d ed. (Dubuque: Kendall/Hunt, 1983), p. 2.

31. For an accurate text of the address, with the audience's applause included, see Franklin D. Roosevelt, "First Inaugural Address," *Contemporary American Public Discourse*, ed. Halford Ross Ryan (Prospect Heights, Ill.: Waveland Press, 1992), pp. 13–17.

32. Quoted in Cabell Phillips, *From the Crash to the Blitz: 1929–1939* (London: Macmillan, 1969), p. 107.

33. See Rosenman, *Working with Roosevelt*, p. 257, and Freidel, *Franklin D. Roosevelt*, p. 359.

34. Rosenman, *Working with Roosevelt*, p. 257; *PPA, 1940*, pp. 607, 608–609.

35. Quoted in Freidel, *Franklin D. Roosevelt*, p. 359.

36. Karl R. Wallace, "The Substance of Rhetoric: Good Reasons," *Quarterly Journal of Speech* 49 (1963): 239–49.

37. *PPA, 1944–1945*, p. 524. For the influence of Groton on FDR, see Laura Crowell, "Roosevelt the Grotonian," *Quarterly Journal of Speech* 38 (1952): 31–36. For an accurate text and an exegesis, see Ryan, "Roosevelt's Fourth Inaugural Address," pp. 157–66.

CHAPTER 2

Harry S. Truman

From Whistle-Stops to the Halls of Congress

DIANA B. CARLIN

Reagan speechwriter Peggy Noonan recounted that in her initial attempt to meet the man for whom she was writing she "first saw him as a foot" before being told that the meeting was canceled. In her fourth month on the job she finally met and spoke with the president—a meeting, which she believed, was arranged merely to appease her, rather than truly to discuss a speech. According to Noonan, some members of the speechwriting staff housed in the Old Executive Office Building went as long as a year without personal contact with the president.[1] It was the staffing process, not the speechwriters, that took a speech draft from the speechwriter to the policy experts to the White House staff to the president and back to the speechwriting office, where it was revised and sent back to the White House for delivery in a "frozen" state that more closely resembled slush than ice cubes.

Noonan's experiences stand in sharp contrast to those among President Harry S. Truman's close advisors, who counted speechwriting among their other responsibilities. The principal writers for Truman carried titles such as special counsel to the president, assistant to the president, or administrative assistant to the president. Many of them attended the daily 9:00 A.M. staff meetings and some sat in on the famous Truman poker games, dined on the *Williamsburg* as it navigated the Potomac, took in the sunshine on presidential vacations in Key West, or logged enough miles on the 1948 campaign train to nearly match those of the namesake of the presidential train car, *The Ferdinand Magellan*.[2] The intimacy of the Truman White House is one of the factors that must be taken into consideration in an attempt to understand the nature of presidential speechwriting in his administration.

This analysis of presidential speechwriting begins with an overview of the system of speechwriting in the Truman administration, followed by a description of the speechwriters and methods of speech preparation based on speechwriters' accounts, Truman's recollections, and an examination of White House speech and personal files. It then moves to an analysis of how the writers' and Truman's processes and philosophies impacted the speeches, including their style and delivery. This chapter concludes by drawing from the case study of speechwriting in the Truman administration some general conclusions about presidential speechwriting.

To explore the dynamics of speechwriting in the Truman administration, this chapter focuses on two types of speeches: State of the Union addresses (1946–52) and whistle-stop campaign speeches (1948 and 1950). The State of the Union is a genre that tests the writing process most stringently. It is one of the most demanding and complex speeches to prepare because it requires input from most of the bureaucracy, is broad in scope, and considers multiple audiences. As it combines characteristics of both deliberative and ceremonial rhetoric, the State of the Union address seeks to review and preview diverse issues and policy initiatives while still attempting to achieve some sense of thematic unity.[3] Truman's whistle-stop speeches stood in sharp contrast to his formal State of the Union addresses: They were partisan and political, rather than policy oriented. They were extemporaneous and tailored for each stop. They became a Truman trademark. The preparation process of such speeches reflected a great deal about Truman, his staff, and his campaign constraints.

The Truman Speechwriting System

The White House staff of the 1940s numbered about twenty-five rather than the hundreds of the twenty-first century. President Truman served as his own chief of staff, and his advisors did not unilaterally make policy.[4] Telegrams, manual typewriters, onion skin second copies, and carbon paper were to the 1946 White House what e-mail, faxes, cellular phones, computers, and photocopy machines are to the contemporary one. Despite the differences in position titles, bureaucratic structure, and technology, the Truman speechwriting system shared many characteristics with today's. It was a committee process, and a "frozen" speech was not really frozen until after the president's ad-lib remarks and editorial changes made during his delivery of a speech were recorded in the "as delivered" text of the address. The nature of presidential speechwriting necessitates a vetting system that includes not only the speaker and writers but also policy, political, and press advisors. As Peggy Noonan discovered, many around the president think they can write a speech because they know how to write, and they listen to speeches.

Judge Samuel Rosenman, who found the Truman process more complex and crowded than the process used when he wrote for President Franklin Roosevelt, commented: "I was trying to write a speech in the presence of a convention! There must have been fourteen people around the table. . . . it takes five times as long to write a sentence with fourteen people around as it does to be alone with him [the president] and one or two others." Rosenman's solution was to say "to all those who were making gratuitous suggestions: 'Now that sounds fine. I wish you would take this yellow pad and go into the other room and write five paragraphs on it.'"[5]

The frustrations speechwriters experience across administrations occur because the process itself is political. Presidential speeches are an enactment of presidential leadership and power, and as such are a product of White House and agency politics that seek to influence the person who makes and, more importantly, publicly articulates policy choices. The process is one that takes place within strict time constraints and among competing demands, especially in the Truman White House where writers had other responsibilities. Thus, change and compromise based on policy considerations and power structures and struggles are unavoidable realities of presidential speechwriting—as are the interpersonal dynamics that can strip a speech of its poetry and punch.

Within this environment the writers, advisors, and president must frame a message that is consistent with the administration's broad goals and specific policy initiatives. The message must reflect the president's personality and language—and even the strengths and weaknesses of the president's delivery. The message must satisfy audience expectations and conventions of form, be supported by research, respond to opponents and critics, and be written with the knowledge that the world will listen and the media will dissect every word.

Kenneth Hechler, a Rosenman protégé who was special assistant to President Truman from 1949–53, described the Truman speechwriting system this way: "Over the years the White House speech-writers—less than half a dozen eager and ambitious historians, political scientists, economists, and lawyers—helped President Truman translate policies into action through the spoken word and also through direct negotiation with movers and shakers of public policy. . . . [T]his outspoken group of dedicated

White House assistants sounded off loud and clear when any staff member felt the President was wrongly advised or could benefit from a fresh viewpoint. Yet there was never any question that Harry S. Truman was in charge."[6]

Other sources corroborate Hechler's description. For example, David H. Stowe noted that speechwriting in the Truman White House was a reflection of Truman's leadership style: "I had the opportunity to tell the President exactly why I felt that . . . [a particular proposal] ran contrary to what he had enumerated, for example, in the State of the Union message. On one or two occasions the President agreed that that was true and asked John [Steelman] to try another approach. This, to me, is a mark of a broad gauged man."[7] In another instance, Charles S. Murphy recalled that when Truman had suddenly added speechwriters for the 1948 whistle-stop tour, he created problems in getting a major speech completed. In attempting to resolve the problem, Murphy told Truman that "he needn't be unduly sensitive about this, that we were all working for him and we would do what he told us."[8]

The Speechwriters

While research and editing were done by a large number of agency personnel and staff, as Rosenman discovered, a small group with considerable continuity did much of the writing in the White House and on the campaign trail. An introduction to the major players resembles a reading from the Old Testament with numerous "begats," because members of the speechwriting team brought on and groomed others.

Truman's first presidential address to Congress was delivered on April 16, 1945, four days after Roosevelt's death. That speech was prepared on the train between Hyde Park and Washington by Rosenman and James F. (Jimmy) Byrnes, a U.S. Senator from South Carolina and later secretary of state. Truman, however, wrote the conclusion that included the biblical quotation of King Solomon and ended with the petition, "I ask only to be a good and faithful servant of my Lord and my people."[9]

Rosenman, who was special counsel to Roosevelt, handed in his resignation after Roosevelt's death, but Truman persuaded him to stay. Rosenman assisted with speechwriting until he resigned in early 1946. But Truman continued to call on him for advice. For example, Rosenman's files show that he was part of the team that wrote and revised the 1947 State of the Union address, early drafts of the 1948 convention acceptance speech, and some formal speeches during the 1948 campaign.

Clark Clifford, who eventually replaced Rosenman, first had a temporary post in the White House as an assistant naval aide to James K.
Vardaman. Clifford had done legal work for Vardaman in St. Louis and
was recruited to the White House when Vardaman accompanied Truman
to the Potsdam Conference in 1945. Rosenman noticed that Clifford had
time on his hands during Vardaman's absence from Washington, D.C.,
and suggested that he should be something more than a "potted plant."
Specifically, he asked Clifford to assist with drafting a speech on universal
military service for Truman to deliver to Congress on his return. When
Truman and Vardaman returned, Rosenman asked for Clifford to remain
and to continue assisting him. Clifford became naval aide when Vardaman
was dismissed, and he replaced Rosenman as special counsel in 1946.[10]

Early on, Clifford was assigned to organize Truman's poker games and
was eventually given a seat at the table. This access helped Clifford to learn
about Truman and his thinking on issues. Clifford oversaw the White House
speechwriting activities for four years: from March 31, 1946 (when he rewrote the speech that an outraged Truman had penned to oppose a railroad strike) until January 31, 1950 (when he left for private law practice).
There is no doubt that Clifford played a prominent role in speech drafting;
however, he may have received more credit on some speeches than he deserved. For example, Eban A. Ayers, a deputy press secretary, later reviewed
his detailed diary of his White House years and commented: "I wrote in
my notes that Clifford is credited with writing the speeches and had a large
part in many of them, if not most of those recently [late 1940s], but much
of the work has been done by others."[11] Notes and speech drafts from the
Truman White House support Ayers' observation.[12]

Just as Rosenman had recruited Clifford, Clifford recruited George M.
Elsey. Elsey had served as naval aide in the Map Room, the top-secret
nerve center for intelligence and communication during the war. Elsey
and others who worked in the Map Room were responsible for condens-
ing volumes of information about the war and for messages between Truman
and Allied leaders. This experience sharpened Elsey's writing skills and his
abilities to comprehend a variety of materials and to synthesize them. Elsey
explained that as Clifford's assistant he "had to do homework in subjects
that I to that point had scarcely even realized existed. . . . there was just no
subject that [Clifford] and I didn't seem to find ourselves involved in."[13]
Elsey served as Clifford's assistant until 1949, when he became an administrative assistant to President Truman.

Clifford also paved the way for Charles S. Murphy to become a member of the speechwriting team. Truman recruited Murphy from the Senate legislative counsel's office where he worked as a bill drafter. As a White House administrative assistant, Murphy bridged the gap between the special counsel's office, which handled policy and planning, and Dr. John Steelman's office, which handled operations—a broadly defined set of responsibilities. Murphy served in the White House from 1947 until Truman left office in 1953. He succeeded Clifford as special counsel in 1950. Murphy selected David E. Bell from the Bureau of the Budget as his assistant. Bell was responsible for speeches and sections of speeches that dealt primarily with economic issues. This included such things as trade and labor, including work on addresses related to strikes. Additionally, Stephen Spingarn referred to Bell as "the natural resources man."[14] Bell served as special assistant to the president in 1947–48, and as administrative assistant in 1951–53.

Joining the speechwriting team in 1948 was David Lloyd, who was originally part of the campaign group from the Democratic National Committee headed by William L. Batt. Lloyd served as "point man" on major speeches after the 1948 campaign. An administrative assistant, he continued to write speeches until the end of the administration. Lloyd was a gifted writer with a special talent for humor that he incorporated effectively and appropriately into campaign speeches and selected presidential addresses. In the fall of 1952, with the Republicans sensing Eisenhower's impending victory over Adlai Stevenson in the presidential election, the Republican Party sent a "truth squad" to hold press conferences wherever Truman spoke. Lloyd provided Truman with a humorous dismissal of the "so-called Republican 'truth squad' who have been limping around in my wake. . . . I wonder if Columbus ever had a truth squad following him around, shouting at the top of his voice: 'The world is flat, I tell you. The world is flat.'"[15]

Leon Keyserling, who served on Truman's Council of Economic Advisors, described the qualities the major players brought to the speechwriting process: "Now in some ways, David Bell and David Lloyd were more 'idea men,' in a conventional sense, than Mr. Clifford was. Clifford was, without equal, the synthesizer and operator. . . . None of these people were non-idea men. It's all relative. Everything in life is a matter of degree. . . . Maybe the much hackneyed and misused word, 'intellectual,' explains it. I would say David Lloyd and David Bell fell more in the classification of 'intellectuals.'"[16]

Other individuals played important roles in research, preparation, and refinement of speeches. They formed a second tier of writers with expertise that complemented the "big picture" view of the principal speechwriters. Ken Hechler, who served as a special assistant to the president throughout the period from 1945 to 1953, was one example of a specialized writer. A Princeton political science professor, Hechler took over the work of the Democratic National Committee's research team after the 1948 election. As he noted in his White House diary, Hechler's most important assignment from the speechwriting team came in 1950 when he was assigned to get some "'calamity-howlers' or 'scare words,' i.e., predictions of despair which sounded silly in light of the facts" and incorporate them into Truman's speeches. He later became the "local color man" for the 1950 whistle-stop tour that Truman took en route to dedicate the Grand Coulee Dam.[17]

David H. Stowe was with the president from 1947 until 1953, first as deputy to the assistant to the president and later as administrative assistant with expertise in education and labor. He worked primarily with Steelman on policy issues. However, during the 1948 campaign, Stowe worked with Murphy on drafts of major speeches. After the campaign, he assisted with State of the Union addresses and economic-related speeches.

Stephen J. Spingarn first worked on speeches while assistant general counsel at the Department of the Treasury from 1946 to 1949. He was then assigned to the White House as assistant special counsel and administrative assistant during 1949–50. Spingarn assisted Stowe on both campaign and policy speeches. His most notable contribution was the initial draft of the Oklahoma City campaign speech on "Communism, Democracy, and National Security," which was intended to "answer Republican charges of communism in government" and show that Truman's Loyalty Program "had proven the loyalty of 99.7 percent of all federal workers."[18] The speech originally called for a comparison to the government being purer than Ivory soap, but the vetting process removed the analogy. Spingarn described himself as one of the "'draft one to draft five men' . . . who would mull this thing over for five drafts and then when we had it in form satisfactory to ourselves, we would sit down with the President and [Press Secretary] Charlie Ross."[19]

Charles Ross, appointments secretary Matthew J. (Matt) Connelly, correspondence secretary William (Bill) Hassett, special assistant Phileo Nash, Joe Short (who succeeded Charlie Ross as press secretary), and Steelman were actively involved in the vetting process and contributed minor changes in the "last, or almost the last, draft." Charles Murphy recalled that this group did "mainly editing . . . [but also] major problems maybe would be brought up. Sometimes it would require major revisions."[20] Ross has been cited by several of the speechwriters in their oral histories as being a stickler for punctuation, especially semicolons! Ross was concerned with what was going to the press, and his contributions were made with that audience in mind.[21]

Matt Connelly kept minutes of cabinet meetings and had a good grasp of what the policy issues were. He occasionally made substantive suggestions, as was the case with the 1950 State of the Union address. During the president's oral reading of a draft to the cabinet, Connelly suggested a change in language calling for federal aid to education, but Truman overruled him after the 1948 Democrat platform was consulted. Speechwriter George Elsey noted in his papers on the address: "Pres. specifically affirmed the language on Federal Aid to Education, after Connelly had asked him to delete reference to the States (Catholics want Fed. Gov't. to give aid directly to Catholics in those states where state laws or State constitutions would prevent states from passing on money)."[22]

Of the group that saw drafts prior to "freezing" the text of a speech, Steelman played a larger role than the others did. Members of his staff were actively involved in speechwriting, and Steelman's name appears on routing slips throughout the process. As one of the major advisors who were "liaison to the President on the economic reports," Steelman was concerned with a broad range of issues, and contributed substantive policy expertise. Leon Keyserling played a role similar to Steelman's by giving help in "two forms: One form would be facts; the other form would be drafts of passages."[23] According to Murphy, Keyserling "was a never-failing source of drafts and materials for a speech on almost any subject, and . . . we frequently called on him for help."[24]

Duke Dumars from the Department of Agriculture was a contact person on agriculture speeches and agriculture sections of addresses such as the State of the Union. Richard Neustadt, who worked in the Bureau of the Budget from 1946 to 1950, made major contributions to sections of speeches while he served in the White House during 1950–53. There were undoubtedly many others from agencies who were regular contacts and who considered themselves part of the team, but were not mentioned by name in the White House files or oral histories consulted for this analysis. One such person was Robert Turner, an assistant to Steelman. When interviewed by Lois J. Einhorn in 1988, he described himself as "a member of the team for writing a speech or a message to Congress when economic matters were involved."[25]

In addition to the White House staff, other writers and researchers were added for the 1948 campaign. William Batt from the Democratic National Committee headed a seven-person team ("the Batt group") that provided background research on both issues and local color. Rosenman was originally scheduled to be on the campaign train, but through some confusion was not on the original passenger list. When it could not be worked out later to include Rosenman, Truman asked Jonathan Daniels to help coordinate the speechwriting process during the campaign.

Truman invited David Noyes and Bill Hillman to assist with speeches on the campaign, and Hillman added Albert Z. (Bob) Carr. According to Murphy, Truman "did this without consultation, if that's the proper word, with the members of the White House staff that worked in this field regularly . . . [and] he did not tell any of us exactly what functions each of us was to perform."[26] The result of these actions was a set of competing speeches for the first major campaign address in Dexter, Iowa. Significant rewriting and compromise followed until roles were clarified. Because of the number of speeches given—140 on the first leg of the whistle-stop trip alone—countless individuals were involved in research, preparation of sections, and vetting throughout the campaign.

In the final months of the whistle-stop tour, news columnist and author John Franklin Carter joined the group on the train. Carter, who also wrote under the name of Jay Franklin, was a welcomed addition because he wrote quickly, and his writing required little editing. After the campaign he fell out of favor because of two articles he wrote which overstated his association with Truman and speculated on rifts between Truman and his foreign policy advisors. Although his tenure was short, Carter did write some of the more humorous material that Truman used in the latter part of the campaign to reinforce his image as "give 'em hell, Harry." The circumstances of his departure from the team underscored his lack of understanding of the role that a team member was expected to play. Truman speechwriters, regardless of whether they were writing speeches to be delivered to Congress or to partisan crowds at a train depot, were considered as part of a team that was supposed to be loyal to the president and to a common purpose without seeking attention for themselves. This attitude enabled them to develop a speechwriting system that remained basically consistent during the administration.

The Speechwriting Process

The speechwriting process for major policy addresses differed sharply from the process of writing Truman's whistle-stop campaign speeches. The contrasting demands of those two different rhetorical situations dictated different kinds of speeches and different modes of speechwriting. Those who drafted Truman's State of the Union addresses and other important policy speeches have given strikingly consistent descriptions of their writing process. It was a system that produced numerous drafts of each address. That process was best described by David Lloyd:

> There are two general types of speech which the President delivers—first, the formal, prepared address; and the second, the informal, extemporaneous speech. Somewhat in advance of major, prepared speeches, the President usually outlines the basic ideas to be expressed therein. There is no formal method used by the President at this preliminary stage. The ideas may be expressed at a staff meeting; in an informal conversation which the President has with one or more members of the staff; through notes which the President jots down; or in the form of a dictated memorandum. From this point on, the White House staff and the administrative departments and agencies share the task of supplying and checking the supporting facts and figures. The President takes a careful hand in setting the tone of the speech, editing various drafts with his own insertions or deletions, and reviewing material suggested by his staff and by the departments and agencies.
>
> No two speeches are alike in the development of this process. Cabinet or Congressional leaders may roll up their sleeves and submit suggestions which are incorporated at various stages of the drafting process. It is extremely rare that a major speech will run through less than six drafts, and the State of the Union and other highly important addresses are more likely to go through twice that number of drafts. . . .
>
> Occasionally, the President will use a few rough notes for his informal extemporaneous remarks. For the most part, however, these informal remarks are delivered entirely "off the cuff."[27]

As a result of the demands of State of the Union addresses, a highly structured committee system emerged for their preparation. In general, calls went out to federal agencies between September and November for suggestions for the address as well as for the printed message and budget.

Sometime in December a memo was circulated based on information received from agencies and from conversations in staff meetings to determine the direction the speech would take. A theme and outline were developed, and drafts were prepared by some combination of the major writers with support from agency contacts. A memo in Clifford's 1948 State of the Union files indicated that seven individuals were responsible for drafting one or more of the fifteen sections of the address. Records for other years had similar divisions of labor.[28]

In addition to a preliminary assignment sheet, a detailed status sheet was prepared on each State of the Union address. Before preparing the status report form, the president and staff would determine the length of the speech and calculate Truman's rate of delivery. The number of words allocated to each section was then determined according to what needed to be emphasized. An excerpt from George Elsey's files for the 1947 address illustrates the method:

Outline	Status	Pending
III. Foreign Affairs (1000) words) Discussion of the importance of United Nations; general report on Foreign relations with reference to political and economic objectives; progress made in peace settlements; need for legislation for Central Intelligence Agency.	Material being prepared	Elsey to prepare draft from State, C.I.G., Treasury, and White House materials.[29]

The Truman White House set December 28 as the standard target date for completion of the first draft of each year's State of the Union address. Since those speeches were typically delivered in January, Truman and his aides had less than a month—some years as little as a week—to revise the speech draft into its final form. Once a draft was completed, it was routed to the appropriate staff and agency contacts for comments. The president did not usually see the speech until about the fifth draft. However, Truman was apprised of issues related to the address during regular meetings with cabinet members and speechwriters. Truman's description of the speech-writing system was similar to other accounts: "After each of these discussions, I again studied the particular draft carefully and made additional changes. Even after the master copy was prepared I would frequently rework many pages. In the hope of making the message as clear and as simply worded as possible, I often made minor changes as late as an hour or so before delivery. Sometimes I would pencil an 'off-the-cuff' remark into the margin just before going on air. . . . Even in formal Presidential addresses I often strayed from the official copy."[30]

Truman gave specific instructions as a speech neared completion. For example, with the 1950 State of the Union address, he sent the speechwriters a memo dictating three changes which were marked for different places in the text:

1. Right here, I want to say that no one appreciates more than I the bipartisan cooperation in foreign affairs which has been enjoyed by this Administration.
2. the establishment of the Columbia Valley Administration, I don't want you to miss that.
3. I think I had better read that over, you interrupted me in the middle. To meet this situation, I am proposing that Federal expenditures be held to the lowest levels consistent with our international requirements and the essential needs of economic growth, and the well-being of our people. Don't forget that last phrase.[31]

Embargoed copies of several State of the Union addresses also included last-minute changes made as Truman did a "read through" and someone made note of them on the press draft for inclusion in the speaking copy. Comparisons of final drafts and embargoed drafts with "as delivered" texts indicated minor changes in some speeches, but there were few major revisions after Truman had a speaking text in hand.[32]

While the writing process for a State of the Union address was a disciplined and lengthy process, that was not always possible with major campaign speeches. For example, during the 1948 campaign, Truman gave a series of major policy speeches interspersed among his brief remarks at the whistle-stops. That combination created a logistical nightmare in the speechwriting process—a problem exacerbated when Truman hired additional campaign writers without specifying their duties. The confusion was eventually resolved by placing Clifford and Elsey on the train to coordinate the whistle-stop speeches and to rework the major speeches with Truman and press secretary Charlie Ross. The regular staff assistants headed by Murphy stayed in Washington, D.C., drafting major speeches and sending them by airplane to a train stop the day before a speech was scheduled for delivery. Murphy also coordinated the Batt group's efforts to collect material for the "local color" and political content of the whistle-stop speeches. According to Murphy, "Elsey and Bell did more of the writing, and . . . Clifford and I did more of the editing and criticizing."[33]

The speechwriting machine for the 1948 campaign, however, also required Truman to play an active role, because the whistle-stop speeches were delivered extemporaneously from outlines and notes from the "local color" briefing book. According to the speechwriters, two factors enabled the whistle-stop system to work: Truman's ability to read the material and remember details, and his ad lib remarks about personal experiences related to the local venue.

The whistle-stop speeches followed a formula that made it easy for Truman to adapt to each location. When summarizing the characteristics of those speeches as a guide for similar brief remarks in the future, speechwriter Charles Murphy noted that each speech contained four parts:

> (1) Friendly local reference, drawn from material supplied by the Batt research group; (2) It was then demonstrated that a vote for [Henry] Wallace or [Strom] Thurmond was really a vote for the Republican ticket, and the real choice was between the Democrats and Republicans; (3) From there the outline documented the concept that Republicans serve the rich and Democrats serve all the people; (4) Finally, the point of the whole campaign was brought home by indicating that "It's a question of whether you'll have enough to eat and to wear. It virtually affects your chance for living in a world at peace."[34]

Oral histories and other accounts of the Truman speechwriting process center on the whistle-stops far more than on the White House process. The challenge that the campaign presented and the team's ability to perform successfully undoubtedly explain the tendency for Truman speechwriters to emphasize the preparation of the brief campaign speeches rather than the more typical process of drafting major policy addresses.

The Rhetorical Product: Content and Style

Critics have noted that there were few, if any, memorable phrases such as those heard in FDR's speeches. One critic referred to Truman's speeches as being "like a musical comedy which doesn't have any tunes you can whistle."[35] The form and style of Truman's speeches—including their deficiencies—resulted from a number of factors, such as: the use of a committee system for writing, the time constraints of the 1948 campaign, and the speechwriters' backgrounds in law, economics, and political science (as opposed to rhetoric and literature).

The writers were undaunted by criticisms of their policy speeches because they saw themselves as concerned primarily with "substance" and secondarily with style. In response to the criticism, Murphy stated that "the primary requirement [of a presidential speech] is accuracy, not style."[36] Thus, the approach to writing presidential speeches was one which viewed content and eloquence as mutually exclusive and which defined eloquence somewhat narrowly as poetic and as appealing to emotions—with a model of Roosevelt's grand style as a primary example. Murphy's attitude reflected Truman's own view that "[p]eople don't go to hear people make speeches for entertainment any more. They have plenty of entertainment on the radio . . . and the movies. What they want are facts and supporting data to prove those facts are correct, and that's all there is to it."[37] However, Truman preferred to minimize the use of statistics "unless they are put in a form which is easily understood."[38]

Truman's preference for direct speech created oratory that Halford Ross Ryan describes as "prosaic." Ryan argues that "inasmuch as Roosevelt gave the nation 'Four Freedoms,' Truman was content with just numbers, to wit his 'Twenty-One Point Message' in 1945 and his 'Point Four' inaugural in 1949." Such criticism should not suggest, however, that Truman lacked any form of eloquence in his words. The fact that Truman was branded as a "give 'em hell" orator demonstrates that he could move an audience. Even Ryan admits that "Truman's unvarnished delivery and diction had a certain effectiveness. When yoked to Cold War rhetoric, Truman's *elocutio* and *actio* proclaimed a pugnacious dynamism, which was lacking in FDR's more suave pronouncements, that well suited the anti-Communist or anti-Republican tone and temper of Truman's addresses."[39]

Both Truman and his writers created a dichotomy between style and substance. That distinction, as well as the writers' lack of rhetorical backgrounds, caused them to pay little conscious attention to the relationship between their words and Truman's personal style. Beyond the desire to be plainspoken and to concentrate on facts, Ayers observed: "I don't think any of those fellows realized—that they were writing Truman's speeches—that they should try to write as Truman would speak. I think that towards the end, or I won't say towards the end, even before that in '48, I think that the bulk in the end was Charlie Murphy's product no matter who worked on it before that."[40]

It is possible, however, that Murphy had spent so much time with Truman that the president's style was absorbed without consciously thinking about it. There is evidence that while the speechwriters did not explicitly analyze what was written as being in Truman's style, there was an awareness of what was not Truman's style. George Elsey remarked to Ken Hechler that one of the whistle-stop speeches Hechler had written in the 1950 congressional campaign was "like the Boss speaks." In his diary, Hechler recorded that Elsey "then told the story about the time someone suggested that Arthur Schlesinger, Jr., be enlisted to help the President with speeches, and David Lloyd had replied that 'Schlesinger does not write on the same conceptual level as the President' . . . [and] he added that anything that Schlesinger wrote for the President would stick out all over as a ghost-written job."[41]

There was one place where Truman's own insertion of his style and his understated eloquence did appear, and that was in his use of spiritual and moral language. Elsey commented that this was an area where Truman "led and the staff followed. The staff did not deliberately compose phrases or paragraphs of this sort, and inject them. This was very much a part of President Truman's own personal belief and feeling." If the staff did not take the initiative to include such references, Truman often did it himself "in longhand near the final draft of a speech."[42]

Such was the case with the 1949 State of the Union Message—Truman's first after winning his own term as president. The speech was one which called for cooperation from both Congress and citizens as the nation confronted the challenges outlined in the address. It is revealing to compare Truman's additions to the speech with the final draft in which his speechwriters had incorporated Truman's language into the speech. This comparison illustrates the difference between the unadulterated Truman style, which was eloquent in both its spirituality and its toughness, and the staff's style, which remained true to Truman's intent but not necessarily to his tone. What resulted was a loss of the melodies to be whistled. In longhand attached to one of the late drafts, Truman wrote ten paragraphs that were filled with biblical and spiritual references, such as:

> On my first appearance before Congress, April sixteenth, Nineteen Forty-five, after I became President, I quoted to you the prayer of King Solomon from the First Book of Kings, Chapter Three, verse Nine—"Give therefore

thy servant an understanding heart to judge the people, that I may discern
between good and bad: for who is able to judge this thy so great people."

There is a paraphrase of this same prayer in the Second Book of
Chronicles, Chapter One, verse Ten—"Give me now wisdom and knowledge, that I may go out and come in before this people: for who can judge
this thy people, that is so great."

I expressed to the 79th Congress a hope for divine guidance, and for
help and cooperation from this august legislative body, and from the people
of the United States.[43]

Interspersed with the solemn phrases were words more characteristic of
the "give 'em hell Harry" tenor of the whistle-stop speeches, or even Jesus'
reaction to the moneychangers in the temple:

> You have learned that the people do not believe in the paid press writers
> and the kept radio commentators. You have learned that the people have no
> patience with the public man who lets the pollsters keep his conscience.
> . . . I have no bitterness in my heart against anyone, not even the opposition
> press and its paid henchmen the columnists and the editors who write ideas
> for pay; nor even the bought and paid for radio commentators. Never in
> the history of the country did a President need the honest help and coop-
> eration of Congress, press and people as I needed help and cooperation in
> September Nineteen Forty-five, just as I need help and cooperation now
> and in the next four years.[44]

By the time the staffing process was finished, Truman spoke the following
words:

> In 1945, when I came down before the Congress for the first time on
> April 16, I quoted to you King Solomon's prayer that he wanted wisdom
> and the ability to govern his people as they should be governed. I explained
> to you at that time that the task before me was one of the greatest in the
> history of the world, and that it was necessary to have the complete coop-
> eration of the Congress and the people of the United States.
>
> Well now, we are taking a new start with the same situation. It is abso-
> lutely essential that your President have the complete cooperation of the
> Congress to carry out the great work that must be done to keep the peace in
> this world, and to keep this country prosperous.
>
> The people of this great country have a right to expect that the Congress

and the President will work in closest cooperation with one objective—the welfare of the people of this Nation as a whole. In the months ahead I know that I shall be able to cooperate with this Congress.

Now, I am confident that the Divine Power which has guided us to this time of fateful responsibility and glorious opportunity will not desert us now. With that help from Almighty God which we have humbly acknowledged at every turning point in our national life, we shall be able to perform the great tasks which He now sets before us.[45]

While it could be argued that calls for cooperation and conciliation would be lost among the *ad hominem* language, Truman's personal version issued a challenge in a far more spirited, honest, and memorable way and called attention to those realities of political life that often stand in the way of cooperation. Leadership is about getting attention as well as fostering cooperation. As Truman remarked: "It isn't polls or public opinion alone of the moment that counts. It is right and wrong, and leadership—men with fortitude, honesty and a belief in the right that makes epochs in the history of the world."[46] Truman's frankness and plain speaking fit his definition, however, his public speaking did not always call attention to his leadership qualities. Recent views of the Truman presidency by both historians and politicians in both major parties acknowledge his strengths, which were undoubtedly exhibited behind closed doors using a language style more similar to his longhand draft than the final version of his 1949 State of the Union address.[47]

The decision to develop a controlled style was made not only as a means of emphasizing substantive policy in clear, unemotional terms but also was based on the assumption that Truman would never compare favorably to FDR no matter what the writers did. It was also believed that Truman's personality, Missouri twang, and plain spokenness did not lend themselves to the grand style. Finally, there was also an acknowledged reality that Truman had trouble reading a manuscript because of his poor vision and limited training with that type of delivery. His speechwriters remarked that Truman's "eyesight was so bad that when he leaned over his manuscript more closely, all you could see was the top of this head,"[48] and that "he read right through punctuation and read whatever was included in the span which his eye caught."[49]

The staff experimented with a variety of ways to make it easier for Truman to read a script. One of his aides reported that "[p]ages with only large type were first used, a teleprompter was tried but did not meet the approval of Mr. Truman. Tape recordings were made at times so that the President might hear himself where improvement could be made."[50] Eventually they settled on short, triple spaced lines with a few words underlined for emphasis.

Truman's weaknesses in delivery were further intensified by a somewhat casual approach to practice. Truman remarked that "[b]efore delivering a speech I like to read it aloud a time or two. . . . In staff conferences on a forthcoming speech, I would sometimes read a draft aloud in pretty much the same manner I expected to use in the actual presentation."[51] But he did not always devote serious time to practice. Records of Truman's schedule and appointments reveal that even for a speech as formal as the State of the Union little official time was set aside for formal practice.[52] Conferences to actually discuss why the writers had written what they did were rare. Keyserling recounted an example of a gaffe in delivery that suggested that Truman had spent little time with the speech and the writers prior to delivery:

> When Truman was in trouble right after the Republican victory [in the 1946 congressional election] there was a Party dinner. . . . Clifford said, "We've really got to have a talk to give the Boss life." In this case I was asked to write it. I wrote a talk and it had a refrain in it every page or so, it would repeat a refrain. . . . Clifford said to me, "This is great; this really has something in it."
>
> Truman gets up at the meeting, and this was before he got his elocution lessons. Well, he read the refrain the first time; every other time he skipped it. Clifford and I were sitting at the same table and we got glummer and glummer because the whole thing fell flat without the refrain. So I said to Clifford later, I said, "Clark, why did the President do that?"
>
> He said, "Well, when the President came to it the second time, he thought it was a typographical error."[53]

When Truman was reading or using his own words, however, he understood that such devices as repeated phrases were not mistakes. In his convention acceptance speech, Truman challenged the Republican Congress to pass legislation to implement the social programs that they claimed to support in the 1948 Republican campaign platform. After he cited each social program, Truman would add: "which they say they are for."[54] Elsey observed: "The manner in which he repeatedly jabbed the Republicans with that line caused wilder and wilder enthusiasm from his audience."[55]

The whistle-stop speeches provided sharp contrasts in language, style, delivery and impact with formal speeches by Truman, especially his State of the Union addresses. The whistle-stop speeches were created by a speechwriting process that let Truman's personality shine through—the Truman who could entertain and energize an audience. To the speechwriters' credit, they understood that a campaign speech was not the same as a policy speech and that a different system was required if Truman was going to instill confidence in his leadership and win votes.

Clifford and others believed that Truman "should stop trying to live up to Roosevelt's rhetoric and start a new form of off-the-cuff speech."[56] That system made Truman a major part of the writing team through his use of extemporaneous delivery. Noting his success on the campaign train, the writers took language Truman used at his whistle-stops and incorporated it into the outlines for subsequent whistle-stop speeches, and sometimes even into the texts of more formal addresses. Those speeches were designed to show the nation the man behind the title. Had the decision not been made to liberate Truman rhetorically on the campaign train, the famous newspaper headline, "Dewey Beats Truman," might have been historic for its accuracy rather than its error.

Murphy and Clifford had made the decision to let Truman be his own "speechwriter" at whistle-stops—to have him extemporize from the outlines and background material provided by the speechwriting team. When Truman was scheduled to address a group of newspaper editors in April, 1948, Murphy and Clifford decided to experiment with the speech. The first part of the speech was prepared through the usual manuscript mode, but the second half was delivered from an outline. Jonathan Daniels, a member of the campaign writing team, summarized what happened when Truman was on his own: "He began an entirely different, extemporaneous, and off-the-record speech of his own, in his own vocabulary, out of his own humor and his own heart. . . . He made the story of his own problems seem one told in earnestness and almost intimacy with each man in the hall. He was suddenly a very interesting man of great candor who discussed the problems of American leadership with men as neighbors. He spoke the language of them all out of traditions common to them all."[57]

Daniels's observation captured the essence of the man—an essence revealed through his language and his own brand of eloquence. His common language pulled no punches and showed no pretense. For instance, in a whistle-stop speech in Fresno, California, Truman told the crowd: "You have got a terrible congressman here in this district. He is one of the worst. He is one of the worst obstructionists in the Congress. He has done everything he possibly could to cut the throats of the farmer and the laboring man. If you send him back, that will be your fault if you get your own throat cut. I am speaking plainly these days. I am telling you the facts."[58] Truman subsequently admitted to a reporter that he feared that his words probably "re-elected the son-of-a-bitch." However, the member of Congress whom he had attacked in that speech did lose his bid for reelection.[59]

And while the feisty side of Truman produced great bluntness, the thoughtful side could produce appealing metaphors. A speech praising Mike Mansfield demonstrated the Truman style at its best. Prompted by an idea from Hechler, Truman told a Montana audience at a whistle-stop speech during his 1950 tour:

> You know, some people will take a look at an acorn and all they can see is just an acorn. But people of Mike Mansfield's type are something differ-ent. They can see into the future. They can see a giant oak tree, with its great limbs spreading upward and outward coming from that acorn.
>
> In Washington there are some men, no matter how hard they try, who can only see little acorns. I don't have to call any names, you know who they are. Even give them a magnifying glass, or even a pair of spyglasses, or even a telescope, they just shake their heads and all they can say is, "I'm sorry, I can't see anything but an acorn there."[60]

Truman followed this thought with a list of important policies that were rejected by members of Congress whom he wanted defeated. The meta-phor resonated with the press in New York City, Baltimore, and Washing-ton, D.C., where Truman was featured in newspaper headlines such as: "TRUMAN RAPS 'ACORN MINDS' OF LITTLE MEN" and "FAIR DEAL OPPONENTS CALLED 'ACORN THINKERS' BY TRUMAN." But his anal-ogy did more than achieve headlines; it also made a point about the vision of his Fair Deal policies.[61]

While Truman's successes on campaign tours did not substantially affect the way his major presidential addresses were prepared or framed, the im-age that Truman projected of himself and the leadership style he exhibited in the whistle-stop speeches allowed him to take office in 1949 on his own terms—rather than as the former vice president to FDR. In the 1948 cam-paign, he not only earned a presidential term in his own right but also acquired a clearer public perception and a greater public acceptance of his persona. As a consequence, the persona that Truman projected through his whistle-stop speeches helped him promote his policy agenda both on the campaign trail and in the halls of Congress.

Implications for Political Speechwriting

Thomas W. Benson, Lois J. Einhorn, Martin J. Medhurst, and other academics in rhetoric and communication have interviewed the speechwriters of various political figures. Through those interviews, they have raised important questions about the scholarly study of speechwriting. Several of those issues provide a means of summarizing what can be learned from this analysis of speechwriting in the Truman White House. Einhorn observes that the "selection of a speechwriting staff represents an important decision for a speaker. Thus, rhetorical critics need to judge whether the speaker selected the best possible ghostwriter or staff of ghostwriters and whether the speaker used the talents of the speechwriting staff in the most effective ways possible."[62] On that score, the Truman White House performed well.

Truman and his staff knew what he had to accomplish through his rhetoric. When Truman succeeded Roosevelt, little was known about him. For example, Francis Heller, a University of Kansas professor who assisted Truman in writing his memoirs, recalled that as a U.S. military officer stationed in the Pacific during World War II, it had been his duty to inform his men that Franklin Delano Roosevelt had died. Someone then asked who was president, and Heller had trouble remembering Truman's name. He recalled that other officers had similar experiences.[63]

Because the public initially knew so little about Truman, there were doubts about his ability to perform the duties of the office. His past connections with a Kansas City political machine and accusations of cronyism added to his credibility problems. He was also following a legend, not only as a speaker but also as a leader. Thus, an emphasis on policy and defensible, well-researched arguments was what Truman needed to bolster public confidence in his abilities. The reality was that the times had demanded that FDR be a charismatic leader and speaker. Truman, however, needed to be a pragmatic taskmaster to help rebuild the world after a devastating war, to cope with crises arising from transforming the country into a postwar economy, and simultaneously to confront Communist expansion and general international political instability. On the campaign trail, Truman needed to project the man who held the office. The system of extemporaneous speeches supported by a highly skilled research team allowed Truman to show that he was in control of the facts while at the same time highlighting his personality and exhibiting his fervor for public service rather than mere office holding. Through Truman's candor and common touch on the campaign train, Americans were encouraged to view the man in the White House as one of them—as someone looking out for their interests.

While the White House speechwriting process created speeches that often masked Truman's fiery personality, it was a system that was representative of Truman's managerial style. Truman was accustomed to working through a system of friends; hence, the individuals who wrote for him became part of an inner circle. That "comfort level" enabled Truman to concentrate on what he needed to do, and he let the staff worry about the details. The men Hechler described as "dedicated" were indeed dedicated to Truman and his political agenda. That did not mean, however, that Truman abdicated responsibility for his speeches. Records indicate that Truman made the final decisions about what went into his speeches. When the speechwriting system did not work to his satisfaction, Truman took charge. For example, on the occasion of his final campaign speech in 1948, Truman ignored the speeches his staff had prepared, and spoke without notes.[64] The fact that some of his major speeches, including his 1948 acceptance speech at the Democratic National Convention, were given from outlines also indicates the type of relationship and decision making that existed among Truman and his aides. Truman sought out the best staff members he could find. He let them have direct access to him and to the inner workings of White House decision making. The objective of the speechwriting process was to try to ensure that the speechwriters' words expressed Truman's thoughts.

The speechwriting process is a reflection of leadership and managerial styles. Recognizing this, Medhurst and Dreibelbis have raised two significant questions about the process of writing speeches for political figures: What is the role of status in the process? And how and by whom are decisions made when there are multiple opinions?[65] The Truman speechwriting system worked because status was not of central importance. The group worked together and went wherever or to whomever it was necessary to get information and answers. Agency personnel were extremely important in speech preparation. Even little-known bureaucrats sometimes played significant roles in providing direction to presidential speeches.[66] The ultimate status, in the speechwriters' views, rested with the president.

From a practical perspective, however, when a speech went through as many as twelve drafts, Clifford and Murphy had the status to make decisions that they believed did not require presidential attention. They tried to do so with a knowledge of the president's desires and within the confines of their roles of as staff members. As Elsey noted:

> The job of staff members is to help the President find out what the facts are; to clarify, where clarification is needed, the opinion and advice of the senior officials of the executive branch; when the President has a sharp view of his own, to advise the President as to whether it's feasible or not to carry it out the way he wants to. . . . An ideal staff member ought not to be a person who has sharp and decided views of his own that he is determined to see carried out. If a staff member is so prejudiced or so opinionated or so determined on a particular matter of foreign policy or defense, he simply can't be trusted to be an effective staff member of the President.[67]

Generally, decisions about speeches were based on the weight of the evidence, which was consistent with the legal and academic backgrounds of the staff. The staff was allowed to argue a point, but Truman made the final decision. The importance of facts in the writing process was underscored by Truman's commissioning of major studies on issues such as communism, foreign policy toward the Soviet Union, and the strategies and issues for the 1948 campaign.

This analysis of speechwriting in the Truman White House suggests the need to study presidential rhetoric from a process perspective. While Truman's speechwriting process worked well for him, it also had its flaws. His staff would have benefited from the presence of someone who understood that content and eloquence are not mutually exclusive and that eloquence takes different forms for different speakers. Truman might have had fewer rhetorical problems if he had received input from aides who better understood the relationship between language and thought, as well as the need for a speaker to prepare to deliver a manuscript speech effectively. The process that evolved during the 1948 campaign of using Truman's own words from one speech in another is what any good speechwriter should do. However, it took Truman's staff three years to modify that aspect of their speechwriting system, and even then it was not used extensively in formal addresses after the election.

Keyserling's off-hand remark about Truman's "elocution lessons" suggests that the speechwriting team, and probably Truman himself, viewed speech practice and techniques to enhance delivery as mere gimmicks that were manipulative and somewhat disingenuous. Truman said that a president's "powers depend a good deal on his success in public relations." However, he also believed that some of what he did as public relations should not be necessary: "I sit here at the President's desk talking to people and kissing them on both cheeks trying to get them to do what they ought to do without getting kissed."[68] Working to achieve a more dynamic delivery, Truman apparently believed, was akin to having to kiss someone, when the words alone should have been sufficient regardless of how they were uttered. The fact of the matter is that Truman sometimes did "kiss people on both cheeks" through the delivery of his speeches. More flourish in his delivery and more attention to the strengths of his personal style would have made the words and substance over which his writers labored more effective.

The most significant lesson to be learned about presidential speechwriting from this case study of the Truman White House concerns who is responsible for presidential rhetoric. Regardless of who writes a speech, the president delivers it and owns it. It is the president who suffers from a speech that does not articulate a vision or respond to critics or define the character of the speaker. A president chooses to deliver the words submitted by writers and other staff members. A president establishes the parameters within which the writers work. When the history of a presidency is dissected, a president's public pronouncements provide some of the major clues to its successes and failures. A president who is judged a successful leader is typically one who inspires through words and actions—and whose words explain and defend actions. Thus, the use of words is one of the defining characteristics of a presidency. As Truman's White House and whistle-stop speechwriting processes demonstrate, the words themselves as well as beliefs about language and its relationship to substantive programs reflect both a president's personality and policies. Hence, the speechwriting process itself provides clues about managerial and leadership styles and how decisions were made in the White House.

For rhetorical scholars to fully understand and interpret the relationship between a president's speeches and the inner workings of the administration and its philosophies, they must look at more than the final rhetorical product. Without access to White House archives as well as a thorough set of oral histories and memoirs from Truman and the writers, solving the speechwriting puzzle would have been impossible.

Based on the historical documents left by Truman and his writers, it can be concluded that unlike Noonan, Truman's speechwriters saw him first and always as more than "a foot." Their knowledge of the man and his thinking came from close personal contact. That personal knowledge was reflected in the speeches they gave him to deliver and in the speechwriting system they instituted for his most important set of speeches—the 1948 whistle-stops. While some of the writers' limitations as rhetoricians made Truman's task of leading the country and getting congressional and public support more difficult, their savvy and understanding of the differences between speeches given in the halls of Congress and on train platforms allowed Truman to win a term of his own and to define who he was as a man and a president.

Notes

1. Peggy Noonan, *What I Saw at the Revolution: A Political Life in the Reagan Era* (New York: Random House, 1990), pp. 49, 51, 65.

2. For studies of Truman's presidential rhetoric, see (listed chronologically): Cole S. Brembeck, "Harry Truman at the Whistle-Stops," *Quarterly Journal of Speech* 38 (1952): 42–50; Ray E. McKerrow, "Truman and Korea: Rhetoric in the Pursuit of Victory," *Central States Speech Journal* 28 (1977): 1–12; John E. Hopkins, "An Investigation of the Speech and Statement Preparation Process During the Presidential Administration of Harry S. Truman, 1945–1953" (Ph.D. diss., Ohio University, 1970); Robert Underhill, *The Truman Persuasions* (Ames: Iowa State University, 1981); Robert L. Ivie, "Literalizing the Metaphor of Soviet Savagery: President Truman's Plain Style," *Southern Speech Communication Journal* 51 (1986): 91–105; Bernard K. Duffy, "President Harry S. Truman and Douglas MacArthur: A Study of Rhetorical Confrontation," *Oratorical Encounters,* ed. Halford Ross Ryan (Westport, Conn.: Greenwood Press, 1988), pp. 79–98; Martin J. Medhurst, "Truman's Rhetorical Reticence, 1945–1947: An Interpretive Essay," *Quarterly Journal of Speech* 74 (1988): 52–70; Halford R. Ryan, *Harry S. Truman: Presidential Rhetoric* (Westport, Conn.: Greenwood Press, 1993); Halford Ryan, "President Harry S. Truman's Inaugural Address, 1949," in *Inaugural Addresses of Twentieth-Century American Presidents,* ed. Halford Ryan (Westport, Conn.: Praeger, 1993), pp. 141–51; Halford Ryan, "Harry S. Truman," *U.S. Presidents as Orators* (Westport, Conn.: Greenwood Press, 1995), pp. 168–89; Carol Gelderman, *All the Presidents' Words: The Bully Pulpit and the Creation of the Virtual Presidency* (New York: Walker, 1997), pp. 36–45; Steven R. Goldzwig, "Civil Rights and the Cold War: A Rhetorical History of the Truman Administration's Desegregation of the United States Army," in *Doing Rhetorical History: Concepts and Cases,* ed. Kathleen J. Turner (Tuscaloosa: University of Alabama Press, 1998), 143–69; Garth E. Pauley, "Harry Truman and the NAACP: A Case Study in Presidential Persuasion on Civil Rights," *Rhetoric & Public Affairs* 2 (1999): 211–41; Robert L. Ivie, "Fire, Flood, and Red Fever: Motivating Metaphors of Global Emergency in the Truman Doctrine Speech," *Presidential Studies Quarterly* 29 (1999): 570–91;

and Garth E. Pauley, *The Modern Presidency and Civil Rights: Rhetoric on Race from Roosevelt to Nixon* (College Station: Texas A&M University Press, 2001), 31–57.

3. Karlyn Kohrs Campbell and Kathleen Hall Jamieson, *Deeds Done in Words: Presidential Rhetoric and the Genres of Governance* (Chicago: University of Chicago Press, 1990), p. 68.

4. David McCullough, *Truman* (New York: Simon & Schuster, 1992), pp. 556, 559.

5. Rosenman quoted in Ken Hechler, *Working with Truman: A Personal Memoir of the White House Years* (New York: G. P. Putnam's Sons, 1982), p. 41.

6. Hechler, *Working with Truman,* pp. 11–12.

7. David H. Stowe, "Oral History" (1963), pp. 19–20, Harry S. Truman Library, Independence, Mo. Hereafter materials from the Truman Library are given as HSTL.

8. Charles S. Murphy, "Oral History" (1969), pp. 138–39, HSTL.

9. McCullough, *Truman,* p. 360.

10. Douglas Frantz and David McKean, *Friends in High Places: The Rise and Fall of Clark Clifford* (Boston: Little, Brown, 1995), p. 41.

11. Eben A. Ayers, "Oral History" (1967, 1970), p. 107, HSTL.

12. For example, Clifford said that he wrote the 1950 State of the Union address, but most of the drafts and memos on that address are located in Elsey's and Murphy's files. Handwritten notes at the top of drafts dated December 16 and 28, 1949, indicate that they were "Redrafted" by Murphy, Elsey, Lloyd, Bell, [and] Spingarn. In addition, Frantz and McKean give two examples of Clifford plagiarizing the work of others and passing it off as largely his own. See George M. Elsey, "State of Union Drafts," Papers of George M. Elsey, Box 38, 1950 January State of Union Drafts Folder 1, HSTL, and Frantz and McKean, *Friends in High Places,* pp. 54–55, 70–74.

13. George M. Elsey, "Oral History" (1974, 1976), p. 17, HSTL.

14. Stephen J. Spingarn, "Oral History" (1967), p. 121, HSTL.

15. Harry S. Truman, "Address at a Columbus Day Dinner in New York City, October 11, 1952," *Public Papers of the Presidents: Harry S. Truman, 1952–53* (Washington, D.C.: Government Printing Office, 1966), p. 804. On Lloyd's writing of this passage and favorable audience reaction, see Hechler, *Working with Truman,* p. 227.

16. Leon H. Keyserling, "Oral History" (1971), pp. 103–104, HSTL.

17. Hechler, *Working with Truman,* p. 130.

18. McCullough, *Truman,* p. 679.

19. Spingarn oral history, pp. 118–19.

20. Charles S. Murphy, "Oral History" (1963, 1969, and 1970), p. 456, HSTL.

21. Ayers oral history, p. 120; and Hechler, *Working with Truman,* p. 239.

22. George M. Elsey, "State of the Union Drafts" [undated], Papers of George M. Elsey, Box 38, Speech File Folder 1950, Jan. 4, HSTL.

23. Keyserling oral history, pp. 105, 102.

24. Murphy oral history, p. 3.

25. Lois J. Einhorn, "The Ghosts Talk: Personal Interviews with Three Former Speechwriters," *Communication Quarterly* 36 (1988): 95.

26. Murphy oral history, pp. 134–35.

27. David D. Lloyd, letter to Miss [Phyllis J.] Glessner, 2 March 1951, Papers of George M. Elsey, Box 54, Oct. 52/1953 January Final Truman Message, HSTL.

28. Clark Clifford, "State of the Union," Folder State of the Union 1-7-48, President's Speech File, Papers of Clark M. Clifford, Box 32, HSTL.

29. George M. Elsey, "Status Report," Dec. 12, 1946, Papers of George M. Elsey, Box 16, Speech File 1947-1-6 State of the Union papers, HSTL.

30. Eugene E. White and Clair R. Henderlider, "What Harry S. Truman Told Us About His Speaking," *Quarterly Journal of Speech* 40 (1954): 39–41.

31. David D. Lloyd, "Press release and typewritten note from President Truman" [undated], Papers of David D. Lloyd, Box 27, President's speech file, State of the Union Jan. 4, 1950, HSTL.

32. For example, see "Original Copy Used by President Harry S. Truman, State of the Union Message, January 8, 1951," Papers of Harry S. Truman, President's Secretary's Files, Box 30, Folder President's Speeches—Original, Jan–Mar 51, HSTL. An "embargoed" speech text was one released to the press prior to presentation by the president, which is available on the condition that journalists will refrain from reporting on the text until a specified date and time—usually the time of actual delivery of the speech by the president.

33. Murphy oral history, p. 3.

34. Charles S. Murphy, "Suggestions for Preparing Outlines for Brief Platform Speeches" [undated], Papers of Charles S. Murphy, Box 1, HSTL.

35. Hechler, *Working with Truman,* p. 223.

36. Murphy quoted in Ibid., p. 223.

37. Truman quoted in Hillman, ed., *Mr. President: The First Publication from the Personal Diaries, Private Letters, Papers and Revealing Interviews of Harry S. Truman* (New York: Farrar, Straus and Young, 1952), p. 65.

38. Truman quoted in White and Henderlider, "What Harry S. Truman Told Us," p. 40.

39. Halford R. Ryan, *Harry S. Truman: Presidential Rhetoric* (Westport, Conn.: Greenwood Press, 1993), pp. 8–9.

40. Ayers oral history, p. 119.

41. Elsey quoted in Hechler, *Working with Truman,* p. 131.

42. Elsey oral history, p. 94.

43. Undated draft of the 1949 State of the Union address, Folder—President's Speeches-Original Jan–Mar 49, Papers of Harry S. Truman, Box 27, President's Secretary's Files 1-47-7-49, HSTL.

44. Ibid.

45. Harry S. Truman, "Annual Message to the Congress on the State of the Union, January 4, 1950," *Public Papers, 1950,* p. 7.

46. Truman quoted in Hillman, *Mr. President,* p. 11.

47. Within a decade of Truman leaving the White House, historians were already ranking him as a "near great" president. Within four decades after leaving office, Truman had become an icon with whom both Democratic and Republican presidential candidates tried to identify. See Richard L. Stout, "A Not-so-great Haberdasher; A 'Near Great' President," *Christian Science Monitor,* April 28, 1983, p. B1;

Leslie H. Southwick, compiler, *Presidential Also-Rans and Running Mates, 1788–1980* (Jefferson, N.C.: McFarland & Company, 1984), pp. 692–93; Bill Bradley, "Restoring Trust in America's Message," *Christian Science Monitor,* May 21, 1996, p. 18; and "Historians Rank Presidential Leadership in New C-SPAN Survey," Feb. 21, 2000 <www.americanpresidents.org/survey/>.

48. Ayers oral history, p. 117.

49. Hechler, *Working with Truman,* p. 66.

50. Phileo Nash, "Memoirs" [undated], Papers of Phileo Nash, Box 1, p. 67, HSTL.

51. Truman quoted in White and Henderlider, "What Harry S. Truman Told Us," p. 41.

52. For example, it was almost January, 1949, before Truman first participated in the planning for the 1947 State of the Union. His first speech conference was on December 30, 1946; he worked on the speech a second time on January 4, 1947. See "Daily Presidential Appointments, September 1946—September 1947," Papers of Matthew J. Connelly, Box 2, HSTL.

53. Keyserling oral history, pp. 99–100.

54. Harry S. Truman, "Address in Philadelphia Upon Accepting the Nomination of the Democratic National Convention, July 15, 1948," *Public Papers, 1948,* p. 409.

55. Elsey quoted in Hechler, *Working with Truman,* p. 83.

56. Hechler, *Working with Truman,* p. 66.

57. Jonathan Daniels, *The Man of Independence* (Philadelphia: J.B. Lippincott, 1950), pp. 347–48.

58. Harry S. Truman, "Rear Platform Remarks in California, September 23, 1948 [Fresno, 8:12 A.M.]," *Public Papers, 1948,* pp. 550–51.

59. Truman quoted in Hechler, *Working with Truman,* p. 96.

60. Harry S. Truman, "Rear Platform Remarks in Montana, May 12, 1950 [Missoula, 7:22 A.M.]," *Public Papers, 1950,* p. 377.

61. Hechler, *Working with Truman,* p. 142.

62. Lois J. Einhorn, "The Ghosts Unmasked: A Review of Literature on Speechwriting," *Communication Quarterly* 30 (1981): 44–45.

63. Francis Heller, remark on a panel on "Truman's Rhetoric" held at the Truman Library as part of the Central States Communication Association Convention, Kansas City, Mo., 1989.

64. Charles S. Murphy, "Some Aspects of the Preparation of President Truman's Speeches for the 1948 Campaign," pp. 85–86, Papers of Charles S. Murphy, Box 50, Confidential File—Speech Prep—48 Campaign/Speech Prep Dec. 6, '48, HSTL.

65. Martin J. Medhurst and Gary C. Dreibelbis, "The Ghost of McGovern," *Communication Quarterly* 26 (1978): 42–43.

66. For example, Benjamin Hardy, a junior officer in the public affairs office of the State Department contributed in important ways to Truman's inaugural address. See Halford Ryan, "Harry S. Truman's Inaugural Address, 1949," pp. 141–51.

67. Elsey oral history, p. 47.

68. Truman quoted in Hillman, *Mr. President,* p. 11.

CHAPTER 3

Dwight D. Eisenhower

The 1954 State of the Union Address as a
Case Study in Presidential Speechwriting

CHARLES J. G. GRIFFIN

*The White House methodology is a reflection—a projection of
the man who occupies the office. It has to work the way he's
comfortable with, or it will not work.*
—Bryce Harlow

The Eisenhower presidency for years presented scholars
with the enigma of a leader whose success as a communicator seemed to
come without apparent ability or effort on his own part. While conceding
that he enjoyed "remarkable rhetorical success," critics dismissed Eisenhower
as idle and ineffectual, a "captive hero" with little direct influence over the
working of his own administration.[1] However, recent studies of the
Eisenhower presidency have begun to unravel this mystery and, while he is
not likely to be ranked him among the great presidential orators, a growing number of scholars acknowledge that Eisenhower was a resourceful
and often effective rhetor—and that his success was no accident, but the
product of calculated effort and hard work.[2]

The rising estimate of Eisenhower's rhetorical skill rests largely on rhetorical analyses of his major addresses and crisis discourse. Critical studies
have done much to dispel the myth of Eisenhower's rhetorical indifference
and to explain the power of his appeal to audiences.[3] What is less well
understood is the speechwriting infrastructure which undergirded this success—the people and procedures which were responsible for coordinating
Eisenhower's words and actions through eight eventful years. This chapter

undertakes a preliminary examination of that infrastructure by using Eisenhower's 1954 State of the Union address as a case study of the presidential speechwriting of his administration.[4] Eisenhower used his second annual message, delivered in January, 1954, to set forth the goals of his presidency and to outline the legislative program through which he hoped to achieve those goals. After providing a narrative of the creation of that address, this essay examines three compositional features of the message and explores the extent to which these features proved broadly characteristic of speechwriting methodology in the Eisenhower White House. Finally, the chapter explores some ways in which White House speechwriting methodology may have reflected as well as sustained President Eisenhower's rhetorical leadership.

Eisenhower's 1954 State of the Union Address

Article II, section 3 of the U.S. Constitution specifies that the president shall "from time to time give to the Congress information on the state of the Union and recommend to their consideration such measures as he may judge necessary and expedient." The annual message, or State of the Union address, is among the most significant and complex undertakings of what some scholars have called the "rhetorical presidency."[5] More than a mere meditation on the nation's current condition, the annual message offers the president's vision of its future and program for realizing that vision. As Karlyn Kohrs Campbell and Kathleen Hall Jamieson observe, in the State of the Union address "one hears a government in the act of creating itself." The complexity of the annual message stems from the very things that contribute to its significance: its peculiar blend of deliberative and ceremonial rhetorical functions and comprehensive accounting of diverse government operations.[6]

Eisenhower's first annual message, delivered mere days after his inauguration in January, 1953, was, of necessity, a fairly cautious document. But he held much greater ambitions for his State of the Union address the following year. Writing to his brother Milton in November, 1953, Eisenhower allowed that "it has been our general intention to use 1953 as a period of study and formulation of programs. We have always felt that the 'Administration Bible' would be brought out for publication in the delivery of the 1954 Message to the Congress." True to this expectation, the fifty-three minute address outlined Eisenhower's legislative agenda in areas as diverse as defense and conservation, housing and postal reform. In his memoirs, the former president recalled that the 1954 State of the Union address embodied "the most massive and comprehensive set of recommendations" of his entire eight years, on which the "entire prestige" of his administration had rested.[7]

Given the importance that Eisenhower himself attached to his 1954 State of the Union address, the story of its composition is not without interest to students of speechwriting in his presidency. The following brief narrative, while necessarily incomplete in some respects, is sufficiently detailed to convey a sense of the process by which the speech was composed and to provide a foundation for discussing the relationship between speechwriting and policy making during the Eisenhower years.

Eisenhower delivered his second annual message before a joint session of Congress and a national television audience at 12:30 P.M. on January 7, 1954. The president's address brought to fruition a process whose roots extended back in time some six months, to late July, 1953. A July 30 memorandum from the president, citing the need to begin planning for the 1954 State of the Union message, directed cabinet secretaries and other key administrators to undertake a "thorough rethinking of the mission of your Department and the means to achieve it." These efforts, Eisenhower directed, should "complement the attention you are giving the 1955 budget in the next six weeks and the formulation of a carefully planned, specific legislative program." The president declared that the new administration had an "historic opportunity" to move the nation forward and to "demonstrate that the goals our people want . . . can be achieved by means other than those that result in making Big Government bigger."[8] He then directed that memoranda summarizing each department's mission-review process reach the White House not later than October 15, 1953.

The work of carving a finished speech from the mountain of material that began to accumulate at the White House in early October required the combined efforts of many individuals, beginning with Eisenhower's chief of staff, Sherman Adams. Adams officially was charged with oversight of all speechwriting projects. But the White House staff over which he presided included a member specifically assigned to speechwriting duties. In the autumn of 1953, that individual was Bryce N. Harlow. Harlow was an experienced speechwriter and political strategist who had only recently taken the position after a stint on the White House congressional relations staff. He was assigned the title administrative assistant to the president.

However, Adams's staff also included other individuals with speechwriting expertise. One of these was Dr. Gabriel Hauge, the president's personal economic advisor. Hauge had written speeches for Eisenhower during the 1952 presidential campaign, but it was his grasp of administration economic policy that made him indispensable to the State of the Union project. Hauge's position and expertise enabled him to coordinate the annual message with the administration's Economic Report and it's Budget Message, which were due to be released at about the same time as Eisenhower's annual message. Thus it was to Hauge, rather than the newly arrived Harlow, that Adams assigned responsibility for the initial planning of the annual message.

On November 6, 1953, Hauge met with the small group of staff members who would be developing the so-called "January documents." In addition to Harlow, who would be responsible for writing the State of the Union address, the group included representatives from Treasury, the Bureau of the Budget, and the Council of Economic Advisors. Hauge's intent was to develop a strategic plan for the three messages and to divide labor accordingly. The three agreed that the annual message would "contain an accounting of our stewardship in the first year, . . . present the main foreign policy and defense programs, and . . . set forth the leading ideas of our economic philosophy and program of the Administration." The speech would be less detailed than the other messages, but would nonetheless present the "principal elements in the legislative program." And it would be held to such a length that "the President could deliver it before Congress in person if he so wished."[9] Harlow, writing his first State of the Union address, emerged from this meeting with several valuable insights into the constraints under which he would be working in the coming weeks.

Armed with this information and with material submitted from some two dozen departments and agencies as a result of the president's July directive, Harlow assembled his own team on November 17, 1953. He divided the complex speech into topic areas, assigning these to staff members with subject competence in the relevant areas. For example, Max Rabb, Eisenhower's special assistant for minority affairs, was given responsibility for drafting portions of the speech dealing with social security, welfare, health, and civil rights. C. D. Jackson, the president's advisor on Cold War psychological operations, was assigned the international affairs sections. Hauge himself was given responsibility for several additional portions of the speech. Seven or eight additional assignments were made. Each writer was supplied background material collected by Harlow and given a tentative word limit for his portion of the speech. Section drafts were to be submitted to Harlow by December 1, 1953.[10]

While awaiting this material, Harlow continued to receive input both directly and indirectly from Eisenhower: "I had several conferences in this period with the President. I started receiving from him short paragraphs. I started receiving from him pages of dictation, ideas. I started receiving in my office people whom he would send over to talk to me about ideas they had expressed to him." Eisenhower's contributions included a three-page draft introduction which, he insisted to Harlow, was simply for "consideration. It is *not* to be accepted merely because I wrote it." A day or two later the president sent along an addendum, directing Harlow to "definitely announce, right after the opening paragraphs, that I am bringing a message of hope." Eisenhower then identified several areas in which the "situation" had "vastly improved" in recent years. He wanted his speechwriter to emphasize the long view, the sense that the nation was moving in the right direction.[11]

Harlow's deadline came and went. But two days later, he had yet to receive most of the section drafts he had requested by December 1, 1953. A glance at the President's calendar for early December offers one possible explanation for the delay. Last minute preparations were under way for the Bermuda summit with British Prime Minister Winston Churchill and French Premier Joseph Laniel, scheduled for December 4–8. Immediately following the summit, the president was to fly to New York for an appearance before the United Nations General Assembly. There he would deliver his historic Atoms for Peace speech.[12]

It was not until December 14, 1953, that Harlow was able to piece together a draft of the entire State of the Union address, minus C. D. Jackson's international section and the conclusion. Now Harlow had a new concern, confiding to Press Secretary James Hagerty that the draft was several pages too long—a problem likely to worsen, since Harlow felt certain that some agencies not mentioned in the draft "will try to get in." Nonetheless, he expressed some satisfaction that "these 8500 words are a compression of approximately 28,000 words which were submitted to me."[13]

Two days later, Harlow sat down to go over his draft with Eisenhower. The two met for an hour and a half. Dozens of changes in substance and style were suggested by Eisenhower and a few by Harlow as well. The president felt that the speech needed more emphasis on "looking ahead, not looking back" and, evidently forgetful of his earlier assurances to Harlow, questioned why his own introduction had not been used. At the conclusion of their session, Eisenhower asked Harlow to travel to State College,

Pennsylvania, in order to go over the entire draft with his brother Milton, then president of Pennsylvania State University.[14]

On December 18, 1953 Adams circulated a "first draft" of the speech to all department and agency heads, as well as a number of other key administration figures. The recipients, more than forty altogether, were advised that the draft was some ten pages too long and were encouraged to submit recommendations for the next revision. "Please do not feel constrained to limit your comments to any particular section of the message," Adams added casually—an invitation, which must have made Harlow cringe.[15]

Between December 18 and December 28, 1953, two additional drafts of the speech were completed. At Harlow's request, John Jessup, chief editorial writer for *Life* magazine, lent his editorial skills to the project. More changes and a fourth draft followed on December 29. On New Year's Day, Harlow and other key staff members assembled in Georgia where the president was enjoying a short vacation. While Eisenhower rested and golfed at Augusta National, the staff labored over draft number five. Press Secretary Hagerty's diary for January 1, 1954, describes a lengthy holiday work session: "In Augusta. Worked on State of the Union message at office at National. Adams, Lodge, Dodge, Martin, Harlow, Morgan, Jessup. President worked in the morning . . . Group worked until 1:30 A.M." A sixth draft followed on January 2, 1954; a seventh the next day.[16]

Eisenhower returned to Washington on January 3, 1954, and the following evening delivered a fifteen-minute talk on national television. "We have had a year of progress and can look ahead with confidence," he began. Then he spoke of his State of the Union message, due to be delivered later in the week. He would not, he said, preview the speech in detail, but he did wish to "review, briefly, the aims and purposes of this administration— in what direction we are headed and how we propose to get there."[17]

On January 6, 1954, the full cabinet met to give the speech a final review. The meeting, a vintage example of Eisenhower's group-centered leadership style, left a vivid impression on Harlow. Years later, he recalled, "The Cabinet met that morning, and I had to read the message to the Cabinet, and the Cabinet was to take notes as I read, and then after I finished, to comment on the message, and the President was to tell me as they commented whether or not to make the change that that Cabinet officer might think desirable." Harlow spent the remainder of that day and all night reworking the speech. "The President gave me some extensive editings late that evening," he recalled, "which I also had to incorporate in, and across and through other changes that had already been made."[18]

By Thursday morning, January 7, 1954, Harlow had completed a "final" draft of the speech. But he was not finished yet. At about 10:30 A.M., Eisenhower and Secretary of State John Foster Dulles notified Press Secretary Hagerty that they had been at work on some new material for possible insertion into the speech. In the end, the material in question was not included in the speech. Finally, the speech was typed in the extra-large print face favored by the president, who made several last-minute editorial changes on his way to the Capitol. At 12:30 P.M., Eisenhower went before a joint session of Congress and a national television audience to deliver his second annual message.[19]

The story of the 1954 State of the Union address offers several important lessons about the speechwriting methodology of the Eisenhower White House. Three aspects of that story warrant especially close attention: (1) the use of a "flexible staffing" system which drew on both formal and informal staff resources during the composition process; (2) Eisenhower's personal involvement in the project; and (3) the deliberate integration of speechwriting and policy-making activities as the speech evolved. The remainder of this chapter explores these features in greater depth and examines the degree to which each was characteristic of the Eisenhower White House speechwriting practice in general.

Flexible Staffing System

In *The Hidden-Hand Presidency*, political scientist Fred I. Greenstein described Eisenhower's "binocular perspective on leadership." Greenstein argued that "Eisenhower ran organizations by deliberately making simultaneous use of both formal and informal organization." On the one hand, he was "highly attentive to finding orderly formal procedures for ensuring that routine or repetitive tasks were carried out reliably, consistently and systematically." At the same time, Eisenhower "placed at least equal emphasis on informal aspects of organizational leadership."[20]

The composition process employed in the 1954 State of the Union address illustrated Eisenhower's penchant for supplementing formal with informal staff resources. Responsibility for the speech rested formally with Adams. According to formal staff procedure, Adams should then have delegated research and writing responsibilities to Harlow, who would, in turn, make assignments of his own. But as we have already seen, Adams adapted to the peculiar demands of the annual message by asking Gabriel Hauge to play an intermediary role between himself and Harlow. Moreover, as work on the speech progressed Harlow augmented his own staff by calling on the help of Hauge, C. D. Jackson, Milton Eisenhower, John Jessup, and others, including the president.

The practice of "flexible staffing" appears to have been characteristic of administration speechwriting methodology throughout Eisenhower's two terms. Adams, who directed the White House staff through August, 1958, offered a more extensive picture of the formal side of the flexible staffing process in his memoirs. Adams described the operation of a "calendar committee," composed of White House Appointments Secretary Thomas Stephens, Press Secretary James Hagerty, the president's personal economic advisor Gabriel Hauge, "and other principal staff members." Eisenhower's practice was to include his chief speechwriter in this group. One obvious result of this move was to bring the speechwriting operation into the mainstream of administration policy making by placing it in the staff chain of command. This facilitated coordination of speechwriting and policy making because it channeled both activities through the same group of individuals. Another, not incidental, effect of this arrangement was to confer upon a presidential speechwriter a certain degree of status, which could prove helpful in his dealings with other senior level administrators.[21]

According to Adams, the calendar committee met regularly to discuss Eisenhower's public appearances. Speaking invitations were carefully screened. Once an engagement had received tentative approval, and the committee had discussed the general objectives and nature of the speech, the head speechwriter was charged with developing a rough draft of the proposed speech. This draft was then brought back to the committee for comment. The process continued until an acceptable draft had been produced. Only then, wrote Adams, would he "pitch" the proposed speech to the president. Eisenhower usually required a few days to mull over the speech, before making his decision. According to Adams, about two-thirds of the president's speaking engagements were handled in this manner. In other instances, Eisenhower himself would initiate the speechwriting process by notifying Adams that he wished to address a particular issue or appear before a particular audience. From that point, the process would work much as before.[22]

Any discussion of the "formal" speechwriting organization within the Eisenhower White House would be incomplete without some discussion, however brief, of the five men who held the head speechwriter position during the life of the administration. The first of these individuals was Emmet John Hughes. Hughes was a journalist by profession, with a background and interest in international affairs. He had been recruited to help draft speeches for Eisenhower during the 1952 presidential campaign by C. D. Jackson, a colleague at Time, Inc. Hughes was a gifted stylist, whose soaring, idealistic prose Eisenhower admired in spite of his own more pragmatic habits of expression. He wrote some of Eisenhower's most eloquent speeches, including both inaugurals and (with Robert Cutler and C. D. Jackson), the moving Chance for Peace, which Eisenhower delivered in April, 1953.

Hughes's tenure as chief speechwriter, however, was destined to be brief. An ardent internationalist, Hughes clashed repeatedly with Dulles, Eisenhower's hawkish secretary of state. He also grew increasingly frustrated with Eisenhower's unwillingness to confront publicly the bellicose Senator Joseph McCarthy. Hughes resigned his post to return to *Time/Life* in October, 1953, although he continued to write for Eisenhower on an occasional basis for several years.[23]

Bryce Harlow succeeded Hughes in September, 1953. Harlow had an extensive background in congressional liaison work, first with the U.S. Army and later in the White House congressional relations office under Gen. Wilton Persons. He approached the speechwriting post from a more sophisticated, pragmatic vantage point than had Hughes. For this very reason, perhaps, he also came rather reluctantly. "I knew what it was," he recalled in an interview years later, "the business of writing speeches for great people is not the most enjoyable work in the world . . . particularly if the person for whom you're writing is a skilled writer himself." Pressed to take the job, Harlow agreed only after gaining Adams's consent that he would be allowed to "spend a great deal of time in the presence of the President so I could understand how he liked to express himself, what he was thinking about, what his concerns were, his chance remarks—understand the client in order to write for the client." As a result, Harlow was given access to most White House activities, including legislative meetings, National Security Council meetings, and press briefings.[24]

Harlow was a savvy and experienced political infighter. "He was all meat and potatoes—solid legislative proposals, tough argumentation, facts and figures and political statistics . . . ," according to one assistant, William Bragg Ewald, Jr. Ewald described the speechwriting technique of his boss as "Harlowizing—writing 'as though you're arguing with somebody,' and driving, polishing, toughening, livening all the way." In addition to Ewald, Harlow was assisted by Kevin McCann and, on an occasional basis, by Charles Moore, Jr., (public relations director for Ford Motor Company) and John Jessup (chief editorial writer for *Life* magazine). Harlow remained as head speechwriter until about January, 1955, when he left to resume work as a congressional liaison. Kevin McCann succeeded Harlow.[25]

McCann was a personal friend of the president. The two had worked together during Eisenhower's tenure at Supreme Headquarters, Allied Powers in Europe (SHAPE) in 1951–52. McCann had been with Eisenhower during his service as president of Columbia University, and during the 1952 presidential campaign. After the election, McCann departed Eisenhower's staff to become president of Defiance College in Ohio. However, he returned to serve the president on a part-time basis in 1953 and full time from 1954 until 1957. Thereafter he was called back periodically, rejoining the administration full time during its final months.

Though he lacked Hughes's soaring style and Harlow's political seasoning, McCann, perhaps more than any of Eisenhower's other head writers, understood his principal. McCann's grasp of Eisenhower's personality and idiom enabled him to write for the president across a broad spectrum of topics. By his own account, he was more "amanuensis" than "ghostwriter."[26]

When McCann returned to academia in October, 1957, Arthur Larson succeeded him. A former law school dean, Larson was already a veteran administration figure, having served first as undersecretary of labor and then as director of the United States Information Agency (USIA). The latter experience, especially, had convinced Larson that "the President of the United States was the most effective single educational medium in the country." Perhaps this is one reason for Larson's ambitious campaign to build up the White House speechwriting staff. He recruited Frederick Morrow, the first African American to serve on the White House speechwriting staff; Malcolm Moos, a political scientist from Johns Hopkins University who joined the staff on a part-time basis in 1957; and Fred Fox, an ordained minister who specialized in ceremonial and short messages. Larson also developed what he called "the White House idea center," a sort of clearing house for creative ideas and action plans culled from newspapers and academic journals, which might be of use in presidential speeches.[27]

Larson, like Harlow, was a seasoned Washington hand. But like Hughes, he could be stubborn and difficult. According to Morrow, his assistant, Larson was totally dedicated to his job, but "wanted to be the sergeant and the commanding officer and everything else . . . ." In the fall of 1958 Larson resigned to head up the newly founded Rule of Law Center at Duke University.[28]

Larson was succeeded by Malcolm Moos, a former professor of political science at Johns Hopkins University and an established figure in Republican intellectual circles. Moos approached the speechwriter's job much differently than the remote, intense Larson. One assistant described him as perhaps "the ideal person for that job. . . . I never saw him flustered, never saw him distraught or burdened or anything of that nature. He always had a wonderful sense of humor, a complete gentleman, a little wisp of a guy—you'd think that a good puff of wind would blow him away—but he sure had a lot of character and a lot of strength about him." Moos himself described the speechwriter's job in simple, pragmatic terms: "I try to find out what the President wants to say, and help him say it in the best way."[29]

Moos presided over the speechwriting operation during the waning days of the Eisenhower administration. Adams was no longer chief of staff, succeeded by "the more easy-going" Gen. Wilton Persons. As a result, Moos enjoyed more informal access to the president than his predecessors did. He was assisted by Capt. Ralph Williams (USN) and a young Stephen Hess.[30]

The five men who held the formal position of head speechwriter during the Eisenhower years differed widely in background, temperament, and management style. Yet, the existence of a formal staff plan that integrated the speechwriting operation into the White House staff system helped to ensure that there would be continuity in the speechwriting operation, despite these differences.

But as the foregoing narrative of the creation of the 1954 State of the Union makes clear, speechwriting methodology in the Eisenhower White House involved the use of informal as well as formal organizational resources. One such resource was the use of "outside" writers to augment the work of the speechwriting staff. The most prominent of these "shadow speechwriters" have been identified already in connection with the 1954 annual message: Gabriel Hauge, C. D. Jackson, and Milton Eisenhower. Though none worked within the formal speechwriting regime, they were men of broad-ranging political and rhetorical expertise whose labors added depth and continuity to the speechwriting process throughout the life of the administration. It would be difficult to overstate their contributions to Eisenhower's rhetorical success.[31]

Other individuals within the administration also contributed to the speechwriting process on a regular basis. For example, it was not unusual for cabinet secretaries and other senior administrators to provide input into speeches relating to their particular areas, much as they did in the 1954

State of the Union project. And for political speeches, significant input often came to the White House from Republican Party officials.[32]

Another aspect of the flexible staffing process was the occasional "subcontracting" of speechwriting projects. That is, in some instances, speeches were developed entirely outside the formal speechwriting structure. Prominent examples include Eisenhower's Atoms for Peace speech (December 8, 1953) and his second inaugural address (January 21, 1957). The former was written by Jackson, with help from Robert Cutler, Eisenhower's national security advisor, and Lewis Strauss, chairman of the Atomic Energy Commission. Eisenhower had Emmet Hughes (by then at *Life* magazine) write his 1957 inaugural. Having been a speechwriter himself during his days as an aide to Gen. Douglas MacArthur in the Philippines, Eisenhower was well aware of the perils of speechwriting by committee. But he also understood the value of teamwork and believed in augmenting formal with informal organizational resources when possible. Through the system of flexible staffing in his speechwriting operation, Eisenhower sought to reap the rewards of teamwork while avoiding its drawbacks.[33]

Involvement by the President

To those inclined to view Eisenhower as a benign and inattentive figurehead, the story of the 1954 State of the Union message must give pause, revealing as it does a president fully engaged in the compositional process. Eisenhower contributed to the inventional aspect of the annual message in several ways. First, his July 30 memorandum to cabinet officers and agency heads effectively delineated the scope of the speech by detailing both the kind of information departments were to submit (i.e., "a thorough rethinking of the mission of your department and the means to achieve it") and the form in which they were to submit it (i.e., mission-review memoranda). Eisenhower also influenced the emerging speech by specifying its length and basic format. According to Harlow, Eisenhower believed that the "ideal" State of the Union message "should be at the most 40 minutes" and felt that the inclusion of too much detail in the annual message "was a mistake, because it would be more likely to confuse than to enlighten the country."[34]

Eisenhower also shaped the speech by furnishing its basic theme. As Harlow later observed: "what the President has to do . . . is to decide what will be the center of emphasis in his message . . . So there's a unifying theme in the entire document. What is the administration seeking fundamentally to accomplish, that is a concerted single purpose, that is comprehensible by the American people, and that makes good sense and will rally the country to that object?" Eisenhower's suggestion to Harlow that the speech convey a message of "hope" and positive momentum provided just such a theme for the State of the Union address. It enabled Harlow to sift through the thousands of words submitted by administration agencies to discover the most relevant and useful contributions.[35]

But Eisenhower's involvement in the speechwriting process went well beyond proffering general advice about scope, format, and theme. Notes from a meeting between the president and Harlow on December 16, 1953, reveal the extent of Eisenhower's willingness to engage in the "nuts and bolts" of message construction. As the two men pored over Harlow's first draft of the annual message, Eisenhower made several broad observations:

1. Needs general tightening up editorially. Use blue pencil.
2. Needs to be cut down considerably.
3. Sections need to be more distinctly marked. Do not be afraid to say "I come now to so-and-so." President said, "you cannot take the human mind from subject to subject . . . as quickly as that." Said he had difficulty deciding what paragraph was about, even in reading.
4. He said he assumed that the order of sections had been carefully considered.[36]

In all, Eisenhower dictated more than thirty specific changes to the text, most of which reflected his desire to make the message more accessible to the average listener. For example, he suggested that Harlow recast phrases such as "substantial reductions in size and cost of Federal government" and "attacks on deficit spending," because "the man we are trying to reach understands 'purchasing power of the dollar'—understands stability in 'the size of his market basket.'" Other changes reflected Eisenhower's desire to emphasize (or de-emphasize) various proposals contained in the speech. He directed Harlow to "[m]ake the section on S. Lawrence Seaway a little stronger. I regard its approval as urgent in the interest of both our economic growth and national security."[37]

Eisenhower's involvement in the 1954 annual message raises the issue of the nature and extent of his participation in the speechwriting process generally. The available evidence suggests that Eisenhower generally entered into the speechwriting process at a later point than he did in the 1954

State of Union. In this regard, Sherman Adams's recollections of the White House speechwriting process seem largely accurate. However, it would be a mistake to conclude from Adams's remarks that Eisenhower took little interest in the speechwriting process. Rather, the president's strategic conception of rhetoric simply required that he be sold on the objective of a speech project before he committed himself to pursue it. Adams recalled ruefully: "I found out early in the game that Eisenhower expected anyone who proposed a speech to him to have the reasons for making it thoroughly thought out. 'What is it that needs to be said' Eisenhower would say. 'I am not going out there just to listen to my tongue clatter.'" Emmet Hughes recalled that Eisenhower rebelled against "the calculatedly rhetorical device. . . . All oratorical flourishes made the man uneasy, as if he feared the chance that some hearer might catch him *trying* to be persuasive." Arthur Larson concluded much the same after coming to work for Eisenhower in 1957: "Every speech must have a Q.E.D.," he recalled Eisenhower insisting. "I don't want to give a speech just to hear my voice. I want to say something."[38]

Capt. Ralph Williams, who served as an assistant to Malcolm Moos, offered his own view of Eisenhower's role in the speechwriting process:

> [Eisenhower] wanted his speeches to come up to him as, to use the military definition, "completed staff work": the whole thing laid out, tailored to the audience with every thing in there that should be said to that audience. . . . He would look at it and at this point he would begin to think about it. But he needed the full text version to stimulate his own thought processes. The more he would read, the more involved—and intensely involved—he would get. He would get completely immersed in the speech before it was over. . . . [H]e would find some things that he would throw out and other ideas that he would think about, and he would scribble them into the marginal notes. He'd call in Ann Whitman and he'd dictate maybe two or three pages of new material. And so, draft by draft, it literally became his very own speech from the beginning to the end.[39]

The 1954 State of the Union speech offers a fair representation of the extent and nature of Eisenhower's involvement once he did enter the speechwriting process. Eisenhower's chief speechwriters were unanimous in their insistence that he was an exacting editor who devoted hours of close study to major speech projects. Hughes, for example, found that Eisenhower possessed "a remarkably quick and exacting faculty for editing." Harlow thought him "an absolutely demanding editor . . . very sensitive to phrasing and emphasis and documentation, a very tough editor." McCann allowed that when Eisenhower "works on a speech . . . you can't recognize the original, because he writes all around it and all over it, fills up the margins, and it becomes almost illegible." Larson noted that Eisenhower "reworked and revised his manuscripts endlessly." And Moos found him "uncannily rigorous" in his attention to speech organization and style. Ann Whitman, Eisenhower's personal secretary, estimated that he spent some "twenty to thirty hours on each major speech."[40]

Eisenhower followed conscious rules of composition in editing the work of his speechwriters. Arthur Larson identified several of the stylistic virtues that Eisenhower expected his writers to observe, which may be paraphrased as follows:

1. Substantiveness: speeches should have valid and necessary objectives.
2. Brevity: speeches should run no longer than absolutely necessary.
3. Simplicity: words should not call attention to themselves.
4. Precision: words should be chosen for correctness and clarity.
5. Accuracy: speeches should avoid unqualified assertions.
6. Dignity: speeches should reflect a level of dignity appropriate to the office of the presidency.

As his involvement in the 1954 State of the Union address makes clear, Eisenhower was willing to go to great lengths to achieve these compositional objectives.[41]

In sum, Eisenhower was at times involved at all levels of the speechwriting process. But his characteristic approach was not to enter into the process until his staff had developed a working speech draft. From that point on, he would fully immerse himself in the project, revising speech texts virtually to the moment of their delivery. In doing so, Eisenhower operated from a conscious set of compositional principles.

Synthesis of Speechwriting and Policy Making

Recent rhetorical scholarship has done much to illuminate Eisenhower's role as a rhetorical strategist who used words as well as policies to further his objectives. Although he was no great orator, he was unusually sensitive to the power of words and to the persuasive implications of his policy decisions. As Martin J. Medhurst has observed, Eisenhower was a master at using "language as action and action as language." The process that led to the 1954 State of the Union exemplifies one facet of Eisenhower's skill as a "strategic communicator": the intentional synthesis of speechwriting and policy-making activities.[42]

It seems clear that Eisenhower regarded the approaching State of the Union as the opening salvo in the coordinated rhetorical and legislative offensive that would define his presidency. After informing his brother Milton that he intended to bring out the "Administration Bible" in his speech, Eisenhower added: "Once we have taken our stand on that program and specified in it the measures on which priority action is mandatory, then, of course, all of us, with me in the lead, will constantly pound the drums for the necessary legislation. I suspect that all kinds of conferences, arguments, speeches and other forms of persuasive action will have to be taken, both clandestinely and publicly, to implement the program." The State of the Union speech, he concluded, was to offer "a very thoughtful and comprehensive program—one that will constitute our platform on which we will take a battling stand."[43]

Eisenhower's memorandum to cabinet secretaries and agency heads on July 30, 1953, affords valuable insight into his strategy for coordinating rhetoric and policy to win the "battle" ahead. By directing administrators to submit mission statements that explained how, through specific legislative and budgetary initiatives, their units would contribute to the goals framing the upcoming annual message, the memorandum effectively linked administration policy making to the speechwriting process. This decision introduced several rhetorical constraints into the policy-making process.

First, Eisenhower's methodology constrained the policy-making process by linking it to the timetable and format of his annual message. The multifaceted nature of the annual message meant that space within the text was at a premium. As a result, both the number of words accorded to a department or agency and the location of those words within the text became matters of contention. Those programs whose contributions to the speech conformed (or could be made to conform) to the theme and stylistic tone of the emerging message simply stood a better chance of inclusion in the speech.

Harlow summed up the policy ramifications of such textual constraints, noting that the "essential theme" chosen by the president for the annual message became the gate through which the "immense aggregations of programs and policies and recommendations and aspirations and desires for places in the sun" had to pass: "Once you establish the theme of this story, then there are all types of experience that flow from it, because by definition it will exclude, as of lesser significance, and relegate to other messages and to lesser documents, matters of intense interest, shall we say, to the Attorney General of the United States or the Secretary of State even. . . ."[44]

Another way in which the compositional requirements of the annual message influenced policy making lay in the area of style. At the November 6, 1953, conference called by Hauge, it had been decided that the annual message would spell out the legislative program "in more or less detail."[45] Those departments whose contributions to the speech failed to recognize this stylistic standard found themselves in difficulty. For instance, on December 9, 1953, Harlow returned material submitted by the Defense Department for the State of the Union speech on grounds that it was "too unspecific in its recital of the accomplishments of the past year . . . and entirely too vague about the program recommended for the calendar year 1954." He continued, "Being vague, it is entirely too long; it should not exceed 1200–1500 words. This portion of the message, critically important as it is, must be hard-hitting and aggressive. I do not feel that, in its present form, it has these attributes. This may be due in large measure to its relative lack of substance." Harlow urged Deputy Secretary of Defense Roger Kyes to prepare a "more authoritative and a more detailed version" of the Defense program as soon as possible.[46]

The methodology of composing the 1954 annual message also integrated speechwriting and policy making by compelling those responsible for these activities to assume some responsibility for one another's work. The most obvious example here is that of Harlow, whose control of the text placed him in the role of "gatekeeper" within the policy-making process. He remarked:

> At one point, I remember, I had a Cabinet officer with me and four waiting to see me, each of them insistent that the area involving their activities be expanded in the State of the Union Message. They were unhappy that their areas had been compressed as much as they had been in the Message, and were in with revised language, demanding that more space be given to their problems; to which I had to respond that the President says he wants this document kept shorter than a two hour speech, and if you want to go beyond what the document as it's shaping [up] includes, you'll have to go see him personally.

Harlow later recalled that the 1954 State of the Union was especially difficult because "it was the first step up to bat of all his new cabinet officers,
with their programs, looking not just to the year ahead, of course. These
programs in the 'State of the Union' messages project over the years ahead."
The cabinet officers, of course, recognized the consequences of having their
programs in the address—or excluded from it. As a result, Harlow explained, there was "an extremely difficult demand on the time available in
that particular message."[47]

And just as Eisenhower's speechwriters were given influence over the
substance of the address, so too his policy makers were given a say about its
form and style. Adams circulated drafts of the speech to department and
agency heads on at least two occasions prior to the final read-through at
the cabinet meeting on January 6, 1954, inviting senior administrators to
put their blue pencils to work. Some did so with a vengeance.[48]

The deliberate synthesis of speechwriting and policy making was a fairly
consistent principle throughout the Eisenhower years. It was encouraged,
certainly, by Adams's tendency to seek the advice of men such as Hauge,
C. D. Jackson, and Milton Eisenhower when developing major speeches.
It was also encouraged by the appointment of head speechwriters from the
administration's policy-making circles—people such as Harlow and Larson.
Yet another factor was Eisenhower's willingness to allow his writers to
pursue rhetorical initiatives, which had significant policy implications.
This willingness was apparent in early speeches such as the Chance for
Peace (1953), and there is evidence that it became more prevalent in the
administration's later years.[49]

Conclusion

Eisenhower's 1954 State of the Union address resulted from a compositional process that exhibited several key features: flexible staffing, presidential involvement, and deliberate integration of speechwriting and policy
making. Each of these features may be viewed as broadly characteristic of
speechwriting methodology in the Eisenhower White House. In concluding, this essay considers briefly some of the implications of the foregoing
analysis for our understanding of Eisenhower's rhetorical leadership.

One conclusion of this study is that Eisenhower's penchant for combining formal and informal organizations extended to the White House
speechwriting operation. Speechwriting responsibilities were fully integrated
into White House chain of command. However, neither Eisenhower nor

his chief of staff hesitated to supplement this formal apparatus with other staff resources when doing so proved expedient. Indeed, on some occasions, they bypassed the formal staff process altogether.

Flexible staffing methodology enabled Eisenhower to realize several advantages. Most obviously, it allowed him to reap the benefits of a clearly delineated staff structure without denying himself access to other resources. It also enabled Eisenhower to apply his philosophy of group-centered leadership to the speechwriting process. By broadening the base of participation in the speechwriting process, without diffusing ultimate accountability for its results, flexible staffing helped to cement the commitment of Eisenhower's subordinates to the final product and to the "White House team," while promoting loyalty to its leader. Third, by drawing on a broad spectrum of viewpoints, flexible staffing enabled Eisenhower to avoid extremes and to maintain the "balanced middle of the road approach" that he favored in both his words and his actions.[50]

A second general conclusion of this essay is that Eisenhower was both willing and well qualified to involve himself in the speechwriting process. His involvement could span the entire composition process, but typically came in its later stages. However, once involved in the process Eisenhower tended to become very involved. This finding raises additional implications for our understanding of Eisenhower's rhetorical leadership. To begin with, it supports the contention that Eisenhower was a leader actively engaged in day-to-day conduct of his administration. It also corroborates the view that while Eisenhower may have had little use for "mere rhetoric," he nonetheless attached great importance to the power of words and worked hard and long to use them effectively. Moreover, the nature of Eisenhower's involvement in the composition process suggests that he understood the role that language played in making his policies appealing to average Americans and in sustaining his popular image as a hero with a common touch. Eisenhower's editorial practices consistently aimed at identifying himself and his ideas with the typical citizen. In sum, Eisenhower was not merely involved in the speechwriting process; he made important contributions to its success.

A third general conclusion of this study is that White House speechwriting methodology both reflected and served Eisenhower's strategic approach to communication by deliberately merging speechwriting and policy-formation activities. White House procedures were designed to ensure coordination between the president's actions and words by: (1) channeling speech projects through a calendar committee (which included policy makers as well as writers); and (2) establishing conditions in which policy makers were allowed to influence the writing process and writers to influence the policy-making process.

The enigma of Eisenhower's rhetorical success will be fully resolved when scholars can account not only for the appeal of his discourse but also for the methods of its production. The findings disclosed in this essay suggest that Eisenhower employed a speechwriting regime, which reflected as well as served his leadership style, lending credence to the view that behind the famous Eisenhower smile resided a shrewd and resourceful rhetorical strategist.

Notes

The author wishes to acknowledge the generous assistance of Mr. David Haight of the Dwight D. Eisenhower Library in Abilene, Kans., along with that of Professors Rachel Holloway and Henry Z. Scheele, whose comments on an earlier version of this chapter were most helpful.

The chapter epigraph is from Stephen J. Wayne and James F. C. Hyde, interview with Bryce N. Harlow, OH 402, May 30, 1974, p. 18, Dwight D. Eisenhower Library, Abilene, Kans. Unless otherwise noted, all unpublished materials are from the Eisenhower Library.

1. See, for example, James David Barber, *The Presidential Character: Predicting Performance in the White House*, 3d ed. (Englewood Cliffs: Prentice Hall, 1985), pp. 134–48; and Marquis Childs, *Eisenhower: The Captive Hero* (New York: Harcourt Brace, 1958).

2. See Fred I. Greenstein, *The Hidden-Hand Presidency: Eisenhower as Leader* (New York: Basic Books, 1982); Anthony James Joes, "Eisenhower Revisionism: The Tide Comes In," *Presidential Studies Quarterly* 15 (1985): 561–71; and Gordon Hoxie, Eisenhower and Presidential Leadership," *Presidential Studies Quarterly* 15 (1985): 561–71.

3. Barber, *The Presidential Character*, p. 138. See, for example, Martin J. Medhurst, *Dwight D. Eisenhower: Strategic Communicator* (Westport, Conn.: Greenwood Press, 1993); and Martin J. Medhurst, ed., *Eisenhower's War of Words: Rhetoric and Leadership* (East Lansing: Michigan State University Press, 1994). For other studies of Eisenhower's presidential rhetoric, see (chronological): Richard E. Crable, "Ike: Identification, Argument, and Paradoxical Appeal," *Quarterly Journal of Speech* 63 (1977): 188–95; Martin J. Medhurst, "Eisenhower's 'Atoms for Peace' Speech: A Case Study in the Strategic Use of Language," *Communication Monographs* 54 (1987): 204–20; Henry Z. Scheele, "The 1956 Nomination of Dwight D. Eisenhower: Maintaining the Hero Image," *Presidential Studies Quarterly* 17

(1987): 459–71; Lawrence W. Haapanen, "Nikita S. Khrushchev vs. Dwight D. Eisenhower" in *Oratorical Encounters: Selected Studies and Sources of Twentieth-Century Political Accusations and Apologies,* ed. Halford Ross Ryan (Westport, Conn.: Greenwood Press, 1988), pp. 137–51; Charles J. G. Griffin, "New Light on Eisenhower's Farewell Address," *Presidential Studies Quarterly* 22 (1992): 469–80; Martin J. Medhurst, "Dwight D. Eisenhower's First Inaugural Address, 1953" and "Dwight D. Eisenhower's Second Inaugural Address, 1957," both in *Inaugural Addresses of Twentieth-Century American Presidents,* ed. Halford Ryan (Westport, Conn.: Praeger, 1993), pp. 153–65, 166–79; Craig Allen, *Eisenhower and the Mass Media: Peace, Prosperity and Prime-Time TV* (Chapel Hill: University of North Carolina Press, 1993); Martin J. Medhurst, "Eisenhower, Little Rock, and the Rhetoric of Crisis," in *The Modern Presidency and Crisis Rhetoric,* ed. Amos Kiewe (Westport, Conn.: Praeger, 1994), pp. 19–46; Martin J. Medhurst, "Reconceptualizing Rhetorical History: Eisenhower's Farewell Address," *Quarterly Journal of Speech* 80 (1994): 195–218; Martin J. Medhurst, "Dwight D. Eisenhower" in *U.S. Presidents as Orators: A Bio-Critical Sourcebook,* ed. Halford Ryan (Westport, Conn.: Greenwood Press, 1995), pp. 190–209; Carol Gelderman, *All the Presidents' Words: The Bully Pulpit and the Creation of the Virtual Presidency* (New York: Walker, 1997), pp. 45–54; Robert L. Ivie, "Dwight D. Eisenhower's 'Chance for Peace': Quest or Crusade?" *Rhetoric & Public Affairs* 1 (1998): 227–43; Martin J. Medhurst, "Text and Context in the 1952 Presidential Campaign: Eisenhower's 'I Shall Go to Korea' Speech," *Presidential Studies Quarterly* 30 (2000): 464–84.

4. This essay examines Eisenhower's speechwriting methodology only as it applied to his formal presidential addresses, a category which included roughly 100–150 speeches a year between 1953 and 1960. It does not examine the preparation of Eisenhower's routine campaign speeches, press briefings, or other informal remarks.

5. James, W. Ceaser, Glen E. Thurow, Jeffrey Tulis, and Joseph M. Bessette, "The Rise of the Rhetorical Presidency," *Presidential Studies Quarterly* 11 (1981): 158–71.

6. Karlyn Kohrs Campbell and Kathleen Hall Jamieson, *Deeds Done in Words: Presidential Rhetoric and the Genres of Governance* (Chicago: University of Chicago Press, 1990), pp. 52, 59.

7. Eisenhower to Milton Eisenhower, Nov. 6, 1953, Ann Whitman File, Speech Series, Box 6 (1); Dwight D. Eisenhower, *Mandate For Change* (New York: Doubleday, 1963), 286–87. According to Bryce Harlow, the man charged with its composition, "If I were to refer anyone to a key document for the Eisenhower period, it would be the 1954 'State of the Union' message, which put together, almost Sears and Robuck Catalogue-ish, an immense and immensely detailed program, which he largely held to the balance of his time in the White House. The fundamentals of it were of course laid out there, as they had to be in his first real 'State of the Union' message." John T. Mason, interview with Bryce N. Harlow, OH 214, March 27, 1967, p. 144.

8. Eisenhower to cabinet secretaries and agency heads, July 30, 1953, Records of Bryce N. Harlow, Box 11 (2); hereafter cited as Harlow Papers.

9. Gabriel Hauge to Sherman Adams, Nov. 9, 1953, Harlow Papers, Box 11 (3).

10. Harlow to DDE, Nov. 17, 1953, Ann Whitman File, Speech Series, Box 6 (1); Harlow to Sherman Adams, Dec. 3, 1953, Harlow Papers, Box 11 (2); Carroll to C. D. Jackson, Nov. 17, 1953, C. D. Jackson Papers: 1931–1967, Box 104 (1); Harlow to DDE, Nov. 17, 1953, Ann Whitman File, Speech Series, Box 6 (1). All references to Dwight D. Eisenhower in correspondence are as DDE.

11. Harlow, OH 214, 141–42; DDE to Hauge, Dec. 1, 1953, Ann Whitman File, Speech Series, Box 6 (1); DDE to Harlow, Dec. 3, 1953, Ann Whitman File, Speech Series, Box 6 (3).

12. Harlow to Sherman Adams, Dec. 3, 1953, Harlow Papers, Box 11 (2); Eisenhower, *Mandate for Change,* pp. 243–51; Stephen E. Ambrose, *Eisenhower,* vol. 2 (New York: Simon and Schuster, 1984), pp. 145–51; Martin J. Medhurst, "Eisenhower's 'Atoms for Peace' Speech: A Case Study in the Strategic Use of Rhetoric," *Communication Monographs* 54 (1987): 204–20.

13. Harlow to James Hagerty, Dec. 14, 1953, Harlow Papers, Box 11 (2).

14. President's Appointment Calendar, Wednesday, Dec. 16, 1953; "Notes by the President on the State of the Union Speech," memorandum of meeting between DDE and Harlow, Dec. 16, 1953, Ann Whitman Files, Speech Series, Box 6 (3); see also, Greenstein, *The Hidden-Hand Presidency,* pp. 66–67.

15. "Personal and Confidential Memorandum," Adams to cabinet secretaries et al., Dec. 18, 1953, Harlow Papers, Box 11 (1).

16. Copies of draft #2 (Dec. 23, 1953) and draft #3 (Dec. 28, 1953) are in Harlow Papers, Box 10 (7), (8); Harlow to Gen. Wilton Persons, Dec. 28, 1953, Harlow Papers, Box 11 (1); a copy of draft #4 (Dec, 29, 1953) is in Harlow Papers, Box 10 (4); a copy of draft #5 (Jan. 1, 1954) is in Harlow Papers, Box 10 (2); Robert H. Ferrell, ed., *The Diary of James C. Hagerty: Eisenhower in Mid-Course, 1954–1955* (Bloomington: Indiana University Press, 1983), p. 1. Besides Adams and Harlow, the individuals named by Hagerty were: Henry Cabot Lodge, Jr. (U.S. ambassador to the United Nations), Joseph Dodge (Bureau of the Budget director), Jack Martin (congressional liaison staff), Gerald Morgan (congressional liaison staff), and John K. Jessup (chief editorial writer, *Life* magazine). The author has been unable to locate a copy of draft #6; however, a copy of draft #7 may be found in Harlow Papers, Box 11 (2).

17. Dwight D. Eisenhower, "Radio and Television Address to the American People on the Administration's Purposes and Accomplishments, January 4, 1954," *Public Papers of the Presidents of the United States: Dwight D. Eisenhower, 1954* (Washington, D.C.: Government Printing Office, 1960), pp. 2–3.

18. Harlow, OH 214, p. 143.

19. Ferrell, *The Diary of James C. Hagerty,* p. 4; Eisenhower's reading copy of the 1954 State of the Union message, January 7, 1954, is in the Ann Whitman File, Speech Series, Box 6 (2). For a published version of the address, see Dwight D. Eisenhower, "Annual Message to the Congress on the State of the Union, January 7, 1954," *Public Papers, 1954,* pp. 6–23.

20. Greenstein, *The Hidden-Hand Presidency,* p. 101.

21. See Charles E. Walcott and Karen M. Hult, *Governing the White House: From Hoover to LBJ* (Lawrence: University Press of Kansas, 1995), pp. 218–19; Sherman

Adams, *First Hand Report: The Story of the Eisenhower Administration* (New York: Harper and Brothers, 1961), pp. 80–83; Greenstein, *The Hidden-Hand Presidency,* p. 106.

22. Adams, *First Hand Report,* p. 81.

23. See William Bragg Ewald, *Eisenhower the President: Crucial Days, 1951–1960* (Englewood Cliffs, N.J.: Prentice Hall, 1981), pp. 223–40; and Emmet John Hughes, *The Ordeal of Power: A Political Memoir of the Eisenhower Years* (New York: Athenaeum, 1963), pp. 88–96.

24. Ewald, *Eisenhower the President,* p. 145; Harlow, OH 214, p. 132.

25. Ewald, *Eisenhower the President,* pp. 145, 148, 150. It is difficult to track down the specific date on which McCann succeeded Harlow, because both men remained on the White House staff. However, a newspaper article dated March 9, 1955, identifies McCann as the chief speechwriter, so the changeover must have occurred before this date. See James Reston, "The White House Staff," *New York Times,* March 9, 1955, 10.

26. Ewald, *Eisenhower the President,* pp. 146–47; McCann, interview with Ed Edwin, Dec. 21, 1966, OH 159, p. 14.

27. Ewald, *Eisenhower the President,* pp. 166, 289–90; Arthur Larson, *Eisenhower: The President Nobody Knew* (New York: Charles Scribner's Sons, 1968), pp. 156, 152–63.

28. Ewald, *Eisenhower the President,* pp. 289–90; see also McCann, OH 159, p. 78; E. Frederick Morrow, interview with Thomas Soapes, Feb. 23, 1977, OH 376, pp. 27, 30.

29. Larson, *Eisenhower,* pp. 161; Capt. Ralph Williams (USN), interview with James Leyerzapf, June 3, 1988, OH 503, pp. 16–17; Moos quoted in Ewald, *Eisenhower the President,* p. 290.

30. Greenstein, *The Hidden-Hand Presidency,* p. 148; see also Williams, OH 503, pp. 13–16, 25.

31. See Robert H. Ferrell, ed., *The Eisenhower Diaries* (New York: W. W. Norton, 1981), pp. 238, 272–73; Adams, *First Hand Report,* pp. 42, 54–55; Ambrose, *Eisenhower,* vol. 2, pp. 203–204, 282, 516–18; Eisenhower, *Mandate for Change,* p. 100; Greenstein, *The Hidden-Hand Presidency,* pp. 149.

32. Harlow, OH 214, pp. 107–108.

33. Medhurst, "Eisenhower's 'Atoms for Peace' Speech," p. 207; Ann Whitman Diary, Dec. 6, 1956, Whitman File, Speech Series, Box 20 (3); Larson, *Eisenhower,* p. 145.

34. Harlow, OH 214, p. 95.

35. Ibid., pp. 93, 95–96.

36. "Notes by the President on State of the Union Speech, Draft #1," Dec. 16, 1953, Ann Whitman File, Speech Series, Box 6 (3).

37. Ibid.

38. Adams, *First Hand Report,* p. 81; Hughes, *The Ordeal of Power,* p. 25; Larson, *Eisenhower,* pp. 146–47.

39. Williams, OH 503, pp. 17–18.

40. Hughes, *The Ordeal of Power,* pp. 24–25; Harlow, OH 214, p. 85; McCann, OH 159, p. 13; Larson, *Eisenhower,* pp. 146, 151–52; Moos, OH 260, p. 27; Whitman estimate cited in Ambrose, *Eisenhower,* vol. 2, p. 346.

41. Larson, *Eisenhower,* pp. 146–49.

42. Martin J. Medhurst, "Ike the Isocratean" (unpublished lecture, Kansas State University, April 20, 1995), p. 20 (manuscript held by the author of this chapter).

43. Eisenhower to Milton Eisenhower, Nov. 6, 1953, Ann Whitman File, Speech Series, Box 6 (1).

44. Harlow, OH 214, pp. 93, 96.

45. Hauge to Sherman Adams, Nov. 9, 1953, Harlow Papers, Box 11 (3).

46. Harlow to Roger Kyes, Dec. 9, 1953, Harlow Papers, Box 11 (1). According to one estimate, Eisenhower's address represented considerably more than an 80 percent reduction of material originally submitted to the White House by departments and agencies; see "7,000-Word Talk a Shadow of Itself," *New York Times,* Jan. 8, 1954, p. 11.

47. Harlow, OH 214, pp. 96–97, 140.

48. Adams to cabinet secretaries and list, Dec. 18, 1953, Harlow Papers, Box 11 (1). For examples of responses to Adams's invitation for senior administrators to edit the speech, see "Suggested Changes in the third draft of the State of the Union message by Gerald D. Morgan," Dec. 29, 1953, Harlow Papers, Box 10 (4); and Hauge to Harlow, Jan. 5, 1954, Harlow Papers, Box 11 (1).

49. See, for instance, Hauge to Eisenhower, Sept. 12, 1957, White House Central Files, Official File, Box 426; and Moos to Eisenhower and Milton Eisenhower, May 24, 1959, "Proposed Speech Calendar for period from June, 1959–January, 1961, White House Central Files, Official File, Box 426.

50. Greenstein, *The Hidden-Hand Presidency,* pp. 115–16; Martin J. Medhurst, "Eisenhower's Rhetorical Leadership: An Interpretation," in *Eisenhower's War of Words,* pp. 291–96.

CHAPTER 4

John F. Kennedy

Presidential Speechwriting
as Rhetorical Collaboration

THEODORE O. WINDT, JR.

In April and May of 1963 Theodore C. Sorensen, special counsel to President John F. Kennedy, delivered the Gino Speranza Lectures at Columbia University, which were subsequently published under the title, *Decision Making in the White House.* Kennedy himself wrote the foreword to the book describing Sorensen as "an astute and sensitive collaborator in the presidential enterprise," and as a "participant, as well as an observer, of important decisions in difficult days."[1] Rarely has an official of a sitting administration spelled out the workings of the executive branch as Sorensen did.[2] Rarer still is the power wielded by a speechwriter to speak about presidential decision making with such authority. These brief lectures, then, may serve as a starting point for an analysis of speechwriting in the Kennedy administration.

Sorensen noted that one important responsibility of a president is "to lead public opinion as well as respect it—to shape it, to inform it, to woo it, and win it." And he continued with the inevitable quotation from Lincoln about the power of public sentiment. Undoubtedly remembering the razor-thin margin by which Kennedy captured the White House, Sorensen found it equally important to cite Jefferson's remark that "great innovations should not be forced on slender majorities."[3]

In his ideal decision model Sorensen placed the "communication" of a presidential decision seventh in his list of eight component steps. However, from a rhetorical perspective, all decisions are not the same. Presaging the notion of "two presidencies," Sorensen noted, "One important distinction should be kept in mind. In domestic affairs, a presidential decision is usually the beginning of public debate. In foreign affairs, the issues are frequently so complex, the facts so obscure, and the period for decision so short, that the American people have from the beginning—and even more so in this century delegated to the President more discretion in this vital area; and they are usually willing to support any reasonable decision he makes."[4] That is an important distinction that bears upon the different kinds of rhetoric an administration can produce.

This chapter begins with Sorensen's observations not only because he was chief speechwriter in the Kennedy administration but because they illustrate the chapter's thesis: This study is less interested in the mechanics of speechwriting or in tracing particular passages in speeches to particular writers and is more concerned with the role of the speechwriter in a presidential administration, especially in the Kennedy administration. The motivation for this focus is, in part, personal. The present author has been a speechwriter for various politicians—at times exhilarated to be in on the action in the middle of policy and political decisions, and at other times enormously frustrated when hired strictly as a wordsmith with no connection to politics and policy—and worse, on several occasions without even a connection to the political figure.

Putting personal reasons aside, the traditional approaches to studying speechwriting—the search for authorship and the concern with the mechanics of speechwriting—are not particularly useful with the Kennedy administration. The collaborators—as Kennedy and Sorensen each called their rhetorical relationship—wrote most of the major presidential speeches. Anyone who has gone through the files in the John F. Kennedy Library will peruse the Sorensen drafts with Kennedy's squiggly handwriting in the margins, between lines, or elsewhere. Beyond that, much has already been written about the process and mechanics of speechwriting in that administration.[5] Therefore, this chapter is divided into two parts: (1) an overview of the process of speechwriting in the Kennedy White House and (2) a discussion of the role and uses of speechwriters in the administration.

The Process of Writing Kennedy's Speeches

As a preface to understanding the mechanics of writing speeches in the Kennedy White House, let us understand something about the general workings of the staff system under Kennedy. Kennedy had come to the White House vowing to "get this country moving again." One major theme of his campaign was an activist presidency. To those ends, the president sought to cut through the bureaucracy of the presidency. He appointed no chief of staff. Evelyn Lincoln, Kenneth O'Donnell, and Theodore Sorensen— each in his or her own way—controlled much of the access to Kennedy. The president directed McGeorge Bundy to dismantle what he considered to be the laborious decision-making machinery of the National Security Council, replacing it with Bundy himself—the first of the strong national security advisors. Ad hoc committees and special task forces—most notably the Executive Committee (ExComm) of the National Security Council—were created to deal with particular problems. He instituted a variety of other management measures that, in the words of James N. Giglio, sought to "unleash the president from the office of the presidency.[6] In so doing, he deinstitutionalized the office and replaced it with a more freewheeling and personalized presidency, using people as the occasion suggested.

The same was true with speechwriting. Kennedy created no Office of Communication nor was anyone named chief speechwriter, primarily because everyone knew Ted Sorensen was "the speechwriter." Instead, Sorensen, the first announced appointee of the new administration, was given the title special counsel to the president with his original primary responsibility being domestic policy. Speechwriting thus became a direct adjunct to policy making. Kennedy appointed Myer Feldman, who, along with Sorensen, wrote many of the messages to Congress; Lee White, who wrote Executive Orders; and Richard N. Goodwin, who specialized in writing speeches on Latin America.

Speechwriting, then, took place within that administrative context. Before considering the actual writing of the speech, one has to remember a political commonplace: deliberative speeches are both a product of and separate from the decision-making process. When a particular problem that needs resolution confronts the president, standard operation is to convene a standing or ad hoc committee or a group of advisors to counsel the president. The arguments various participants put forward for policy options provide a rich inventional resource for the speechwriter, provided that the writer is present to hear the arguments or has access to all the documents. After the failed Cuban Bay of Pigs invasion in April of 1961, Sorensen had added foreign policy to his repertoire of responsibilities in domestic policy. As a result, he was fortunate enough to be intimately involved in most discussions of major issues.

The Berlin "crisis" during the summer of 1961 illustrates this point. After the Vienna Summit meeting and Khrushchev's *aide-memoire,* the administration divided into two groups about the appropriate response to what it considered a provocative threat by Khrushchev. One group, symbolized by Arthur Schlesinger, Jr., advocated a diplomatic response consistent with his understanding of his conversation with his Russian diplomatic friend, Georgi Kornienko.[7] Dean Acheson, former secretary of state under Harry Truman, headed a hard-line group advising Kennedy. Acheson argued that "until this conflict of wills is resolved, an attempt to solve the Berlin issue by negotiation is worse than a waste of time and energy. It is dangerous. This is so because what can be accomplished by negotiation depends on the state of mind of Khrushchev and his colleagues."[8] Acheson sought to bolster his interpretation of the crisis with the dubious argument that Russian leaders always sought to "test" new presidents. Although Kennedy did not accept some of Acheson's more provocative recommendations, he did make "testing of wills" the theme of his speech on July 25, 1961: "West Berlin is all of that. But above all it has now become—as never before—the great testing place of Western courage and will. . . ."[9] And anyone who has studied the deliberations on the Cuban missile crisis will immediately notice some lines of argument emanating from the discussion of ExComm.

In considering the actual speechwriting process in the Kennedy White House, one needs to recognize that practically anyone could be involved in some of the minor speeches. For example, in early April of 1963 Norman Cousins went to the White House to discuss his forthcoming meeting with Khrushchev and concluded the day writing the president's brief speech on culture to high school students in the Rose Garden.[10]

With major speeches, Kennedy was very much involved in their development from the outset to the final version—which he sometimes amended or extended even as he delivered it. Kennedy would begin the process by outlining the speech. James Golden has described the method:

> The outline he presented in these sessions went beyond a generalized statement describing the major emphasis or thrust of the arguments. Often it included a request for a compelling introduction, a list of suggested main points, and the approximate length of the speech. Similarly, it sometimes contained specific instructions to his assistants as the following: (1) find an appropriate quotation from F.D.R. or Mr. Dooley; (2) ask Billy Graham to submit some relevant Biblical citations; (3) obtain a list of the names of Irish-American soldiers who fought in the battle of Texas independence; (4) study the content and format of the Inaugural addresses of

all the presidents; (5) analyze Lincoln's Farewell at Springfield and his Gettysburg Address; (6) study earlier Kennedy public statements in order to avoid major inconsistencies and to establish a continuity of thought; and (7) contact leading academicians for fresh ideas.[11]

Most significant among these was studying previous public statements. Believing as he did that "[e]very speech put his career on the line, reflecting choices for which he would be praised or blamed," he directed people to gather and study prior statements carefully so as to achieve consistency in his positions.[12]

The actual writing process took several forms in each step of the process. Because the Kennedy White House functioned in a freewheeling manner, the people involved in the writing of a particular speech might have been specifically chosen for the task, or they might have been enlisted for no other reason than that they happened to be hanging around that day.

The first order of business was gathering information for the speech. If it were a major speech, Sorensen would assign it to himself. Since he had been present at discussions over the policy, he would have access to arguments and information, though, of course, he could call up additional information as the drafting began.[13] The alternative method was to assemble a group of people who had expert knowledge about a particular problem and have them meet to discuss the speech or to submit ideas concerning the issue at hand. Dr. Robert Turner, Kennedy's assistant secretary of the Bureau of the Budget and a former Truman speechwriter, described a typical group meeting: "Ted [Sorensen] would have a conference with other people on the White House staff and the Council and the Bureau of the Budget and key staff people from other agencies. Sometimes we'd have twenty people in the room talking over the problem of what the speech or message was to be about. That might be a three or four hour meeting; it might be continued the next day. We'd go over all the angles of the issue. Then, Ted would go off by himself."[14] That fairly well describes the group process except for the romantic ending of Sorensen trudging off as the solitary speechwriter to turn various recommendations into a magical whole.

Sorensen may have made initial drafts in solitude, but he did not always work alone. As one draft was replaced by another, additional people came into the process, primarily high-level officials with authoritative positions. For example, Dean Rusk noted that, though Sorensen was principal writer of the Cuban missile crisis speech, "[Robert] McNamara, [McGeorge] Bundy, and I all worked with him in crafting a carefully constructed speech."[15] Drafts were circulated among the appropriate departments or agencies for suggestions.

Despite assistance by others, Sorensen was Kennedy's speechwriter. Sorensen's method of composition was twofold. Apparently, when time permitted, he wrote drafts in longhand on legal-size tablets. Turner explained the other method: "[Sorensen] would go off by himself with four secretaries. He'd dictate to one for an hour, to the second for an hour, to the third for an hour, and to the fourth for an hour and come up with a draft. Then he would send a copy down to key staff people for their comment. We would go over the draft with our own subordinates, and we would come in with written or oral comments. But he made the final decisions."[16] Turner concluded that the President did not get involved until the last stage of the process. Sorensen tells a different story: "We [Kennedy and Sorensen] always discussed the topic, the approach and the conclusions in advance. He always had quotations or historical allusions to include. Sometimes he would review an outline."[17]

Of course, the truth lies somewhere between the two. After all, Turner was in the Bureau of the Budget and thus did not have a great deal of information about the inner workings of the White House. On the other hand, Sorensen has spent his post-assassination career attempting to persuade people that "Kennedy was the true author of all his speeches and writings."[18] The image of Kennedy spontaneously spouting "historical allusions" and "quotations" must be tempered by knowledge of the various commonplace files in the White House that included a humor file, a quotation file, and so on.[19] The truth of the matter seems to be that Kennedy got involved whenever he felt like getting involved—whether it was at the outset of the process, in the middle of it (reviewing outlines or preliminary drafts), or after a speech had gone through several drafts. But that he was intimately involved in each of the major speeches and most of the others is indisputable.

Sorensen described in some detail the kind of speech he sought to write for Kennedy. His words are worth quoting at length, despite his occasional hyperbole:

> Our chief criterion was always audience comprehension and comfort, and this meant: (1) short speeches, short clauses and short words, wherever possible; (2) a series of points or propositions in numbered or logical sequence,

wherever appropriate; and (3) the construction of sentences, phrases and paragraphs in such a manner as to simplify, clarify and emphasize.

The test of a text was not how it appeared to the eye, but how it sounded to the ear. His best paragraphs, when read aloud, often had a cadence not unlike blank verse—indeed at times key words would rhyme. He was fond of alliterative sentences, not solely for reasons of rhetoric but to reinforce the audience's recollection of his reasoning.

Sorensen remarked that Kennedy loved precision in the words he used, but when equivocation was required, he preferred equivocal words to "ponderous prose"—a not unsubtle jab at Eisenhower.[20]

Kennedy's role was that of editor, as James Golden pointed out. Once he received a draft, he either went over it with the writer or worked on it separately while the writer rewrote. He scribbled in his almost illegible hand words and phrases as he struck out others. Kennedy's editing might extend right up to the moment the speech was delivered or beyond.

Kennedy's justly famous speech on civil rights on June 11, 1963 (after Governor Wallace had "stood in the schoolhouse door") was one of those occasions when the speechwriting process continued during the speech itself. Since that speech had to be written quickly to catch up with events, Sorensen and others were trying to complete a first draft by early afternoon, and spent the remainder of the day dictating words, phrases, paragraphs while the president met with Averell Harriman, Edward R. Murrow, and others. Kennedy joined the writers about two hours before air time to help in the effort. But up to four minutes before air time for this televised speech, it was not complete and both Kennedy and Sorensen were furiously dictating. (Evelyn Lincoln, Kennedy's personal secretary, had to type more than five hundred new words during the last few minutes.) When he went on the air he still did not have a complete manuscript. He extemporized, from a memo by Louis Martin, the section: "The Negro baby born in America today . . . has about one half as much chance of completing high school as a white baby born in the same place on the same day. . . ."[21] And he ad-libbed the conclusion: "We have a right to expect that the Negro community will be responsible, will uphold the law, but they have a right to expect that the law will be fair, that the Constitution will be color blind, as Justice Harlan said at the turn of the century."[22]

Kennedy exercised his editorial prerogatives more extensively with a speech prepared by Arthur Schlesinger for delivery in October 3, 1961, celebrating the publication of the first four volumes of the John Quincy

Adams papers. Schlesinger noted that Kennedy discarded the first half of the speech and improvised while adapting and improving the second half of the remarks the Harvard professor had prepared for him.[23]

Of course, the ultimate act of editorship is rejecting a speech altogether and "winging it." Kennedy often did this with minor ceremonial remarks or campaign speeches. But on one occasion it could have had disastrous consequences. Sorensen had prepared a long manuscript for his speech at the Berlin Wall, but Kennedy rejected it. Instead, he gave a short speech. In the process, he inserted two half-pages to the manuscript, including the Latin and German words: "civis Romanus sum," "Ich bin ein Berliner" and "Lass sie nach Berlin kommen"—with several of these words spelled out phonetically.[24] His remarks electrified the crowd with his commitment, but he astonished his aides with his belligerence. Kenneth P. O'Donnell and David F. Powers noted that: "Kennedy's fighting speech in Berlin, as magnificent as it was, actually was a grave political risk, and he knew it. Such a heated tribute to West Berlin's resistance to Communism could have undone all of the success of his appeal for peace and understanding with the Soviets in his American University speech two weeks earlier. He was carried away . . ."[25]

The most offending line in the speech—"And there are some who say in Europe and elsewhere we can work with the Communists. Let them come to Berlin."—directly contradicted his call for American-Soviet cooperation less than two weeks before. Kennedy rectified this harsh language when Sorensen wrote a softer statement into his speech at the Free University later that afternoon. The "softer" or clarifying statement read: "As I said this morning, I am not impressed by the opportunities open to popular fronts throughout the world. I do not believe any democrat can successfully ride that tiger. But I do believe in the necessity of the great powers working together to preserve the human race." Kennedy had so muddled his meaning that he baffled his listeners. West German Chancellor Konrad Adenauer was so confused that he remarked: "I'm worried. Does this mean that Germany could have another Hitler?"[26]

There was one notable exception to the chaotic routine of producing public addresses in the Kennedy White House. One address was a secret speech drafted only by Sorensen and Kennedy, who worked on it together and separately. It was kept from the cabinet, departments and agencies until the last minute. And it was one of his best speeches. That was Kennedy's "peace" speech at American University on June 10, 1963. Sorensen drew his information for the address from Norman Cousins, McGeorge Bundy,

Carl Kaysen, his brother, Tom, as well as others, all of whom were sworn to secrecy. Kennedy did not want his new policy—that Sorensen rightly called the "first Presidential speech in eighteen years to succeed in reaching beyond the cold war"—to be distorted or diluted by officialdom's "usual threats of destruction, boasts of nuclear stockpiles and lectures on Soviet treachery."[27] Sorensen began circulating drafts of the speech only two days before the scheduled delivery of it, which left precious little time for officials to water it down with diplomatic qualifications and bureaucratic euphemisms.

In sum, in the Kennedy White House there was not one process for producing speeches, but a variety of approaches that usually depended on the occasion, the topic, time constraints, and the purpose the speech was to serve.

The Kennedy Speechwriters

William Safire's description of a speechwriter as a type of "ghostwriter" similar to a "phrasemaker" or a "wordsmith" hardly does justice to the writers who worked for Kennedy, though each could turn a phrase and each had a way with words. Even Safire's definition of speechwriter—"a ghost who operates out in the open"—is a pale definition of the various responsibilities that Sorensen handled.[28] Kennedy's speechwriters were substantive men with substantive responsibilities beyond their speechwriting chores. John Kenneth Galbraith is a case in point. He added to Kennedy's inaugural address the phrase "Let us begin," as well as a rough version of never fearing to negotiate, but never negotiating out of fear. He also contributed to State of the Union addresses and various economic speeches. But he was also the author of nine books and was a professor of economics at Harvard before assuming his duties as Ambassador to India in the administration. A gifted stylist who wrote both books on economics and works of fiction, Galbraith wrote for Kennedy only occasionally because his views were too liberal, and his rhetorical sensibilities too limited.[29]

Richard Goodwin, at twenty-eight, was the least experienced among Kennedy's writers. Culled from a list of potential speechwriters that had been drawn up when Kennedy decided to run for president and Sorensen's writing duties became too extensive for one person, the brash Goodwin quickly proved his mettle, though he had never written a speech prior to his tryout.[30] He could write as Kennedy spoke. He and Sorensen became the only two writers to accompany Kennedy throughout the 1960 presidential campaign.

Once in the White House, working under Sorensen with the title assistant counsel to the president, Goodwin decided he did not want to be a speechwriter and assigned himself to the Latin American task force, which would become his specialty over the next year or so. He had coined the phrase "Alliance for Progress"—although Sorensen deprecatingly said that they had already decided on an alliance and Goodwin merely added "progress."[31] Goodwin wrote Kennedy's major address of March 13, 1961, on the Alliance for Progress. When talking with the president about the speech, Goodwin averred that he might not be able to get agreement from the task force on policy. According to Goodwin, the president replied: "I don't care if everyone agrees. You know what our thinking is. That's the only agreement you need—with me." Kennedy went on to instruct him that he did not want the speech to be strictly an anti-Castro speech: "Just throw Castro in with the other dictators. I don't want them to think the only reason we're doing this is because of Cuba."[32] As was his procedure, Kennedy spent hours rewriting the final text with Goodwin and additional hours practicing the Spanish that Goodwin had inserted into the address. According to Goodwin, even when he left the White House for the State Department in late 1961, he continued to write Kennedy's major speeches on Latin American policy (with the exception of speeches on Cuba)—a practice he continued when he moved to the Peace Corps in July, 1962.

Two things are important about Goodwin. First, he was the most versatile writer in the White House, easily making the transition from the Kennedy to the Johnson administration where he wrote the Great Society speech, the "We Shall Overcome" civil rights speech, and numerous early speeches justifying Johnson's Vietnam War policies. Second, he was involved in policy and decision making throughout his stay in the Kennedy administration. Therefore, he had the benefit of knowing the exact arguments that justified policy and was able to incorporate the rhetorically effective ones into speeches.

When Goodwin left the White House, Arthur Schlesinger, Jr., tried to replace him. But it did not work. His speeches were "too Stevensonian," and by his own admission Kennedy mistrusted his efforts.[33] Yet, he continued to produce drafts for literary or historical occasions, such as the Adams speech, and for the United Nations, where presumably his Stevensonian cadences would not be offensive to the U.S. ambassador Adlai Stevenson.

That brings us to the single most important figure in the speechwriting efforts of the administration, Theodore C. Sorensen. Sorensen joined Kennedy's staff as legislative assistant shortly after Kennedy was elected to the U.S. Senate. He began his speechwriting activities when he produced a St. Patrick's Day speech that admirably suited both Kennedy's Boston idiom and his Irish constituents' ears.[34] He followed up with a compelling address to the Senate justifying Kennedy's support for the St. Lawrence Sea Way, a risky proposition for a freshman Senator from Massachusetts since all elected officials from that state had voted against it for the past twenty years. From that point on Sorensen was "the speechwriter."

During Kennedy's Senate years Sorensen performed every conceivable duty for Kennedy from legislative assistant and speechwriter to advance man and traveling companion. Gradually they merged into one with Sorensen repeatedly being referred to as Kennedy's "alter ago." The merger went beyond the vaunted style of Kennedy's speeches. By his own admission, Kennedy had been greatly influenced by his father's conservatism, and when he got to the Senate, he had neither a political philosophy or a liberal reputation. As he himself said, "I had just come out of my father's house at the time and these were the things I knew."[35] At another time he admitted he had few liberal tendencies: "Some people have their liberalism 'made' by the time they reach their late twenties. I didn't. I was caught in crosscurrents and eddies. It was only later that I got into the stream of things."[36] Sorensen, on the other hand, came from a politically liberal family. Sorensen's liberalism coalesced with Kennedy's pragmatic realism to the point that "no one—not even Sorensen—was sure just where his thoughts left off and Kennedy's began."[37]

Trying to untangle what was Kennedy's and what Sorensen's is comparable to trying to untangle what was Nixon's and what Kissinger's in that administration's foreign policy. Sorensen even came to imitate Kennedy's personal style: "he used 'hahf' for half and 'mo-weh' for more—pronunciations he never learned on the plains of Nebraska. He also came to gesture as Kennedy did, jabbing the air with one forefinger while he held the other hand in the side pocket of his jacket. He even compromised his opposition to alcohol, developing a taste for Heineken's beer and an occasional daiquiri—Kennedy's two favorite drinks."[38]

The Kennedy-Sorensen collaboration—and each described their relationship as such, rather than as speechwriter to president—provided unique resources for the writer-advisor-counselor. Kennedy's absolute trust in Sorensen allowed Sorensen to speak with authority to members of the administration. Conversely, being totally devoted to Kennedy, Sorensen's only thoughts were advancing the fortunes of the president. Sorensen was often in the envious position of sitting in on important decisions, so that he well knew the arguments for a policy. At the same time, Sorensen was confident, even jealous, of his special relationship with the president, which enabled him to select those arguments most suitable to Kennedy's public persuasive case. Other than the president, no one could truly overrule him and thus he did not have to "clear" speech drafts with the political or policy-making officials in the administration, as speechwriters normally must do.

Patrick Anderson with a keen insight observed that Sorensen exercised one of the few powers that a good speechwriter has: he "could put ideas before Kennedy and force him to accept or reject them; he could seize upon Kennedy's good intentions and translate them into specific policies."[39] This was Sorensen's contribution to Kennedy's thinking during his Senate days. It served him well also in the White House.

The most dramatic example of this came during the Cuban missile crisis. When members of ExComm deadlocked on whether to recommend a blockade or an air strike, Sorensen was dispatched to write two speeches, each justifying a different option. Unable to write these speeches, Sorensen returned to the group with a series of questions—questions that clarified the issues and eventually led to a compromise policy that won nearly unanimous support and became Kennedy's policy.[40] It is questionable whether any other modern presidential speechwriter has had the influence to do what Sorensen did.

Conclusion

The striking feature of presidential speechwriting in the Kennedy White House was that the freewheeling and ad hoc nature of that White House permitted both the president and his speechwriters to protect the writing process from being severely compromised by the ill-effects of "committee writing." Rather than following a rigid process, the presidential speeches of the Kennedy administration were written in a variety of methods that depended on the circumstances of each address. To an important extent, then, the process of speechwriting in a particular White House will depend on the president's style of management.

Because Kennedy's management style permitted Sorensen to be so intimately involved in Kennedy's writing, no discussion of JFK's speechwriting would be complete without saying something about authorship of the Kennedy-Sorensen materials. Herbert Parmet has probably done the best job of describing who wrote *Profiles in Courage*.[41] But the speeches are another matter. Most assume that Sorensen brought the "glory of words" to Kennedy.[42] To buttress this conclusion, critics generally cite Kennedy's tepid speeches before Sorensen came on board. Thus, Sorensen is given primary credit for the evolution of Kennedy's oratorical style. But that answer may be too simplistic. Just as their ideas coalesced, so too did their style. And since Kennedy's earlier efforts are cited to give credit to Sorensen, one might just as easily cite Sorensen's post-assassination writings (most notably *The Kennedy Legacy* and *A Different Kind of Presidency*)[43] to give some credit to Kennedy, because in those books Sorensen's writing does not sparkle as do his speech texts in collaboration with Kennedy.

The Kennedy-Sorensen collaboration produced such moving presidential addresses that even so severe a critic of those speeches as Patrick Anderson had to admit that they "not only won elections, but inspired a generation of Americans."[44] That occurred because Kennedy placed great value on public words, whether written or spoken, to move a nation—to borrow the title of Roger Hilsman's book.[45] JFK and Sorensen wanted their speeches not only to be instrumental in gaining support for policies but also to be enduring as linguistic monuments to the Kennedy administration.

Notes

1. John F. Kennedy, "Foreword" in Theodore C. Sorensen, *Decision Making in the White House: The Olive Branch or the Arrows* (New York: Columbia University Press, 1963), pp. xiii–xiv.

2. Certainly, these lectures had political and public relations value to Kennedy, especially since Sorensen (and Kennedy also in his foreword), stressed the limitations of presidential power. This theme helped to justify (or rationalize) Kennedy's slender record for the first two and a half years of his administration. These lectures were given before Kennedy's bold move for legislation on civil rights and his advocacy of the test ban treaty, the two major achievements of his administration. However, at the time, Sorensen's lectures were viewed as an insightful glimpse into the White House and his thesis contrasted greatly with what Thomas Cronin has criticized as the "textbook presidency" of the 1950s and 1960s, which portrayed the president as a superman. For example, see Thomas Cronin, *The State of the Presidency*, 2d ed. (Boston: Little, Brown and Company, 1980), pp. 75–95.

3. Sorensen, *Decision Making in the White House*, pp. 46, 48.

4. Ibid, p. 48. For a subsequent academic discussion of the "foreign policy presidency" as contrasted with the "domestic policy presidency," see Aaron Wildavsky, "The Two Presidencies," *Trans-action*, vol. 4, no. 2 (Dec., 1966): 7–14.

5. For rhetorical studies of Kennedy, see (chronological): Donald L. Wolfarth, "John F. Kennedy in the Tradition of Inaugural Speeches," *Quarterly Journal of Speech* 47 (1961): 124–32; James L. Golden, "John F. Kennedy and the 'Ghosts'," *Quarterly Journal of Speech* 52 (1966): 348–57; Wayne Brockriede and Robert L. Scott, *Moments in the Rhetoric of the Cold War* (New York: Random House, 1970), pp.

79–117; Harry Sharp, Jr., "Campaign Analysis: Kennedy vs. Big Steel" in *Explorations in Rhetorical Criticism,* ed. G. P. Mohrmann, Charles J. Stewart, and Donovan J. Ochs (University Park: Pennsylvania State University Press, 1973), pp. 32–50; Roderick P. Hart, *Verbal Style and the Presidency: A Computer-Based Analysis* (Orlando, Fla.: Academic Press, 1984), pp. 94–108; William C. Spragens, "Kennedy Era Speech Writing, Public Relations, and Public Opinion," *Presidential Studies Quarterly* 14 (1984): 78–86; Theodore O. Windt, Jr., "Seeking Détente with Superpowers: John F. Kennedy at American University," *Essays in Presidential Rhetoric,* 2d ed. (Dubuque, Iowa: Kendall/Hunt, 1987), pp. 135–48; David Henry, "Senator John F. Kennedy Encounters the Religious Question: I Am Not the Catholic Candidate for President," *Oratorical Encounters: Selected Studies and Sources of Twentieth-Century Political Accusations and Apologies,* ed. Halford Ross Ryan (New York: Greenwood Press, 1988), pp. 153–73; Justin Gustainis, "John F. Kennedy and the Green Berets: The Rhetorical Use of the Hero Myth," *Communication Studies* 40 (1989): 41–53; Martin J. Medhurst, "Rhetorical Portraiture: John F. Kennedy's March 12, 1962, Speech on the Resumption of Atmospheric Tests" in Martin J. Medhurst, Robert L. Ivie, Philip Wander, and Robert L. Scott, *Cold War Rhetoric: Strategy, Metaphor, and Ideology* (New York: Greenwood Press, 1990), pp. 51–68; Theodore O. Windt, Jr., *Presidents and Protesters: Political Rhetoric in the 1960s* (Tuscaloosa: University of Alabama Press, 1990), pp. 17–87; Vito N. Silvestri, "Background Perspectives on John F. Kennedy's Inaugural Address," *Political Communication and Persuasion* 8 (1991): 1–15; Kevin W. Dean, "'We Seek Peace—But We Shall Not Surrender': JFK's Use of Juxtaposition for Rhetorical Success in the Berlin Crisis," *Presidential Studies Quarterly* 21 (1991): 531–44; Moya Ann Ball, *Vietnam-on-the-Potomac* (Westport, Conn.: Praeger, 1992), pp. 1–106; Theodore O. Windt, Jr., "President John F. Kennedy's Inaugural Address, 1961," *Inaugural Addresses of Twentieth-Century American Presidents,* ed. Halford Ryan (Westport, Conn.: Praeger, 1993), pp. 181–93; Denise M. Bostdorff, *The Presidency and the Rhetoric of Foreign Crisis* (Columbia: University of South Carolina Press, 1994), pp. 25–55; Enrico Pucci, Jr., "Crisis as Pretext: John F. Kennedy and the Rhetorical Construction of the Berlin Crisis," *The Modern Presidency and Crisis Rhetoric,* ed. Amos Kiewe (Westport, Conn.: Praeger, 1994), pp. 47–71; Steven R. Goldzwig and George N. Dionisopoulos, *"In a Perilous Hour": The Public Address of John F. Kennedy* (Westport, Conn.: Greenwood Press, 1995); Vito N. Silvestri, "John Fitzgerald Kennedy," *U.S. Presidents as Orators,* ed. Halford Ryan (Westport, Conn.: Greenwood Press, 1995), pp. 210–27; Carol Gelderman, *All the Presidents' Words: The Bully Pulpit and the Creation of the Virtual Presidency* (New York: Walker, 1997), pp. 54–63; and Denise M. Bostdorff and Daniel J. O'Rourke, "The Presidency and the Promotion of Domestic Crisis: John Kennedy's Management of the 1962 Steel Crisis," *Presidential Studies Quarterly* 27 (1997): 343–61; Vito N. Silvestri, *Becoming JFK: A Profile in Communication* (Westport, Conn.: Praeger, 2000).

6. James N. Giglio, *The Presidency of John F. Kennedy* (Lawrence: University of Kansas Press, 1991), p. 30.

7. See Arthur Schlesinger, Jr., *A Thousand Days: John F. Kennedy in the White House* (Boston: Houghton Mifflin Press, 1965), pp. 380–94.

8. Quoted in Richard Reeves, *President Kennedy: Profile of Power* (New York: Simon and Schuster, 1993), pp. 190–91.

9. John F. Kennedy, "Radio and Television Report to the American People on the Berlin Crisis, July 25, 1961," *Public Papers of the Presidents of the United States: John F. Kennedy, 1961* (Washington, D.C.: Government Printing Office, 1962), p. 534. Hereafter, this publication series is cited as *Public Papers* (year).

10. Reeves, *President Kennedy,* p. 510.

11. James L. Golden, "John F. Kennedy and the 'Ghosts'," p. 351.

12. Theodore C. Sorensen, *"Let the Word Go Forth": The Speeches, Statements, and Writings of John F. Kennedy, 1947–1963* (New York: Delcorte Press), p. 2. Sorensen took the standard speechwriter's position when he also wrote: "John Kennedy was the true author of all of his speeches and writings. They set forth his ideas and ideals, his decisions and policies, his knowledge of history and politics."

13. A notable example of when discussions were not helpful to drafting a speech occurred when he encountered "writer's block" while drafting the Cuban missile crisis speech. Unable to write, he returned to discussions among ExComm to get some new ideas and arguments. But he found them still wrangling over the two final policies—a blockade or an air strike. As a result, they were no help at all. See Robert Smith Thompson, *The Missiles of October: The Declassified Story of John F. Kennedy and the Cuban Missile Crisis* (New York: Simon and Schuster, 1992), p. 232. Also see Theodore C. Sorensen, *Kennedy* (New York: Harper and Row, 1965), pp. 692–93.

14. Lois J. Einhorn, "The Ghosts Talk: Personal Interviews with Three Former Speechwriters," *Communication Quarterly* 36 (1988): 98.

15. Dean Rusk as told to Richard Rusk, *As I Saw It* (New York: W. W. Norton, 1990), p. 234.

16. Einhorn, "The Ghosts Talk," p. 98.

17. Sorensen, *Kennedy,* p. 60.

18. Sorensen, *"Let the Word Go Forth,"* p. 2.

19. Benjamin Bradlee noted that Kennedy began "collecting rhetoric in a small, black leather book before the war." Cited in Henry Fairlie, *The Kennedy Promise* (New York: Dell, 1974), p. 72. 20. Sorensen, *Kennedy,* pp. 60–61.

21. I take this version from Reeves, *President Kennedy,* pp. 521–22. However, Reeves is mistaken to attribute the one section solely to a memorandum from Louis Martin. Kennedy had used practically the same words in his opening statement in his first television debate with Vice President Nixon and in some subsequent campaign speeches.

22. John F. Kennedy, "Radio and Television Report to the American People on Civil Rights, June 11, 1963," *Public Papers, 1963,* p. 471.

23. Schlesinger, *A Thousand Days,* p. 691. Also see John F. Kennedy, "Remarks at a Luncheon Marking the Publication of the First Four Volumes of the Adams Papers, October 3, 1961," *Public Papers, 1961,* pp. 634–37.

24. Draft of Berlin Speech, Box 60, Papers of Theodore C. Sorensen, John F. Kennedy Library, Boston. (Subsequently, citations from this collection will be to the Sorensen Papers.) For the speech text as delivered, see John F. Kennedy, "Remarks in the Rudolph Wilde Platz, June 26, 1963," *Public Papers, 1963,* pp. 524–25.

Kennedy's last-minute change also created a humorous gaffe, for his improper phrasing of "Ich bin ein Berliner" (rather than Ich bin Berliner) meant "I am a jelly doughnut" in colloquial German. See Silvestri, "John Fitzgerald Kennedy," p. 219.

25. Kenneth P. O'Donnell and David F. Powers with Joe McCarthy, *"Johnny, We Hardly Knew Ye": Memories of John Fitzgerald Kennedy* (New York: Pocket Books, 1973), p. 417.

26. John F. Kennedy, "Address at the Free University of Berlin, June 26, 1963," *Public Papers, 1963,* p. 529; Reeves, *President Kennedy,* p. 536.

27. Sorensen, *Kennedy,* pp. 730–31. For drafts of the speech, see Speech File, Box 72, Sorensen Papers.

28. William Safire, *Safire's New Political Dictionary: The Definitive Guide to the New Language of Politics,* rev. ed. (New York: Random House, 1993), p. 281.

29. Galbraith was enlisted to write a draft of Johnson's November 26, 1963, speech before a joint session of Congress after the assassination. He noted: "I had drafted out a liberal program; it was pretty bad. [Schlesinger] . . . correctly said that this was not what the occasion called for." John Kenneth Galbraith, *An Ambassador's Journal* (Boston: Houghton Mifflin, 1969), p. 593.

30. Richard N. Goodwin, *Remembering America: A Voice from the Sixties* (Boston: Little Brown, 1988), p. 63.

31. Ibid., pp. 108–109; and Sorensen, *Kennedy,* p. 533.

32. Goodwin, *Remembering America,* pp. 147–48.

33. Schlesinger, *A Thousand Days,* p. 690.

34. Michael Medved, *The Shadow Presidents: The Secret History of the Chief Executives and Their Top Aides* (New York: Times Books, 1979), p. 264.

35. Quoted in Patrick Anderson, *The President's Men: White House Assistants of Franklin D. Roosevelt, Harry S. Truman, Dwight D. Eisenhower, John F. Kennedy and Lyndon B. Johnson* (Garden City, N.Y.: Doubleday, 1968), p. 278. Sorensen echoed this sentiment: "It seemed to me in 1953 that an inner struggle was being waged for the spirit of John Kennedy—a struggle between the political dilettante and the statesman, between the lure of luxury and lawmaking." Sorensen, *Kennedy,* p. 27.

36. Quoted in Fairlie, *The Kennedy Promise,* p. 67.

37. Ibid.

38. Medved, *The Shadow Presidents,* p. 249.

39. Anderson, *The President's Men,* p. 337.

40. Thompson, *Missiles of October,* pp. 232–33.

41. Herbert Parmet, *Jack: The Struggles of John F. Kennedy* (New York: Dial, 1980), pp. 312–33.

42. Pierre Salinger, *With Kennedy* (Garden City, N.Y.: Doubleday, 1966), p. 66.

43. Theodore C. Sorensen, *The Kennedy Legacy* (New York: Macmillan, 1969); Theodore C. Sorensen, *A Different Kind of Presidency: A Proposal for Breaking the Political Deadlock* (New York: Harper and Row, 1984).

44. Anderson, *The President's Men,* p. 346.

45. Roger Hilsman, *To Move a Nation: The Politics of Foreign Policy in the Administration of John F. Kennedy* (Garden City, N.Y.: Doubleday, 1967).

CHAPTER 5

Lyndon B. Johnson

From Private Deliberations
to Public Declaration—
The Making of LBJ's Renunciation Speech

MOYA ANN BALL

Lyndon Baines Johnson took his oath of office on *Air Force One,* with its blinds closed, engines running, and with the casket of a slain young president behind a curtain. The death of President Kennedy was not that of a monarch after which the crowd would cry, "the King is dead; long live the King!"[1] Johnson had lived under the shadow of John F. Kennedy for three years. While Kennedy enjoyed the spotlight, Johnson was given headlines such as "Whatever Happened to Lyndon Johnson?"[2] and "LBJ: Who's That?"[3] An anecdote, found in one of speechwriter Richard Goodwin's files at the Johnson Presidential Library, recalled how Vice President Johnson went to a luncheon at the Willard Hotel, which refers to itself as the hotel of presidents. The luncheon was not listed on the hotel's bulletin board, so Johnson approached a young woman at the reception desk. "I am the Vice President," he began. The young woman smiled sweetly and inquired, "may I ask of what?"[4] When he became president, the circumstances of Kennedy's death, and the following three days of national mourning, robbed Johnson, yet again, of any immediate recognition.

Yet, by some accounts, President Johnson rose to the occasion,[5] and it may well be that the first few weeks of his presidency were his finest, for he held his country and government together in a time of deep trauma and crisis. In his first speech to Congress, the new president began in an uncharacteristically humble way: "All I have I would have given gladly not to be standing here today. The greatest leader of our time has been struck down by the foulest deed of our time. Today John F. Kennedy lives on in the immortal words and works he left behind."[6]

Then, reminding his audience of Kennedy's inaugural address in which he had said, "Let us begin," Johnson emphatically declared, "today, in this moment of new resolve, I would say to my fellow Americans, let us continue." According to Karlyn Kohrs Campbell and Kathleen Hall Jamieson, this speech satisfied human and institutional needs, eulogizing Kennedy, legitimizing Johnson as president, and serving to carry forward the dead president's policies.[7] Patricia Witherspoon carefully traced the preparation of this important speech, suggesting that Theodore Sorensen, John Kenneth Galbraith, and McGeorge Bundy were its principal draftsmen, with input from other advisors, including Hubert Humphrey who added the famous phrase, "let us continue."[8]

Fifty-two months and ten days after delivering this speech, the man who had won a landslide presidential election in 1964, began another speech to the nation with, "Tonight, I want to speak to you of peace in Vietnam and Southeast Asia," and ended with the surprising announcement, "Accordingly, I shall not seek, and I will not accept, the nomination of my party for another term as your President."[9] Afterwards, the Washington, D.C., bureau chief for the *Chicago Tribune* stated, "history may record the speech as his finest hour. He never delivered a speech better, but did we see tears in his eyes at the close?"[10] Larry Berman, who has traced Johnson's handling of the Vietnam War, suggests that Johnson was a "Rip Van Winkle who had gone to sleep in November 1963 . . . and awoke in March 1968."[11] John Patton, describing this transformation, writes that LBJ's renunciation speech of March 31, 1968, "makes a move from strategic to moral considerations."[12] In some respects, the moral imperatives for the 1963 and 1968 speeches were the same: a situational exigency which demanded a rhetorical response to unify a nation splintered by the tragedies of violence at home and abroad. Other scholars have noted how Johnson believed that unity was a great resource of the American people and how he persistently sought a norm of consensus.[13] Reflecting on his March 31 renunciation speech and divisions and hostilities among Americans, Johnson wrote: "I wanted to heal some of these wounds and restore unity to a nation."[14]

Shared situational exigencies, however, are not the only reason for bracketing the two speeches together as the introduction to this essay. As Kenneth Burke remarked: "we use words; words use us."[15] Actually, Burke's idea is ancient, having its roots in Homer's observation that "violent thoughts lead to violent words and, eventually, violent deeds,"[16] attesting to the intimate relationship between thinking, speaking, and acting. Isocrates, too, implied that speaking can help train a moral consciousness and that the arguments we use to persuade others in public are the same arguments employed on our own thoughts.[17] In other words, to speak in public has a self-persuading effect.[18] The feminist author, Susan Faludi, has written also about the transforming effect of speaking in public. Until giving a dreaded speech at the Smithsonian Institute, Faludi felt she had not proved herself: "Until you translate personal words on a page into public connections with other people, you aren't really part of a political movement; . . . women need to be heard not just to change the world, but to change themselves."[19]

When Lyndon Johnson proclaimed the words "let us continue," he cemented himself to courses of action in foreign as well as in domestic policy which can partly account for his speech of March 31, 1968. LBJ's first speech to Congress reflected how he was haunted by the Kennedy persona. Paul Henggeler has written at length about the effect of the "Kennedy Mystique" on Johnson, and elsewhere I have examined how Johnson, always more comfortable with domestic than foreign policy, was greatly influenced in his decision making by the Kennedy appointees, Robert McNamara and McGeorge Bundy prior to July, 1965.[20] In several ways, the public proclamation of "let us continue" became a self-persuasive prophecy impacting private deliberations in a myriad of ways.

If speaking in public has a transforming, consciousness-raising effect on the speaker, then people who write the words spoken by a president have a rhetorically powerful, policy-making role. This chapter illustrates that point by focusing on the making of LBJ's renunciation speech of March 31, 1968. Reflecting on the announcements made in that speech, Johnson said, "No President, at least not this President, makes a decision until he publicly announces that decision and acts upon it. When did I make the decisions that I announced the evening of March 31, 1968? The answer is 9:01 P.M. on March 31, 1968, and they are the same decisions I would make in retrospect."[21] I want to quibble with that statement. Obviously, until he (and someday, she) opens his or her mouth in public to declare his or her intentions, a president always will have the option of changing his or her mind. Regarding the announcements made in the March 31 speech (the beginning of de-escalation, halting of bombing, and his decision not to seek reelection), Johnson resembled more of a Gulliver-like figure—a great giant held down on all sides by a myriad of restraints—than a man in command of his decisions.[22]

A careful examination of the making of the March 31 address reveals a mosaic of external and internal constraints, resulting in the tentative step toward de-escalation and the decision not to seek re-election. To that end, this chapter demonstrates how the historical context composed of events, people, and public responses impacted the private deliberations of Johnson and his advisors, resulting in the rhetorical response on March 31, 1968. This essay is concerned less with the finished product (the speech) than with the mosaic of interactions involved in the eventual need for it. Thus, the need for a public statement became a key decisional period in the private deliberations of the Johnson administration.

Historical Context

To understand the development of the speech, it is necessary first to understand its historical context, both long-range and immediate. As vice president, Johnson had argued against a proposed coup against South Vietnam's prime minister Ngo Dinh Diem.[23] When he became president, he inherited the chaotic repercussions of the assassinations of Diem and his brother, Ngo Dinh Nhu, including a revolving turnstile of incompetent South Vietnamese leaders as well as a stated commitment to the fate of South Vietnam. Until early 1965, Johnson resisted further military expansion in South Vietnam. In February, 1965, the United States began an overt program of reprisal bombings against North Vietnam, and in July of that year Johnson announced the decision to increase greatly the number of U.S. ground forces in Vietnam. Throughout the remainder of 1965 and 1966 the war continued to expand in an incremental fashion, so that by the end of December, 1966, approximately 860,000 tons of bombs had been dropped on North Vietnam.[24] The massive bombing had little effect on the resolve of the North Vietnamese. Ironically, that situation fulfilled the predictions of secret war games that had been played in both the Kennedy and Johnson administrations.[25]

According to speechwriter John Roche, it was during 1966 that the "Kennedy crowd" undermined Johnson. Roche reported: "the whole crowd swung from being the greatest bunch of crusaders for world freedom . . . and domino players and everything else, to all of a sudden, bang! They went the other way"—a defection which was a "body blow" to Johnson.[26] In early March, 1967, Robert F. Kennedy gave a speech on the Senate floor

in which he called for an "honorable settlement" and a halt to the bombing.[27] This was the man who, as attorney general, had actively encouraged
the coup against Diem. At that point in time, Diem and his brother, Nhu,
had signaled they were willing to have talks with the North Vietnamese
and that they thought the United States was becoming too active in their
affairs.[28] Likewise, in late 1965 McGeorge Bundy told President Johnson
that a "tissue paper" could not be put between his (LBJ's) and Robert
Kennedy's stances on Vietnam.[29]

Besides the "Kennedy crowd defection," there were other crises and
changes to be dealt with in 1967. In June there was the Arab-Israeli War. In
September Nguyen Van Thieu was elected president of South Vietnam,
and Prime Minister Nguyen Cao Ky became vice president. The South
Vietnamese candidate who finished second, Truong Dinh Dzo, had favored a halting of the bombing and negotiation,[30] indicating that a large
number of voters were willing to compromise with the Communists. On
September 29, 1967, Johnson made an important speech that came to be
known as the "San Antonio Formula." The speech made public peace over-
tures that had been initiated privately under the secret code names of
Marigold and Sunflower.[31] It was well received by the American public but
rebuffed by the North Vietnamese.

In the meantime, riots had wreaked havoc in American cities. On October 21, 1967, approximately twenty thousand angry anti-war demonstra-
tors marched on the Pentagon. In November former president Dwight D.
Eisenhower publicly called for a limited invasion of North Vietnam, while
Senator Eugene McCarthy announced his intention to challenge Lyndon
Johnson in the Democratic Party's presidential primary elections. By the
end of the year there were about 485,000 U.S. troops in South Vietnam,
and the number of U.S. soldiers killed there had reached 16,021. As of
December, 1967, LBJ had lost many of his White House aides: Press Secretary George Reedy had gone to the Struthers Research Corporation; Special Assistant Horace Busby had left to practice law; Special Assistant Jack
Valenti was heading up the Motion Picture Association; Press Secretary
Bill Moyers was working for *Newsday;* Special Assistant for National Security Affairs McGeorge Bundy had gone to the Ford Foundation; and Secretary of Defense Robert McNamara had announced his intention to direct
the World Bank.

Compounding the internal turmoil caused by the loss of key advisors
were two events in January, 1968, that further shook the administration.
On January 23, North Korea seized the U.S. Navy ship, the USS *Pueblo,*

resulting in the call-up of fourteen thousand reserves to strengthen the U.S. position in South Korea. Then, beginning January 30, the North Vietnamese launched the Tet Offensive, a military action that took its name from the Vietnamese New Year holiday—traditionally a time for family reunions and celebrations. The North Vietnamese attacked five of South Vietnam's major cities, thirty out of forty-four provincial capitals, and sixty-six district towns. During February, Walt Rostow reported that American casualties reached an all-time high with 1,012 killed in thirteen days.[32] The North Vietnamese had secured a psychological rather than a military victory, for fifty-eight thousand of their own troops were killed.[33] The American public's confidence in its military and government had been badly shaken. The North Vietnamese had demonstrated that they were more in number, more daring, and more resolute than the United States had imagined. As a military response to this realization, Gen. Earl G. Wheeler submitted a bleak report at the end of February, and Gen. William Westmoreland requested 205,179 additional troops.[34]

On March 1, 1968, Clark Clifford became the new secretary of defense. On March 12, Eugene McCarthy received 42.2 percent of the Democratic Party votes in the New Hampshire presidential primary. On March 16, Robert Kennedy announced his candidacy for the presidency, causing Lyndon Johnson to comment that he was "forever trapped between the two Kennedys."[35]

Hence, the external constraints prior to LBJ's renunciation speech of March 31, 1968, included a rapidly deteriorating situation in Vietnam, other international crises, deserting advisors, a gathering of challengers for the 1968 presidential election, rioting in American cities, and an American public that was increasingly disillusioned with its military and government. Not to be discounted either were external constraints that involved concerns about the president's health and the volatile nature of Johnson's relationship with the news media, which Kathleen Turner aptly called Johnson's "dual war."[36]

The Speechwriting Organization

The preceding discussion illustrates that political decisions and presidential speeches do not occur in an historical vacuum. They do not occur in an organizational vacuum, either. To trace the making of LBJ's speech of March 31, 1968, it is necessary to understand the organization of speech writing in the Johnson administration as well as the communication surrounding the speechwriters. While president, Johnson gave 1,636 speeches, including 110 addresses on international conflicts. He presented sixty-seven of those foreign policy speeches in Washington, D.C., but he also traveled extensively in order to argue his case on Vietnam before the American people (thirty-one speeches) and outside the United States (twelve speeches). That does not even take into account 150 other multitopic speeches which prominently featured Vietnam.[37] Obviously, President Johnson was not the author of them all. Such ghostwriting raises both ethical and scholarly issues.[38] Harry McPherson, one of Johnson's closest aides and a principal architect of LBJ's "San Antonio Formula" speech and his speech of March 31, 1968, later defended speechwriting on several grounds: (1) If presidents wrote their drafts, they would have little time for anything else. (2) Presidents do not know how to write "presidentialese"—that "exalted language" in which great public issues should be discussed. (3) Speechwriters do not last long if they don't know what the president wants to say. (4) The final product of a major address belongs to the president more than the writers.[39] With his final point, McPherson overstated his case. As this chapter demonstrates, a major presidential speech is painstakingly manufactured by a mosaic of events and people inside as well as outside the White House.

In the beginning of the Johnson presidency, Theodore Sorensen, President Kennedy's extraordinarily gifted writer, remained to coordinate major policy statements. Prior to his departure in 1964, he recommended that the task of drafting speeches be better planned, less concentrated, and that the new Special Counsel, with the help of Jack Valenti, solicit an initial draft in advance from the agencies with jurisdiction over the subject matter of the speech.[40]

After Sorensen departed, Bill Moyers, Horace Busby, and Jack Valenti formed the core of the speechwriting operation. Press Secretary George Reedy prepared some public statements, as did Liz Carpenter who had the dubious distinction of being the in-house "gag" writer.[41] When Sorensen left, Richard Goodwin returned from a Kennedy-imposed exile in the Peace Corps.[42] Goodwin, who is thought to have coined the term, "the Great Society,"[43] was described by McPherson as "probably the best writer to serve a President since Roosevelt's day."[44] According to Valenti, speechwriters and other advisors worked on each of Johnson's major presidential speeches for weeks, with an important speech going through ten to fifteen drafts. Valenti also noted that the president wanted "a newsworthy item in every speech, not just a lot of blather."[45]

The final product of a speech resembled a mosaic in that it had its origin in various departments, agencies, outside sources, chief speechwriters, minor speechwriters, and, sometimes, in the rather minimal input of Lyndon Johnson himself.[46] The Johnson White House created hierarchies of influence among the speechwriters, including ad hoc writing groups that were designed more to keep certain aides busy than to provide serious input. For instance, Richard Neustadt wrote to McGeorge Bundy in November, 1964, about an "ad hoc second level committee for paper drafts," ending his memorandum with, "I am glad to build paper mache machinery if that's what these animals desire."[47]

Between July, 1965, and December, 1966, Bundy, Moyers, Reedy, and Valenti resigned. After the departure of Valenti, Robert E. Kintner, former president of NBC, took over the responsibility of managing the speechwriting operation. According to John Roche, the Kintner system was a "flop." Roche blamed Kintner for creating a vacuum in the speechwriting operation, recalling: "there was this guy sitting in the basement in the corner room whom I took to be the White House bookmaker. His name was Kintner. . . . I figured he was taking bets. I didn't know what else he did. He looked like a bookie . . . [he was] an unpleasant man who kissed Johnson's ass with an assiduousness that could only nauseate the onlooker."[48]

Not surprisingly, Kintner eventually resigned, after which Marvin Watson, Jim Jones, and Charles Maguire coordinated speechwriting assignments every Thursday before handing them out on Fridays. Drafts of speeches were returned to Maguire, who then sent them on to writers Harry McPherson and John Roche. Even though this seemed to be a more clearly defined organizational scheme, McPherson alluded to a function that still was loosely structured and poorly coordinated when he stated, "frequently, you didn't know how many people were writing on a certain subject, particularly a speech."[49] Perhaps he was thinking of the 1968 State of the Union Message which he called a "disaster," and a "terrible experience," because "other people got brought in, everybody but the cook got brought in to make it more personal or human or whatever."[50]

During that period, Lyndon Johnson made one of his few contributions to the speechwriting system. Maguire reported in a memorandum to the speechwriters: "It is a small thing, but there is a large flea in the President's ear about word counts. . . . [H]e says too many speeches are coming through without the count clearly marked at the top right hand corner."[51] Obviously, the length of a speech was important, but LBJ's concern also reflected organizational norms in the Johnson White House, which emphasized quantification.[52]

Organizational norms reflect shared expectations of right action which bind together the members of a group and regulate their behavior. They can be either productive or unproductive in any group's functioning. What is particularly noticeable about the communication of the speechwriters is that they shared a norm of conflict and rivalry that, in fact, was endemic to the Johnson White House. Valenti referred to the norm, saying, there was "warfare" which was a "normal virus that infects every White House" with an "interplay of egos and a clashing of ambitions."[53] His metaphors are significant, because "viruses" and "infections" signal organizational sickness, not health. Metaphors illuminate relationships, reflecting and inviting conformity to certain behaviors, and intensifying our perceptions of behavior and events. Thus, metaphorical use can be a key indicator of organizational norms.

Interestingly, speechwriter John P. Roche wrote about what he called the "Pneumonia Memorandum," explaining that "the military remind me of physicians who had a cure for pneumonia but not for the common cold, so they had a vested interest in the patient with the cold getting pneumonia."[54] Incidentally, bombing was prescribed as the cure for pneumonia. Not surprisingly, the memo was not well received by McNamara. These medical metaphors are intriguing because they reflect a major language construct that dominated much of the Vietnam discussions. The language of the White House advisors portrayed the decision-making group as on a "healing mission" in South Vietnam.[55] As military battles were waged in South Vietnam, private wars were waged in the corridors of the White House. The presidential "healers" needed to heal themselves. Similarly, George Christian, in talking about the White House and human relations, referred to a "bear pit" in which man was pitted against man.[56] The "bear pit" metaphor had been used by Rostow to describe Vietnam so, yet again, the inner-workings of the White House became a mirror image of the Vietnam War.[57]

To different degrees, speechwriters were caught up in skirmishes for power. According to Valenti and Roche, Moyers had an "intelligence operation," a "network of informers," which was part of a "private presidential operation."[58] Valenti also noted that Moyers and Horace Busby "clashed early" because Busby would rather "philosophize than brutalize."[59] Another speechwriter, Peter Benchley, recalled how the staff, as well as the public, were divided into factions of hawks and doves, involving a great deal of "personal conflict and rivalry," which was compounded by the "feeling that controlling the utterance of the President of the United States is a very great power. . . ."[60] Benchley went on to say that the imposition of taste and judgment on the writing of another person was bound to hurt some egos.

That some speechwriters' egos were sensitive and that they distrusted each other were reflected in the ways they fought possessively over their written words. Valenti described how, driving to the Capitol for Johnson's first State of the Union message, Sorensen insisted on clutching the only copy of the speech. When Valenti asked if he could hold it, Sorensen refused because he was afraid Valenti would change some of the words.[61] Goodwin, too, was anxious to protect the "sanctity of his paragraphs" against the onslaught of Valenti and "even the President."[62] Before Johnson's inaugural address in 1965, McGeorge Bundy informed the president, "Dick Goodwin is getting almost as tenacious about his favorite language as Ted Sorensen used to be."[63]

There were power struggles over the use of words and, sometimes, struggles for access to the president. In 1966, a White House Fellow named Richard Copaken was at odds with Kintner over his desire to see Johnson. According to Kintner, "few do [see the president]; Maguire didn't under J.V., does so rarely now." Later, Kintner told Maguire that Copaken was "very brash, pushy, and immature."[64] With approximately ten speechwriters vying for both the use of their words and for access to the president, conflict was inevitable. Certainly, some speechwriters felt unappreciated and discontented.[65] It did not help that discontent when other aides complained about them to the president. Will Sparks told George Christian that he had sent a letter to the president from a lady in Minnesota who thought the president's speechwriters were "full of baloney." Sparks had attached a note to the letter, informing the secretary to tell Johnson, "I agree with everything the lady says—including her comments on the speech writers."[66]

In sum, the speechwriting operation was a fluid mosaic of conflicting personalities, word-wars, rivalries, and power ploys. That conflict influenced the final speech products in a variety of ways. With policy decision on both Vietnam and domestic issues, Johnson habitually chose a middle-way out of conflict. The tendency to reach for a compromised solution was most prevalent in the presence of a great deal of conflict.[67] How did this affect the speechwriting operation? It resulted in speeches that were more bland, watered-down, and less reflective of the personality of the man who would deliver them.[68]

The competitive atmosphere in the speechwriting operation was compounded by confusion concerning how best to explain Vietnam to the
American people. According to George Christian, Johnson habitually
"down-played" Vietnam because he did not want the war to "mess up his
domestic policy."[69] Subsequently, Johnson walked a tightrope between his
desire for peace on the one hand and his refusal to withdraw from Vietnam on the other. Denise Bostdorff shows that in the Gulf of Tonkin
"crisis" in 1964, Johnson attempted to balance strength with restraint, keeping him trapped in a moderate policy. To do so, he altered the meaning of
peace and defense so that both constituted limited military involvement.[70]
Thus, Johnson confused the meaning of the concepts when he joined peace
with a defense of freedom. Real peace would have involved withdrawal
and an absence of war, whereas a real defense of freedom would have demanded a complete military commitment. After a temporary "pause" in
bombing, Johnson continued to join "peace" and "war" when he stated:
"The end of the pause does not mean the end of our own pursuit of peace."[71]

This repeated association of contradictory concepts contributed to the
confusion among the American people. At the end of 1965, reflecting the
same mental muddle of the White House, a poll showed that a majority of
people "supported a military build-up," but "favored a negotiated settlement."[72] In 1966, Johnson was informed, "The public are [sic] absolutely
confused about Vietnam."[73] This confusion was reinforced not only by the
Gulf of Tonkin incident but also in LBJ's subsequent speech given at Johns
Hopkins University in April, 1965. According to McPherson, the speech
sent a confusing message to the public: we mean to win, but victory is not
our goal. The speech also argued that the men in Hanoi are a serious threat,
but we must make peace with them.[74]

The confusion of the public reflected the confusion in the White House.
Writing to the president in 1966, McGeorge Bundy referred to the "right
and brave" course in Vietnam and how the Vietnam effort must continue
"both in battle and in the work of peace."[75] Secretary of State Dean Rusk
believed that the only way to send messages to Hanoi was to take action
because a "formal warning" has the "danger of sounding like a threat" and
on the other hand "sounding like indecision and weakness."[76] Congressional frustration over the mixed message on Vietnam had prompted Senator
Richard Russell of Georgia, among others, to urge in 1966 that the United
States either "get it over or get out."[77]

If the internal White House war and confusion were not enough strain
on the speechwriting process, the man who delivered the words was also a

serious rhetorical obstacle. It is well known that Lyndon Johnson was more comfortable communicating in person with small groups, rather than with the public at large. John McCone, former director of the CIA, recalled: "anytime you're in contact with President Johnson, you're impressed with his personality and his vision and his persuasiveness."[78] He was not so persuasive in public. Frederick Dutton, writing to Bill Moyers in 1964, urged him to make sure that Johnson was seen on TV talking to small groups. He argued: "The President is not at his most effective on television when speaking in outdoor settings, where he is often either too quiet or too strident."[79] Apparently, this rhetorical problem had not changed much by 1966 when Sparks remarked: "The President has been using his present rather evangelical style for 35 years, and it is going to be hard to convince him that it doesn't get him anywhere."[80] Even when the speechwriters gave Johnson what they thought was a faultless script, he still managed to change its meaning with his delivery and gestures. After hearing him give a speech in May, 1966, McPherson rebuked Johnson for causing confusion and distrust with a speech delivery that contradicted the message of his address:

> I felt it was harsh, uncompromising, over-militant. It seemed you were trying to beat Fulbright's ears down before an audience of Democrats who, I am told, had earlier applauded him strongly. . . . The speech does not read as bad as it sounded. The combination of tone, emphasis, and frequent glances down at Fulbright made it (for me) wrong. There was nothing of Baltimore or subsequent assurances that we want to negotiate an honorable way out. . . . [W]henever it touched on foreign policy it was militant—if not in language, then in delivery.[81]

McPherson expressed his frustration with what he termed Fulbright's "vapid sophomoric bitching," but warned Johnson: "he cannot be shouted out of existence."[82]

If Johnson's delivery was an obstacle, so was his persona. Simply put, the public no longer trusted him. Scholars have suggested that a president's principal source of influence is public support, and public support depends on his popularity.[83] Johnson had defeated Barry Goldwater in the 1964 presidential election by portraying himself as the peace candidate and portraying Goldwater as the war candidate. When Johnson subsequently escalated the Vietnam War, much of the public concluded that he had intended to expand the war all along—that he had concealed his true intentions in order to win the election.[84] After spending his 1966 vacation in

Rhode Island, McPherson told Moyers that the people with whom he had talked did "not trust LBJ."[85] Three days before Johnson gave his address on March 31, 1968, he was told: "people resent Johnson more than they resent the war."[86] Four days after that speech, the *Washington Star* ran the headline: "Johnson's Political Exit is Hard to Believe," underneath which was written, "the Lyndon we have known is no Richard II—'with mine own hand I give away my crown': save your obituaries, boys; and see how they read in September."[87]

The preceding sections provide an overview of the ways in which constraints both outside the Johnson administration and inside the Johnson White House influenced presidential speechwriting in general. Those constraints also affected the creation of the specific speech of March 31, 1968, in which LBJ renounced his ambitions for another term as president of the United States.

Private Deliberations Become Public Declaration

The seeds of the March 31 speech were sown long before the need for it became apparent. As Johnson spoke Kennedyesque words on November 27, 1963, he was setting the stage for a King Lear-like tragedy in which a successful short-term strategy would reap long-term defeat. Within less than two years, the LBJ White House was consumed with pushing and pulling between advisors who, sometimes ahead of Johnson and sometimes in step with him, marched toward the overt widening of the Vietnam War. During the following years, LBJ's frustrations, stubbornness, and even paranoia seemed to cement him to the middle-of-the-road policy of a "limited" war.

In particular, two speeches by Johnson foreshadowed his address of March 31, 1968: the Johns Hopkins University speech on April 7, 1965, and the San Antonio address on September 29, 1967. At Johns Hopkins University LBJ faced more than a thousand faculty members and students and an extended television audience of about 6 million.[88] Basically, it was a peace speech designed to reverse the heavy flow of critical mail from the public regarding the bombing of North Vietnam in February, 1965. McGeorge Bundy had outlined the original draft and then passed it on to Goodwin, Valenti, and others. Incidentally, the privilege of writing a "first draft" was a power well-recognized by Bundy.[89] The speech offered a "carrot and stick" formula for future talks with North Vietnam, a formula which had been reiterated constantly in the private communications between LBJ and his advisors.[90] By all accounts, the speech had its intended effect. The heavy flow of critical mail was reversed, and Hanoi responded with a lengthy speech that included four points as a basis for negotiation.[91]

The effect of the speech, however, was only temporary. There was no negotiation, and the war was greatly widened in July. Even so, the public announcement of an intent for peace cannot be discounted. Unfortunately, at the same time that Johnson was talking about peace (in private as well as in public), he was also committing himself to war. At a meeting in 1966, Johnson stated, "There are island hoppers who jump from issue to issue and there are those who would put a bag of cement on the back of the men running the race. . . , [but] we are committed and we will not be deterred."[92] Just five months later, however, Robert McNamara began to "wobble," writing to Johnson: "I see no reasonable way to bring the war to an end soon. Enemy morale has not been broken. . . . .[They have] adopted a strategy of keeping us busy and waiting us out."[93] Still, the bombing program was expanded in April, 1967. In May, McNamara sent a controversial memo to the president, suggesting that it was time to change their objectives in Vietnam.[94]

In July, 1967, a secret peace initiative (under the code name "Pennsylvania") used then professor Henry Kissinger as a messenger, offering to stop the bombing if Hanoi would enter into productive discussions with the United States.[95] To give credibility to this offer, Johnson publicly repeated it on September 29 in a major speech which came to be known as the "San Antonio Formula." There is some confusion regarding the authorship of that speech. Berman contends that McNamara wrote the speech with the assistance of Assistant Secretary of Defense Paul Warnke and Deputy Secretary of Defense Paul Nitze.[96] Turner suggests that the idea for the speech originated with economist Albert Carr, who shared it with McPherson. Then, in the typical speechwriting procedure of the Johnson White House, McPherson wrote one draft even as Special Assistant for National Security Affairs Walt Rostow wrote another.[97] It seems likely that both versions are correct. A memo from McPherson to Johnson outlined the need for two speeches to explain how the United States became involved in Vietnam, why, and what the future looked like. A note attached to that memo indicates that Johnson agreed and had instructed that "everyone [get] to work full time" on the address during the next few days.[98]

A draft of the San Antonio speech included the statement: "This evening I want to talk to you about the dominant issue of the day—the struggle in Vietnam." But Johnson crossed out that line and changed it to read:

"I want to talk to you about Vietnam"[99]—a revision that reflected Johnson's wish that the Vietnam War was not the dominant issue of his presidency. The speech drafts also quoted John F. Kennedy from 1961: "We are Americans, determined to defend the frontiers of freedom, by an honorable peace if possible, and by armies if arms are used against us."[100] Those words by Kennedy were a part of Johnson's stubborn commitment to the fate of Vietnam. Withdrawing from Vietnam was not an "honorable peace," as far as Johnson and most of his advisors were concerned.

Accordingly, the San Antonio speech stressed that the goals of the United States were to help South Vietnam find freedom while at the same time protecting U.S. interests. It signaled a willingness to talk to Hanoi, but only under certain conditions. Reactions to the speech at home were favorable, but not in Hanoi. A cable to the White House read: "Communist North Vietnamese today dismissed President Johnson's latest appeal for peace as 'nothing new' and said there can be no talks on the Vietnam War until the U.S. unconditionally stops bombing. . . . Radio Hanoi referred to the 'vague' terms of the San Antonio speech as a 'faked desire' for peace."[101] McPherson, calling himself the "principal architect" of the speech, said it was a "pretty good apologia."[102] The news media described the speech as "a crucial turning point."[103] Years later, the writers of the National Security Council's history of LBJ's speech of March 31, 1968, would agree. That study concluded that the March 31 speech both reaffirmed the "San Antonio Formula" and reactivated the offer in the Johns Hopkins University speech for North Vietnam to participate in the economic development of Southeast Asia.[104]

Even as Johnson was proposing the San Antonio Formula, however, he was aware that the North Vietnamese were planning a massive winter-spring offensive.[105] At about the same time, McNamara aired his doubts about pursuing the bombing program at a luncheon meeting on October 31, 1967.[106] At another meeting, however, Johnson was advised not to withdraw from Vietnam, although George Ball who had always been against any escalation, also suggested restricting bombing to an area around the demilitarized zone.[107] McGeorge Bundy, who had been at the same meeting, later wrote to the president about the need for a "visible de-escalation," ending his letter with, "I think we should search for it."[108]

On January 13, 1968, perhaps thinking about the forthcoming State of the Union address, McPherson suggested that a future speech should offer a "practical extension of the San Antonio Formula," and stressed that Clark Clifford, soon to be appointed secretary of defense, especially agreed with him. Accordingly, in the 1968 State of the Union speech, Johnson reiter-

ated the formula as a basis for any decision to halt the bombing.[109] Previously, Johnson had excised a long section of the State of the Union message which dealt with Vietnam, saying that he wanted to keep it for another time, and asking McPherson to prepare another speech.[110] For the
draft of this new speech, McPherson began to discourage the use of the
phrase "San Antonio Formula" because "it might make it hard for N.V. to
come to the table" because of their previous public rejection of that offer.
Johnson responded on the bottom of McPherson's note: "That's fine. Bear
that in mind in writing."[111]

On January 29, 1968, the United States began a truce in deference to
Tet. Enemy attacks began shortly after midnight with the American Em-
bassy in Saigon coming under attack on January 31. Sam Adams writes
that the Tet Offensive and its subsequent reporting on television showed
the Viet Cong as such a potent and skillful force that the American people
realized they had been "conned by double talk."[112] The Tet Offensive
shocked Johnson and his advisors. According to McPherson, the origins of
the March 31 speech actually took place early in February when, McPherson,
LBJ, and Rostow thought of ways in which to address the situation.[113]
Other primary sources, though, indicate that Rostow had sent Secretary of
State Dean Rusk a "rough working outline" of a speech on January 31. On
that outline, Rostow indicated his reservations about any additional peace
moves when he wrote: "The San Antonio Formula—as far as any President can go: rock bottom!"[114]

During the month of February, 1968, at least three drafts of the speech
responding to the Tet Offensive were written. The first draft was written
sometime during the first week of February, because on February 5 Marvin
Watson informed Johnson that Horace Busby's reaction to the speech draft
had been "lukewarm," that it was "not convincing," and that Congress
should be the venue of the address.[115] Eleven days later, U Thant informed
Johnson, through Walt Rostow, that Hanoi would talk if the bombing
stopped but that they would not submit themselves to the assumptions of
the San Antonio Formula.[116] In the meantime, Gen. William Westmoreland
had dropped a "bombshell" when he requested an additional 205,000
troops—a request that McPherson called "unbelievable" and "futile."[117]
On February 28, Johnson asked Clark Clifford to head up an intensive
working team to consider the request. On March 1, Clifford took over the
Department of Defense from Robert McNamara.

In a cabinet room meeting on March 4, 1968, Clifford recommended a
new strategy for Vietnam—but not a peace initiative—saying that his team

was divided over the bombing policy.[118] In the same meeting, Treasury Secretary Henry Fowler had given a "brutal description" of the fiscal implications of a further military build-up, and Rusk ventured that bombing perhaps could be stopped during the rainy season, to which Johnson had replied in a typical fashion, "get on your horse on that one."[119] According to Johnson, it was Rusk who, the next day, suggested that a paragraph on limiting bombing be added to the proposed speech.[120]

The dismal atmosphere in the White House deteriorated still further when Westmoreland's request for more troops was leaked to the *New York Times,* whose resulting story stirred up considerable dissent. Adding insult to Johnson's injury, the 1968 New Hampshire primary election showed that LBJ had only a small lead over Eugene McCarthy—at that point his only openly declared challenger for the presidential nomination of the Democratic Party. On March 14, 1968, Dean Acheson suggested a "progressive disengagement" from Vietnam.[121] While meeting with Clifford and Sorensen that same day, Robert Kennedy offered a deal: he would not run for the presidency, if LBJ admitted his error in Vietnam.[122] Two days later Kennedy announced his candidacy. The next week LBJ delivered an extemporaneous speech in Minneapolis in which he asked the country to join him in a "total national effort to win the war"—a remark that gave some credence to those who wanted to hold Johnson fully responsibility for the Vietnam War. The speech created an uproar both within and without the White House.[123.]

By this time, the proposed speech for March 31, 1968, had gone through at least four drafts. The draft that Johnson saw on March 20 began: "I speak to you tonight in a time of grave challenge to our country."[124] In a meeting that same day, Clifford had stated emphatically that the administration needed to wind down the war.[125] On March 25, Rusk wrote to Johnson, "my own mind is very close to McPherson's about a possible peace move."[126] That day, Rusk had met in his Department of State dining room with a group of former statesmen, dubbed the "Wise Men." After that lunch meeting, Johnson had asked one of the attendees, McGeorge Bundy, to summarize the group's views. Accordingly, Bundy told Johnson that Dean Acheson urged disengagement with six of the men in favor, and four preferring the status quo.[127] That same day, Rostow received a gloomy memorandum from George Carver, Jr., special assistant for Vietnam affairs at the CIA, reporting the increasing strength of the North Vietnam Army.[128]

In his meticulous work on Senator Mike Mansfield, Gregory A. Olson notes that this senator who had persistently and privately dissented against

the war met with the president on March 27, 1968, and that after the meeting, Mansfield thought that Johnson had changed his mind.[129] Also, on
March 27, Clifford told Rusk, Rostow, McPherson, and William P. (Bill)
Bundy that the speech (then in its seventh draft) was "wrong!" He continued: "The speech is more of the same. The American people are fed up
with more of the same." He went on to suggest that the administration
consider "winding down the war." McPherson recalled that Rusk and
Rostow did not react negatively, even when Clifford asked McPherson to
write "alternative draft #1."[130] Much later, McPherson was to recall: "I left
the State Department [that night] wanting to holler. Whom could I talk
to? Celebrate with? No one."[131] By 10:00 P.M. that evening, McPherson had
written the new draft, marked it "1A," and sent it to Johnson. By the next
morning, LBJ had decided to go with the new draft. Significantly, the first
sentence of draft 1A read: "Tonight, I want to speak to you of the program
of peace in Vietnam. . . ."[132] Hence, in the course of a week the speechwriting
process had transformed a war speech on the "grave challenge" in Southeast Asia into a peace speech on Vietnam.

During the next two days, four more drafts were written. On Saturday,
March 30, 1968, a group composed of Johnson, Nicholas Katzenbach,
Clifford, Bill Bundy, Rostow, Christian, and McPherson worked on it all
day. (By this time, Rusk was on his way across the Pacific.) At the end of
that meeting, McPherson had suggested that the speech needed a new
"peroration," to which Johnson replied, "I may even add one of my own."[133]
Actually, Johnson's peroration had been in the making for several months.
In August, 1967, Johnson had told Governor John Connally that he did
not intend to run again, and George Christian was asked to write a statement for possible use in December. Of course, Johnson had decided that
was not the right time; instead, he toyed with the idea of using it in his
State of the Union address on January 17, 1968.[134] Clifford recalled how
Johnson had asked him in the fall of 1967 to write a memorandum concerning President Truman's decision not to seek re-election in 1952, saying
casually, "I may do the same thing as Truman"—a comment which Clifford
had not taken seriously.[135]

Apparently, Horace Busby had taken the president seriously, for in January, 1968, he wrote to Johnson advising him to avoid any impression of
"self-pitying." He continued, "I think it possible that making yourself a
'lame duck' might have unforeseeable serious consequences abroad without offsetting gains at home. . . . [but] if you do what is right for yourself,
it will be right in the history books."[136] Although Johnson's decision not to

seek re-election was a surprise to most, Jim Rowe had informed LBJ on March 28, that the "Kennedy people" were talking about the possibility.[137] George Christian, Tom Johnson, and Horace Busby polished the draft of Johnson's peroration for his speech on March 31, 1968. Perhaps fearing that her husband was leaving room to change his mind later, Lady Bird Johnson changed the phrase, "I have no desire to accept the nomination" to "I will not accept the nomination." Later, she preferred Christian's phrasing of "I shall not seek, and I will not accept the nomination of my party for another term as your President."[138]

On March 30, 1968, at 9:30 P.M., McPherson, apparently unaware that President Johnson had his own ending to the speech, informed him: "Here is the closing peroration. It does not light up the sky with rockets. Clark Clifford feels strongly—I-would-say-vi-o-lent-ly—that it should not light up the sky. He argues that if you come on with a strong "we must resist aggression" line at the end of a peaceful initiation speech, people will say, "ah—now here comes the real Johnson. Old Blood and Thunder"; and that the purpose of the speech will be lost. I agree with him.[139]

LBJ continued to revise the address almost to the time of its presentation. On Sunday, March 31 at 2:06 P.M., Johnson requested seven copies of his secret peroration, with the admonition, "show it to no one."[140] Clark Clifford, invited to the White House for dinner that evening, was shown the new ending as Johnson dressed for the occasion. During the day, Johnson had Charles Maguire cut the speech's length.[141] Additionally, Johnson had changed the phrase "guard against divisions and all its works" to "guard against divisiveness and all its consequences," expressing at the same time that he particularly liked the phrase, "clear the American Agenda."[142] At 8:15 P.M. the new ending was added to the TelePrompTer, and at 9:00 P.M. President Lyndon Baines Johnson began his address with the words, "Tonight, I want to speak to you of peace in Vietnam and Southeast Asia."

Despite the reservations expressed by the *Washington Star,* reactions to the speech were overwhelmingly positive. The Dow Jones Index jumped twenty points, and a poll of fifty-seven major news editors and columnists showed that forty-three approved, and only five disapproved.[143] Rejoicing was mixed with regret as indicated by the following assortment of newspaper headlines: "Johnson Called Man of Courage"; "The Liberation of Lyndon Johnson"; and "Publishers and Comedians Hurry to Alter Anti-Johnson Material."[144] Apparently, Johnson approved of the speech, too: later that year, seventy thousand booklets of the speech were distributed at a cost of over $30,000.[145]

On April 3, 1968, Hanoi sent a message that it was ready to talk. Clark Clifford contended that the importance of Johnson's speech was not its offer to Hanoi but its effect on the United States. In Clifford's view, the speech marked an end to a war of escalation, and the first step, however ambiguous, toward de-escalation and disengagement.[146] Both the Kennedy and Johnson administrations had missed opportunities to withdraw in 1963, in 1964, and in 1965. Each opportunity was followed by a slow and deadly increase in the widening of the war. Unfortunately, the decisions to gradually de-escalate and disengage had similar results. During approximately eight weeks following LBJ's speech, 3,700 Americans were killed in Vietnam, and 18,000 more were wounded—not to mention the enormous losses suffered by the military forces of North Vietnam and by civilians.

Conclusion

The preceding discussion demonstrates the complexity of presidential speechwriting. Speeches are written within a collage of constraints—both those internal to the White House and those external to the presidential administration. Within that context, speechwriting is a policy-making activity in which various writers may serve the president well or ill. Looking back on the LBJ White House of 1963 to 1965, McPherson noted that Johnson's rhetoric "outdistanced the facts." The blame for Johnson's inflated speeches, McPherson believed, rested "not mostly [with] Johnson." Instead, McPherson placed the blame on "Goodwin, and also Moyers . . . the exuberance was mostly speech writers."[147] That exuberance was shown in a memorandum that Moyers wrote to Johnson in 1965. Moyers suggested that it was his job to implement policy that had been decided by the president, but he went on to urge Johnson to make a speech, saying, "The world is waiting for you to speak . . . once lost, such a moment comes again only when the fates decide so."[148]

Moyers's choice of words—as well as this chapter's account of the speech of March 31, 1968—suggests that at least a part of the power of speechwriters and other advisors who urge the need for a speech resides in that classical concept of *kairos*. Isocrates, a speechwriter himself, told his student, Nicocles, to grasp the appropriate moment to speak. In his treatise "Against the Sophists," he stated, "it is not possible for speeches to be good if they do not partake of the opportune moments, and the appropriate and novel."[149] Moyers, then, was following in the steps of classical rhetoricians when he stressed the right "moment," and he was exercising presidential power even if it was tempered by his reference to Johnson's decisional responsibility.

Unlike Moyers, Goodwin never tried to camouflage his role. His advice to McPherson was this: "Wait until the last moment before submitting a draft to the President and the bureaucracy. In that way . . . you can make your ideas almost a fait accompli."[150] McPherson confirmed that when he was trying to moderate Vietnam speeches, he was actually trying to moderate Vietnam policy.[151] Even those who were not speechwriters knew the power of writing ideas in the form of a speech. For instance, McGeorge Bundy told Johnson that he had cast foreign policy "in the form of a speech," simply to see "how it might work."[152]

The crucial decision to alter the substance of LBJ's speech of March 31, 1968, was steered by the alliance of Clifford and McPherson who actively campaigned to alter the speech as well as policy. The need for a speech only accentuated the need for a new policy. Moreover, in the steps leading to the speech, McPherson seemed to hold a unique position in his relationship to Johnson, being comfortable enough to tell the president he was "wrong." McPherson was honest at other times, too. After a trip to Vietnam in 1967, he wrote this: "If I were a young peasant living in a hamlet, and had had none of my family hurt or killed by the VC; if I saw that the ridiculous Vietnamese educational system would almost certainly deny me the chance to go beyond the fifth grade . . . I would join [the Viet Cong]."[153] Less than two weeks before LBJ's renunciation speech, he told the president: "when you say 'stick with it in Vietnam,' . . . you are saying, stick with a situation that shows signs of growing worse, . . . you ask people to continue to support an administration that was in office while the Vietnam War grew. . . . [Y]our culpability or lack of it is beside the point."[154] Clifford and McPherson's campaign for the president's mind was aided also by a montage of events and input from other people. The need for a speech, however, defined the need to arrange the external and internal constraints into a decision.

This study also reveals the tension between private deliberations and public declarations. Essentially, speechwriters are mediators between the private and public realms, even as speechwriting must mediate between thinking and speaking, and rhetoric seeks to mediate between past, present, and future. Speechwriters try to bridge the gap between policy and the public, the government and the people. Roderick P. Hart contends that "how one behaves in public may bear only faint resemblance to how one behaves in private," and that "that difference makes no difference at all in many cases."[155] Yet, this study reveals a strong connection between private decision making and public rhetoric. For example, the confusing public statements about peace and war are illuminated by discovering that they were constant echoes of private communication within the White House. Consequently, the ambiguity of Johnson's speeches, at times, had more to do with personal and organizational confusion than with any purposeful attempt to deceive the American public. The fact that LBJ's delivery changed the meaning of his speeches indicates that there was a discrepancy between content and oral style—between the phrasing of the words and the temperament of the man. That discrepancy was responsible, in part, for the public's distrust of Johnson.

Similarly, examining the private communication of presidents and their advisors during the speechwriting process also demonstrates how some speeches, once made public, further constrain their decisions, affecting their private deliberations. The Johns Hopkins University and the San Antonio speeches are examples of the phenomenon where private deliberations affect public declarations, which affect subsequent private deliberations. Those two speeches resonated with the private communication of President Johnson and his advisors from early 1965 all the way to LBJ's speech of March 31, 1968. Perhaps more importantly, LBJ's speeches resonated with the speech that John F. Kennedy had made in 1961 ("We are Americans, determined to defend the frontiers of freedom by an honorable peace."),[156] and with Robert F. Kennedy's partial reiteration of JFK's theme in 1967.[157] As a consequence, Lyndon Johnson and many of his advisors were cemented into a vain search for a way out of Vietnam that would not be a withdrawal. Johnson's own presidential declaration of "let us continue"[158] in November, 1963, had set him on that course. The search for that "honorable" peace proved fruitless. So, instead of withdrawing U.S. troops, President Lyndon B. Johnson withdrew himself.

Notes

1. Louis Heren, *No Hail, No Farewell* (New York: Harper and Row, 1970), pp. 8–9.
2. Ward S. Just, "What Ever Happened to Lyndon Johnson?" *The Reporter,* Jan. 17, 1963, p. 27.
3. Kenneth Crawford, "LBJ: Who's That?" *Newsweek,* Feb. 11, 1963, p. 39.
4. Anonymous Document, "Quips and Witticisms," Box 11, Office Files of Richard N. Goodwin, Lyndon Baines Johnson Library, Austin, Tex. All unpublished materials cited in this chapter (including oral history interviews) are from the Lyndon Baines Johnson Library, Austin, Tex.

5. See Merle Miller, *Lyndon: An Oral Biography* (New York: G. P. Putnam and Sons, 1980), pp. 316–17.

6. Lyndon B. Johnson, "Address Before a Joint Session of Congress, November 27, 1963," *Public Papers of the Presidents of the United States: Lyndon B. Johnson, 1963–64* (Washington, D.C.: Government Printing Office, 1965), Book I, p. 8. Hereafter, this publication series is cited as *Public Papers* (year).

7. Karlyn Kohrs Campbell and Kathleen Hall Jamieson, *Deeds Done in Words: Presidential Rhetoric and the Genres of Governance* (Chicago: University of Chicago Press, 1990), p. 41. Also see Kurt Ritter, "Lyndon B. Johnson's Crisis Rhetoric after the Assassination of John F. Kennedy: Securing Legitimacy and Leadership" in *The Modern Presidency and Crisis Rhetoric*, ed. Amos Kiewe (Westport, Conn.: Praeger, 1994), pp. 73–89.

8. Patricia D. Witherspoon, "Let Us Continue: The Rhetorical Initiation of Lyndon Johnson's Presidency," *Presidential Studies Quarterly* 4 (1987): 531–40.

9. Lyndon B. Johnson, "The President's Address to the Nation Announcing Steps to Limit the War in Vietnam and Reporting his Decision Not to Seek Reelection, March 31, 1968," *Public Papers, 1968–69*, Book I, p. 476.

10. Walter Trohan, "Report from Washington: LBJ Did Best, But Reaped Only Blame and Abuse," *Chicago Tribune*, April 2, 1968, section 1, p. 2.

11. Larry Berman, *Lyndon Johnson's War: The Road to Stalemate in Vietnam* (New York: W. W. Norton, 1989), p. xi.

12. John H. Patton, "An End and a Beginning: Lyndon B. Johnson's Decisive Speech of March 31, 1968," *Today's Speech* (1973): 33–41.

13. Dan F. Hahn, "Archetype and Signature in Johnson's 1965 State of the Union," *Central States Speech Journal* 34 (1983): 236–46.

14. Lyndon Baines Johnson, *The Vantage Point* (New York: Holt, Rinehart and Winston, 1971), p. 427.

15. Kenneth Burke, *Language as Symbolic Action* (Berkeley: University of California Press, 1966), pp. 44–55.

16. Richard Leo Enos, *Greek Rhetoric Before Aristotle* (Prospect Heights, Ill.: Waveland Press, 1993), p. 7.

17. Isocrates, "Against the Sophists" and "Antidosis" in *Readings in Classical Rhetoric*, ed. Thomas W. Benson and Michael H. Prosser (Davis, Calif.: Hermagoras Press, 1988), pp. 43–52.

18. See Roderick P. Hart, *The Sound of Leadership: Presidential Communication in the Modern Age* (Chicago: University of Chicago Press, 1987), p. 91. Hart notes that, according to social scientists, people will rearrange their attitudes in the direction of lies they tell to keep cognitive tension in check. Hart also observes that during the course of his presidency, Johnson seemed more and more committed to his Vietnam War policies.

19. Susan Faludi, "Speak for Yourself," *New York Times Magazine*, Jan. 26, 1992, p. 29.

20. See Paul R. Henggeler, *In His Steps: Lyndon Johnson and the Kennedy Mystique* (Chicago: Ivan R. Dee, 1991); Moya Ann Ball, *Vietnam-On-The-Potomac* (New York: Praeger, 1992); and Moya Ann Ball, "The Phantom of the Oval Office: The John F. Kennedy Assassination's Symbolic Impact on Lyndon B. Johnson, His Key Advisers, and the Vietnam Decision-Making Process," *Presidential Studies Quarterly* 24

(1994): 105–19. For additional studies of Johnson's presidential rhetoric, see (chronological): Robert H. Hall, "Lyndon Johnson's Speech Preparation," *Quarterly Journal of Speech* 51 (1965): 168–76; David Zarefsky, "President Johnson's War on Poverty: The Rhetoric of Three 'Establishment' Movements," *Communication Monographs* 44 (1977): 352–73; Richard A. Cherwitz, "Lyndon Johnson and the 'Crisis' of Tonkin Gulf: A President's Justification of War," *Western Journal of Speech Communication* 52 (1978): 93–104; Lee Sigelman and Lawrence Miller, "Understanding Presidential Rhetoric: The Vietnam Statements of Lyndon Johnson," *Communication Research* 5 (1978): 25–56; David Zarefsky, "The Great Society as a Rhetorical Proposition," *Quarterly Journal of Speech* 65 (1979): 364–78; David Zarefsky, "Lyndon Johnson Redefines 'Equal Opportunity': The Beginnings of Affirmative Action," *Central States Speech Journal* 31 (1980): 85–94; Cal M. Logue and John H. Patton, "From Ambiguity to Dogma: The Rhetorical Symbols of Lyndon B. Johnson on Vietnam," *Southern Speech Communication Journal* 47 (1982): 310–29; David Zarefsky, "Subordinating the Civil Rights Issue: Lyndon Johnson in 1964," *Southern Speech Communication Journal* 48 (1983): 103–18; Roderick P. Hart, *Verbal Style and the Presidency* (Orlando, Fla.: Academic Press, 1984), pp. 108–26; Kathleen J. Turner, *Lyndon Johnson's Dual War: Vietnam and the Press* (Chicago: University of Chicago Press, 1985); David Zarefsky, *President Johnson's War on Poverty* (Tuscaloosa, Ala.: University of Alabama Press, 1986); Kurt Ritter, "President Lyndon B. Johnson's Inaugural Address, 1965," *Inaugural Addresses of Twentieth-Century American Presidents,* ed. Halford Ryan (Westport, Conn.: Praeger, 1993), pp. 195–207; Kenneth S. Zagacki, "Lyndon Baines Johnson," *U.S. Presidents as Orators: A Bio-Critical Sourcebook,* ed. Halford Ryan (Westport, Conn.: Greenwood Press, 1995), pp. 228–48; Roderick P. Hart and Kathleen E. Kendall, "Lyndon Johnson and the Problem of Politics: A Study in Conversation," in *Beyond the Rhetorical Presidency,* ed. Martin J. Medhurst (College Station: Texas A&M University Press, 1996), pp. 77–103; Carol Gelderman, *All the Presidents' Words: The Bully Pulpit and the Creation of the Virtual Presidency* (New York: Walker, 1997), pp. 63–75; Garth E. Pauley, "Presidential Rhetoric and Group Politics: Lyndon B. Johnson and the Civil Rights Act of 1964," *Southern Communication Journal* 63 (1997): 1–19; Garth E. Pauley, "Rhetoric and Timeliness: An Analysis of Lyndon B. Johnson's Voting Rights Address," *Western Journal of Communication* 62 (1998): 26–53; and Garth E. Pauley, *The Modern Presidency & Civil Rights: Rhetoric on Race from Roosevelt to Nixon* (College Station: Texas A&M University Press, 2001), pp. 159–99.

21. Johnson, *Vantage Point,* p. 424.

22. David Mervin, "The Bully Pulpit II," *Presidential Studies Quarterly* 25 (1995): 19–21.

23. Moya Ann Ball, "A Case Study of the Kennedy Administration's Decision-making Concerning the Diem Coup of November, 1963," *Western Journal of Speech Communication* 54 (1990): 557–74.

24. Ronald H. Spector, *After Tet: The Bloodiest Year in Vietnam* (New York: Vintage Books, 1993), p. 11.

25. See Ball, *Vietnam-On-The-Potomac,* pp. 93, 129, 130, 134, 153.

26. See John P. Roche, Oral History (Interview I by Paige Mulhollen, July 16, 1970), p. 10. Depoe has described how, between 1966 and 1968, Arthur Schlesinger, Jr., attempted to unify dissent against Vietnam; see Stephen Depoe, "Arthur

Schlesinger, Jr.'s 'Middle Way Out of Vietnam': The Limits of 'Technocratic Realism' as the Basis for Foreign Policy Dissent," *Western Journal of Speech Communication* 52 (1988): 147–66.

27. Robert F. Kennedy, "Vietnam," *Congressional Record*, 90th Cong., 1st Sess., Mar. 2, 1967, vol. 113, part 4, p. 5281.

28. See Ball, "A Case Study of the Kennedy Administration's Decision-making," p. 565.

29. McGeorge Bundy to the president, Sept. 14, 1965, "Vols. 12–14," Box 4, Bundy Memos to President, National Security File. Hereafter materials from this collection are cited as NSF.

30. Berman, *Lyndon Johnson's War,* p. 79.

31. Robert S. McNamara, *In Retrospect: The Tragedy and Lessons of Vietnam* (New York: Random House, 1995), p. 247.

32. Letter, Rostow to president, Feb. 12, 1968, "3/31 Speech Volume 2, Tabs A–Z," Box 47, NSF.

33. Clark Clifford, *Counsel to the President: A Memoir* (New York: Random House, 1991), pp. 469–75.

34. Memorandum, Gen. Earl G. Wheeler to the president, Feb. 27, 1968, "March 31 Speech," Box 47, NSC History, NSF.

35. Clifford, *Counsel to the President,* p. 505.

36. See Johnson, *Vantage Point,* pp. 425–27; Turner, *Lyndon Johnson's Dual War.*

37. Hart, *Sound of Leadership,* pp. 8, 92.

38. Ernest G. Bormann, "Ghostwriting and the Rhetorical Critic," *Quarterly Journal of Speech* 46 (1960): 284–88.

39. Harry C. McPherson, *A Political Education: A Washington Memoir* (Boston: Little, Brown and Company, 1972), p. 326.

40. Theodore C. Sorensen to the president, Jan. 10, 1964, "Sorensen, Theodore," Box 12, Office of the President File.

41. See Fred Panzer to Liz Carpenter, March 14, 1968, "March 31 Speech," Box 5, EX SP 3/01/68, White House Central File (WHCF).

42. Valenti recalled how Goodwin, who had clashed with Sorensen, was exiled from the Kennedy White House and eventually became Sargent Shriver's writer at the Peace Corps. Jack Valenti, Oral History (Interview V by Joe B. Frantz, July 12, 1972), p. 2. For more on Goodwin, see the chapter on John F. Kennedy in this volume.

43. Emmette S. Redford and Richard T. McCulley, *White House Operations: The Johnson Presidency* (Austin: University of Texas Press, 1986), p. 68.

44. McPherson, *A Political Education,* p. 327.

45. Valenti, Oral History (Interview IV by Joe B. Frantz, March 3,1971), p. 31.

46. McPherson, *A Political Education,* p. 327.

47. Richard Neustadt to Bundy, Nov. 11, 1964, Box 7, Name File—Neustadt, NSF.

48. Roche, Oral History (Interview I), p. 38.

49. Harry McPherson, Oral History (Interview III by T. H. Baker, Jan. 16, 1969), p. 4.

50. McPherson, Oral History (Interview III), p. 11.

51. Charles Maguire to McPherson and Roche, "SP 10/19/67–12/28/67," Box 4, EX SP, WHCF.

52. See Ball, *Vietnam-on-the-Potomac,* pp. 149–50.

53. Valenti, Oral History (Interview V), pp. 17, 19.

54. Roche, Oral History (Interview I), p. 73.

55. Repeatedly, Johnson and his advisors used imagery that depicted them as on a medical mission in South Vietnam; see Ball, *Vietnam-on-the-Potomac,* pp. 132–33.

56. George C. Christian, Oral History (Interview by Joe B. Franz, Feb. 27, 1970), tape 3, p. 4.

57. Walt W. Rostow to Jack Valenti, Jan. 29, 1966, "January 1966," Box 17, Files of McGeorge Bundy, NSF.

58. Roche, Oral History (Interview I), p. 21; and Valenti, Oral History (Interview V), p. 14.

59. Valenti, Oral History (Interview V), p. 6.

60. Peter Benchley, Oral History (Interview by Thomas Harrison Baker, Nov. 20, 1968), p. 8.

61. Valenti, Oral History (Interview II by Joe B. Franz), pp. 28–29.

62. Valenti, Oral History (Interview V), p. 6.

63. McGeorge Bundy to the president, Jan. 18, 1965, "Vols. 5–8," Memos to the President, NSF.

64. Robert E. Kintner to Charles Maguire, Sept. 29, 1966, "RC Richard Cophaken," Box 10, Office Files of Charles Maguire.

65. See, for instance, Benchley, Oral History.

66. Will Sparks to George Christian, Sept. 12, 1967, "SP 8/01/67–9/12/67," Box 12, EX SP 6/01/67, WHCF.

67. See David Zarefsky, *President Johnson's War on Poverty,* p. 204; and Ball, *Vietnam-on-the-Potomac,* pp. 153–54.

68. Bormann argues that "ghostwriting" has similar consequences; see Bormann, "Ghostwriting and the Rhetorical Critic," pp. 284–88.

69. George Christian, Special Oral History (Interview by David Culbert, Sept. 17, 1979), p. 9.

70. Denise Bostdorff, *The Presidency and the Rhetoric of Foreign Crisis* (Columbia: University of South Carolina Press, 1994), pp. 62–64.

71. Lyndon B. Johnson, "Statement by the President Announcing Resumption of Air Strikes on North Vietnam, January 31, 1966," *Public Papers, 1966,* Book I, p. 115.

72. Haynes Redmon to Bill Moyers, Dec. 27, 1965, "BDM Memos September 1965—March 1966," Box 11, Office Files of Bill Moyers.

73. Eric Goldman to the president, July 11, 1966, "Goldman, Eric," Box 5, Office of the President File.

74. McPherson, *A Political Education,* p. 394. Also see Lyndon B. Johnson, "Address at Johns Hopkins University: 'Peace Without Conquest,' April 7, 1965," *Public Papers, 1965,* Book I, pp. 394–99.

75. McGeorge Bundy to the president, 1966 [otherwise undated], "Bundy," Box 3, Name File—Rostow, NSF.

76. Walt Rostow to the president, June 8, 1966, "Vietnam 2 EE 1965–67," Box 74–75, Countries—Vietnam.

77. Bill Moyers to the president, May 3, 1966, "Aides Memos on Vietnam," Box 1, Reference File—Vietnam.

78. John A. McCone, Oral History (Interview by Joe B. Franz, Aug. 19, 1970), p. 2.

79. Frederick Dutton to Bill Moyers, Sept. 26, 1964, "Aides Memos," Box 53, Office Files of Bill Moyers.

80. Will Sparks to Robert E. Kintner, May 26, 1966, "Good Speech and Pointers File," Box 13, Office Files of Charles Maguire.

81. Harry C. McPherson to the president, May 13, 1966, "McPherson, Harry," Box 7, Reference File—Vietnam.

82. Ibid.

83. Benjamin I. Page and Robert Y. Shapiro, "Presidential Leadership Through Public Opinion" in *The Presidency and Public Policy Making,* ed. George C. Edwards III, Steve A. Shull, and Norman A Thomas (Pittsburgh, Pa.: University of Pittsburgh Press, 1985), p. 33.

84. Mitchell Lerner, "Vietnam and the 1964 Election: A Defense of Lyndon Johnson," *Presidential Studies Quarterly* 25 (1995): 751–66.

85. Harry C. McPherson to Bill Moyers, Aug. 4, 1966, "Vietnam (1 of 2)," Box 28, Office Files of Harry McPherson.

86. Charles D. Roche to the president, March 27, 1968, "Vietnam [2 of 2]," Box 32, Office Files of Marvin Watson.

87. Clipping from the *Washington Star,* April 4, 1968, "L.B.J.—Reactions to 3/31/68 Speech," Box 401, Office Files of Fred Panzer.

88. See Turner, *Lyndon Johnson's Dual War,* pp. 111–33.

89. McGeorge Bundy to Jack Valenti, Oct. 12, 1965, "October 1965," Box 5, Files of McGeorge Bundy, Aides File, NSF.

90. See Ball, *Vietnam-on-the-Potomac,* p. 133.

91. See Memorandum for the Record [no author indicated], April 13, 1965, "McB vol. 9, 10, 11," Box 3, Memos to President, NSF; and Dick Goodwin to the president, April 22, 1965, "4/26/65–5/5/65," NSF-Defense, EX ND/CO312.

92. Summary Notes of 557th NSC Meeting, May 10, 1966, 5:45 P.M., "May 10, 1966," Box 2, Meetings File, NSF.

93. Robert S. McNamara to the president, Oct. 14, 1966, "Vol. 4," Tab 47, Box 2, NSC Meetings File, NSF.

94. McNamara, *In Retrospect,* p. 234.

95. Clifford, *Counsel to the President,* p. 453.

96. Berman, *Lyndon Johnson's War,* p. 83.

97. Turner, *Lyndon Johnson's Dual War,* p. 194.

98. Harry McPherson to the president, Aug. 25, 1967, "Vietnam—1967," Box 53, Office Files of Harry McPherson.

99. Draft, "Folder 2, 9/30/67 Speech," Box 247, Statements of LBJ.

100. Undated Note, Folder "9/30/67," Box 247, Statements of LBJ; and see John F. Kennedy, "Address in Seattle at the University of Washington's 100th Anniversary Program, November 16, 1961," *Public Papers of the Presidents of the United States: John F. Kennedy, 1961* (Washington, D.C.: Government Printing Office, 1962), p. 727.

101. Cable from Hanoi, 10/03/67, Folder "9/30/67," Box 247, Statements of LBJ.

102. Harry McPherson to W. Brubeck, Oct. 19, 1967, Folder "9/30/67," Box 247, Statements of LBJ. For the speech text as presented, see Lyndon B. Johnson, "Address on Vietnam Before the National Legislative Conference, San Antonio, Tex., Sept. 29, 1967," *Public Papers, 1967,* Book II, pp. 876–81.

103. See, for example, Burbank [Calif.] Daily Review, Nov. 7, 1967, p. 2A.

104. March 31, 1968, Speech History, p. 1, "Volume I," Box 47, NSC History, NSF.

105. March 31, 1968, Speech History, p. 2, "Volume I," Box 47, NSC History, NSF.

106. Clifford, *Counsel to the President,* p. 457.

107. Ibid., p. 454.

108. McGeorge Bundy to the president, Nov. 10, 1967, Box 1, Reference File on Vietnam.

109. Albert H. Cantril, Jr., to Harry McPherson, Briefing Book on Vietnam, Box 61, Office Files of Harry McPherson; also see McPherson to president, Jan. 13, 1968, "Memoranda for President, 1968," Box 53, Office Files of Harry McPherson.

110. McPherson, *A Political Education,* p. 423.

111. Harry C. McPherson to the president, Jan. 27, 1968, "Memoranda for President, 1968," Box 53, Office Files of Harry McPherson.

112. Sam Adams, *War of Numbers: An Intelligence Memoir* (South Royalton, Vt.: Steerforth Press, 1994), p. xii.

113. McPherson, Oral History (Interview IV by T. H. Baker), Tape 1, p. 6.

114. Walt Rostow to Dean Rusk, Jan. 31, 1968, "3/31 vol 7," Box 49, NSF.

115. Marvin Watson to the president, Feb. 5, 1968, "SP 1/23/68–2/29/68," Box 4, EX SP 6/1/68, WHCF.

116. Walt Rostow to the president, Feb. 16, 1968, "March 31 Speech, Volume 3," Box 47, NSC History, Speech, NSF.

117. McPherson quoted in Clifford, *Counsel to the President,* p. 484.

118. Quoted in the NSC History of March 31 Speech, p. 22, "March 31 Speech," Box 47, NSC History, NSF.

119. Fowler and Johnson quoted in Clifford, *Counsel to the President,* p. 495.

120. Johnson, *Vantage Point,* p. 400.

121. Memorandum for Record, Dean Acheson's Proposal, Summarized by W. W. Rostow, "3/31 Speech Vol. 4," Box 48, NSC History, NSF.

122. Clifford, *Counsel to the President,* p. 505.

123. Lyndon B. Johnson, "Remarks to Delegates to the National Farmers Union Convention in Minneapolis, March 18, 1968," *Public Papers, 1968,* Book I, p. 410; and Clifford, *Counsel to the President,* p. 507.

124. McPherson, Draft, 3/20/68, "Folder #5," Box 271, LBJ Statements.

125. Clifford quoted in McPherson, *A Political Education,* p. 431.

126. Dean Rusk to the president, March 25, 1968, "3/31 Speech," Box 49, NSC History, NSF.

127. Clifford, *Counsel to the President,* p. 517.

128. George A. Carver, Jr., to Walt Rostow, March 26, 1968, "3/31 Speech," Box 49, NSC History, NSF.

129. Gregory A. Olson, *Mansfield and Vietnam: A Study in Rhetorical Adaptation* (East Lansing: Michigan State University Press, 1995), p. 194.

130. McPherson, Oral History (Interview IV), Tape 1, p. 17.

131. McPherson, *A Political Education,* p. 437.

132. Alternative Draft #1, p. 1, "3/31/68 Speech," Box 273, Statements of LBJ.

133. McPherson, *A Political Education,* p. 437.

134. Tom Johnson to the president, March 20, 1969, "3/31/68 Address," Box 274, Statements of LBJ.

135. Clifford, *Counsel to the President,* pp. 524–25.
136. Horace Busby to the president, Jan. 15, 1968, "3/31/68 Address," Box 274, Statements of LBJ.
137. Memorandum, Jim Rowe to president, March 28, 1968, "Jim Rowe," Box 30, Office Files of Marvin Watson.
138. Johnson, *Vantage Point,* p. 429.
139. McPherson to the president, 3/30/68, 9:30 P.M., "March 31," Box 274, Statements of LBJ.
140. Anonymous note attached to Horace Busby's handwritten draft, "3/31/68 Original Draft," Box 274, Statements of LBJ.
141. Redford and McCulley, *White House Operations,* p. 166.
142. Anonymous note attached to Horace Busby's handwritten draft, "3/31/68 Original Draft," Box 274, Statements of LBJ.
143. Spector, *After Tet,* p. 23; and clipping from the *Washington Star,* April 4, 1968, "L.B.J.—Reactions to 3/31/68 Speech," Box 401, Office Files of Fred Panzer.
144. Newspaper clippings in "Reactions to March 31, 1968 Speech," Box 401, Office Files of Fred Panzer.
145. Undated Memorandum, Folder "March 31 Address," Box 9, Office Files of Charles Maguire.
146. Clifford, *Counsel to the President,* p. 530.
147. McPherson, Oral History (Interview III), Tape 1, p. 13.
148. Bill Moyers to the president, June 21, 1965, "Memos to the President 1/65–6/65," Box 11, Office Files of Bill Moyers.
149. See Isocrates, *Panegyricus; and, To Nicocles,* Stephen Usher, ed. and trans. (Warminster: Aris and Phillips Ltd., 1990), p. 135, as well as James L. Kinneavy, "Kairos: A Neglected Concept in Classical Rhetoric," *Rhetoric and Praxis,* ed. Jean Dietz Moss (Washington, D.C.: Catholic University of America, 1986), p. 80.
150. McPherson, *A Political Education,* p. 327.
151. McPherson, Oral History (Interview III), Tape 1, p. 17.
152. McGeorge Bundy to the president, Dec. 27, 1964, "Bundy, McG," Box 1, Office of the President Files.
153. McPherson to the president, June 13, 1967, p. 9, "Vietnam—1967 (Part 2)," Box 29, Office Files of Harry McPherson.
154. McPherson to the president, March 18, 1968, "Memoranda for President (1968) 3 of 3," Box 53, Office Files of Harry McPherson.
155. Hart, *The Sound of Leadership,* p. xxiii.
156. John F. Kennedy, "Address in Seattle at the University of Washington's 100th Anniversary Program, November 16, 1961," p. 727.
157. Robert F. Kennedy, "Vietnam," *Congressional Record,* 90th Cong., 1st Sess., Mar. 2, 1967, Vol. 113, Part 4, pp. 5279–84.
158. Johnson, "Address Before a Joint Session of Congress, November 27, 1963," p. 9.

CHAPTER 6

Richard M. Nixon and Gerald R. Ford

Lessons on Speechwriting

CRAIG R. SMITH

With the overthrow of Thrasybulus in 467 B.C., the is-
land of Sicily restored democracy but suddenly was plagued with lawsuits
concerning land claims. The government ruled that petitioners were to
present their own cases without the aid of counsel. The more inventive
Sicilians rushed to the offices of Corax and his former pupil Tisias, and
employed them to write speeches for the petitioners. The art of speechwriting was born and carried on by such illustrious teachers as Lysias,
Isocrates, and Quintilian. In the modern era, speechwriters are thought of
more as stylists; they rarely teach delivery, and TelePrompTers have made
memoria obsolete.

This examination of speechwriting in the Nixon and Ford administrations relies largely on personal interviews and experiences of the author.[1]
Based on that primary data as well as other scholarship and published memoirs, this chapter explores the Nixon and Ford speechwriting operations in
terms of the following themes. First, to what extent did the education of
each president contribute to his speaking skills and his determination to
make the text his own?[2] Lincoln's serious study of Shakespeare's plays and
the *King James Bible* helped him master *decorum,* the art of meeting and
creating expectations, and *ornatus,* the art of functional adornment. Franklin
Roosevelt's tour of duty as editor of the *Harvard Crimson* made him into a
detailed editor of the drafts produced by his speechwriters. And Ronald
Reagan's entertainment career gave him an ear for a good line—a circumstance that made him his own best speechwriter and also trained his voice

for the electronic media. In a like manner, Nixon and Ford brought their own experiences to the enterprise of presidential speechwriting.

A second theme emerges from an examination of the composition of acceptance speeches for national conventions and their relationship to the structure of the writing operation.[3] They are the most anticipated and viewed speaking events of the political campaign. Furthermore, if the candidate is not the incumbent president, he takes a greater hand in the acceptance speech. It is important to ask then, to what extent does the writing of the acceptance speech inform the speechwriting process that follows in the White House?[4]

A third theme centers on how speechwriters gain credibility and influence with the president.[5] From George Washington to the current president, speechwriters have helped to craft presidential messages with varying degrees of success and influence. Alexander Hamilton's and James Madison's suggestions for President George Washington often were incorporated into his speeches. William Seward influenced the rhetoric of Abraham Lincoln and Andrew Johnson. Judson Welliver, who served as a "literary secretary" for Presidents Warren Harding and Calvin Coolidge, was the first full-time presidential speechwriter. Some speechwriters, such as Theodore Sorensen, not only had a significant impact on the president's rhetoric but were also able to influence policy matters.[6]

Reflecting on what is reported from the investigation of these themes, this chapter concludes by focusing on the priority of rhetorical strategies surrounding the presidential speechwriting process. It argues that scholarship on presidential rhetoric tends to neglect the importance of delivery as a dimension of speechwriting, while stressing style, organization, and invention. This is ironic since it is delivery of speech that defines us as human beings and it is delivery that is the necessary though not sufficient condition of an effective public speech.

The Education of the President as Orator

By the time Richard Nixon made his second run for the presidency in 1968, he was an experienced orator. At Whittier College he had been trained as an intercollegiate debater and orator. His skills in argumentation were undoubtedly sharpened at Duke Law School and in his short-lived tenure as a prosecutor in the district attorney's office in Whittier. Political oratory, particularly campaign debating, seemed to come naturally to him. In 1946, for example, he easily defeated Jerry Voorhis, the incumbent member of

Congress from Whittier, in part because of his debating skill. A year later in McKeesport, Pennsylvania, when he took on another freshman congressman—one John Kennedy of Massachusetts—Nixon out scored the young Kennedy on debating points.[7] In 1948, Nixon sharpened his interviewing skills when he cross-examined Alger Hiss, formerly a high-ranking State Department official, and then dealt with a hostile press in the first of his many crises. In 1950, exercising an overkill in negative campaigning that would forever alienate him from most of the news media, Nixon defeated liberal Congresswoman Helen Gahagan Douglas for a seat in the Senate.

Nixon's meteoric rise to power almost came to an abrupt end in 1952 when, as he ran for vice president, he was accused of maintaining a "slush fund." While delivering an apologia on television, he abandoned his script and ended with an extemporaneous plea thereby saving his place on the ticket with Eisenhower and demonstrating his skill at adapting to public sentiment.[8] Nixon also would learn from his losses, which would significantly change his approach to invention and delivery. In 1960, Nixon learned how crucial polling was to audience adaptation in modern America. Kennedy's pollster Louis Harris had divided the American public into 480 categories. Kennedy's team then crafted different appeals for those various combinations of groups they met along the campaign trail. Nixon also discovered that television, which had served him so well in 1952, would penetrate not only his top layer of skin to reveal a persistent dark shadow, but highlight his pale, nervous, and haggard visage.

With the advent of color television, Nixon came back, not only tanned and ready for the new cameras, but equipped with a self-deprecating humor that cooled him in the age of Marshall McLuhan.[9] The Nixon campaign would capture the Republican nomination and provide its candidate with the opportunity to consolidate support. And by that time Nixon had honed his delivery skills while holding his writers to a very high standard.[10]

Gerald Ford's education did not include any extensive training for speaking other than law school. In fact, he lost his campaign for class president in high school. At the University of Michigan, he was a football star, not a star speaker. At Yale, where he finished in the top third of a very impressive law class, he learned legal argument and developed a healthy respect for evidence and audience analysis, but did not distinguish himself as an orator.

Ford served in the U.S. House of Representatives for twenty-five years and as its minority leader from 1965 to 1974, during which time he gave

530 speeches at Republican fund-raisers alone. Like many in Washington, Ford succumbed to the flattery of party regulars and believed that he was a good speaker. He became vice president with the resignation of Spiro Agnew and president shortly thereafter with the resignation of Nixon. Like Harry Truman, whom Ford admired, he ascended to the presidency with less preparation for national speechmaking than his predecessor. But unlike most executives, his speaking style would evolve dramatically while he was president.

With the help of his old friend and vice presidential chief of staff Bob Hartmann, Ford began his presidency by crafting a speech worthy of Truman's best moments. Ford told the waiting nation that its "long national nightmare . . . [was] over"; it was time for a "little straight talk among friends."[11] Ford's desire to be honest and forthright would for a time overcome his sometimes inarticulate nature. However, his lack of training as an orator and a writer eventually disadvantaged him.[12] Nixon's rhetorical education, on the other hand, seemed to serve him well. He was able to critique his speechwriters directly without the use of an intermediary.

The Writing Process

Nixon's acceptance speech at the 1968 Republican National Convention illustrated his success in adapting his discourse to multiple audiences. That circumstance reinforces the point that audience analysis, speechwriting, and speech delivery are highly interdependent processes. In June Nixon began to outline his acceptance speech on his famous yellow legal pads, a process he would continue as president.[13] Nixon had access to polling data while working on a draft at Montauk, Long Island in July. His pollsters not only ranked important issues such as the Vietnam War, crime, and inflation, and voter preferences for solutions to each problem, but they also focused on such intangible qualities as leadership, trust, and "ruthlessness." The data from the polls were converted into a profile of the target audience accompanied by a series of two-page position papers. This practice would continue through the end of his administration.

There are those who deny Nixon's heavy reliance on poll data—notably Martin Anderson who was in charge of policy development. But all other Nixon aides who were interviewed reported that Nixon used polls extensively. Indeed, polling data was to Richard Nixon what eucalyptus leaves are to a koala bear. By overlaying the poll-generated profiles of national and delegate audiences, Nixon's political advisors could exploit points where issue-positions converged. Thus, on crime, Nixon could talk about appointing a tough new attorney general, appointing more conservative Supreme Court justices, and spending more on law enforcement, thereby appealing to a majority of voters. On Vietnam, which divided the national audience, he could avoid solutions that would exacerbate the split by claiming he did not want to interfere with the ongoing peace talks in Paris. Thus, the crucial section of the speech developed this way: First, Nixon detailed the issue by acknowledging home viewers' conceptions of the war as frustrating and misguided. Second, he issued a disclaimer that since "there's a chance that current negotiations may bring an honorable end to that war, . . . we will say nothing during this campaign that might destroy that chance." Third, he praised American troops for courage and the "loyal opposition" Republicans for supporting the administration so that America could present a united front at the bargaining table. Fourth, Nixon implied that he supported an "honorable and negotiated" end to the war but kept his suggestions vague on this score.[14]

Nixon's position on the Vietnam War overcame the division revealed by polling data and functioned to secure adherence among the national and delegate audiences. He cemented his persuasion with a moving peroration that exploited the tension between the American nightmare of a young boy growing up and dying in the jungle of some foreign land and the American dream of achieving success embodied in Nixon himself.[15] He was so pleased with the results of the address that he used several of its segments for campaign commercials.[16]

Nixon's judicious use of issue-position rhetoric would serve him well during his tenure as president. After every speech he delivered on the Vietnam question, his approval ratings rose. And, in the 1972 campaign, he exploited the fact that he led George McGovern on fifteen out of sixteen major issues in public opinion polls.[17] In short, Nixon's national pulse taking became a hallmark of his rhetoric. Audience adaptation and authoritative delivery served him well.

As work began on Ford's acceptance address for the 1976 Republican National Convention, suggestions from friends poured in; Hartmann filed away statements and phrases he believed might prove useful at the Kansas City Convention. By June, Ford found himself fighting for the nomination while running 30 to 33 percentage points behind his likely Democratic Party opponent Jimmy Carter. Ford narrowed the gap with his speeches celebrating the bicentennial of the Declaration of Independence and closed it further when he cinched the nomination over Ronald Reagan.

In August, writers crafted a version of the acceptance speech containing many more stylistic devices than Ford had ever used. Earlier successes with them in speeches commemorating the bicentennial seemed to have eased Ford's mind about employing them in the acceptance speech. Hartmann also insisted that the speech needed to make a headline with its first few lines. After consulting with Stu Spencer, his chief political advisor, Ford decided to challenge Carter to a series of presidential debates, the first since 1960. The ploy worked, exciting the crowd and baiting the media. Carter's campaign organizers, particularly those drafting his acceptance speech, had sought to transcend issues in an effort to hold together the broadly based special interests of the Democratic Party. Carter talked about competence, honesty, and his religious faith. Ford's advisors believed that if they could get Carter into a debate, he would be forced to take specific stands on issues that would alienate some in the Democratic Party, break apart his coalition, and reveal him as less conservative than he claimed to be.

As to the substance of his acceptance speech, Ford made clear what many Republicans knew: he was in fact more conservative than Nixon, and perhaps the most conservative president since Herbert Hoover. This was an important point to stress because from the beginning of the primary season Carter also had portrayed himself as a conservative. To win the election, particularly in crucial southern swing states, Ford had to retain the support of conservative southern Democrats whom Nixon had so carefully courted.

Ford claimed that "the issues are on our side" but it was the delivery and style of his acceptance speech that finally made that clear to the American public. He rehearsed his speech not once, but five times, using live television cameras in the convention hall. It was easily the best delivered speech of his career and earned applause sixty-five times in forty minutes. As one newspaper reported: "Far and away the best stroke [at the convention] was Jerry Ford's personal accomplishment at the podium Thursday night. . . . [I]t was the finest oratory heard by a party that had summoned all its best campaigners to Kansas City."[18]

Ford's acceptance speech contained more memorable lines than most of his political speeches. For example, he encapsulated his service to the nation in phrases marked by homeotuleton and alliteration: "To me, the Presidency and Vice Presidency were not prizes to be won, but a duty to be done. . . . My record is one of specifics, not smiles. . . . We will build on performance, not promises; experience, not expedience. . . ."[19] The speech proved to be the most effective of his career, and its impact in terms of poll data was striking. Had he been re-elected, there is little doubt that he would have continued to rehearse major speeches and be receptive to more highly stylized drafts. In short, his successful acceptance affected his presidential speechwriting operation, short-lived though it was. It is to these speechwriting processes that we now turn.

White House speechwriting operations can be very complicated, and the Nixon operation proved no exception.[20] Writing was the product of collaboration informed by the president, his press office, the research staff which supported the writers, political consultants, cabinet, and other executive offices. While these groups provided speechwriters with almost unlimited resources, Martin Anderson focused the policy development operation. Like the speechwriters, Anderson knew that these groups could threaten the writer's own voice. A speech draft often had trouble surviving the "staffing" process. National Security Advisor Henry Kissinger explains how he played the staffing game:

> In addition to a folder of speeches, Nixon had voluminous briefing books prepared for him by my staff and the State Department. They included an overall conceptual paper that explained our objectives, the strategy for achieving them, and their relationship to our general foreign policy. In addition there were talking points for each country, discussing the issue likely to be raised and biographical material about the leaders he would meet. . . . [T]he talking points . . . were broken into the issues the various leaders were likely to raise; they listed the suggested responses and warned about sensitive topics to avoid.[21]

Kissinger's candid comment reveals that presidential speechwriters have to guard against those who provide the president with information thereby becoming speechwriters themselves.

Early in both the Nixon and Ford White Houses, cabinet members or their assistants and undersecretaries would submit entire speeches. During election campaigns, political consultants felt free to alter drafts of speeches once they were on the road with the candidate. But a year into each administration, speechwriters, using their researchers as loyal servants, had gained the upper hand. In the case of the Nixon administration, this was because of the talent of the writers and their ability to wield language in ways that impressed Nixon. It was also because of the talent of James Keough who adroitly administered the speechwriting operation. His counterpart in the Ford administration was Robert Hartmann whose dogged protection of the speechwriting operation guaranteed his writers direct access to the president.[22]

This is not to say that cabinet-level contributions were ignored, for they could come to dominate a speech during a crisis. For example, Nixon's very important April 30, 1970, address on the military incursion into Cambodia relied on reports from Henry Kissinger's Special Action Group, the CIA, and the Defense Department.[23] The intramural debates of the Special Action Group were particularly influential because they were summarized for Nixon, allowing him to choose evidence and arguments that impressed him. In like manner, Ford's address to the nation on the Mayaguez crisis relied extensively on Defense Department information and was constructed for the most part in the White House operations room.

Researchers provided a layer of internal support for speechwriters and were responsible for ensuring the accuracy of drafts. Like their predecessors in the Nixon White House, Ford's researchers had access to remarkable resources, including the Library of Congress, various executive agencies, and a library in the Old Executive Office Building near the speechwriters' offices. In addition, researchers were motivated by the fact that they might, with some luck, be promoted to writers. Researchers were abreast of current affairs because, in both administrations, they were responsible for compiling the daily summary of news items about the president.[24]

The political operation was vital to the speechwriting process because it, along with schedulers, provided speechwriters with much needed audience analysis. After Nixon won the nomination in 1968, he instituted a twenty-four hour tracking poll that kept his staff unusually well informed on the issues and the positions people took on them.[25] Ford discontinued this practice when he became president with adverse consequences because it prevented his writers from staying current on the nature of the audiences Ford faced.[26]

Nixon's speechwriting staff was one of the largest in White House history:[27] Pat Buchanan (who joined Nixon's private staff in January, 1966), William Gavin, and William Safire were conservatives who could write effective political punch lines.[28] During the White House years, Safire worked mostly on domestic speeches, particularly economic ones.[29] Ray Price, who joined Nixon's team in late 1967, was the most philosophical and liberal of the group.[30] He stylized Nixon's major speeches, including the acceptances, inaugurals, State of the Unions, and the resignation address.[31] Price also wrote most of Nixon's radio campaign speeches of 1968 and 1972. Early in Nixon's second term, he was "shifted for a while to a special consultancy in the hope that he could do some leisurely and productive long-term thinking for the President," but as the Watergate scandal grew, he was recalled to his speechwriting assignment.[32] Lee Huebner, who had been an award-winning debater as an undergraduate at Northwestern University in the late 1950s and early 1960s, was a utility hitter who focused on arguments and issues. The Jesuitical John McLaughlin filled a similar role when he joined the speechwriting staff in 1972.

No speechwriting staff has ever been more successful after leaving the White House than Nixon's—a fact that is all the more remarkable considering the disgrace of their leader.[33] Buchanan became communications director for the Reagan administration, a television talk show personality, and a candidate for president. Safire became a syndicated columnist for the *New York Times.* Huebner was editor of the *Herald-Tribune,* the paper that keeps Americans in touch with their country while they travel abroad. And John McLaughlin launched one of the most successful political talk programs on television—*The McLaughlin Group.* The post-presidential careers of the Ford writers pale by comparison. Hartmann retired. Robert Orben, who had contributed humor to Ford's speeches, continued to write comedy. Pat Butler became a lobbyist for the Times-Mirror Company. David Borstin tried his hand at playwriting. And the present author continued to bob in and out of the academic community and up and down in the political world.

Once Nixon became president, he did not participate as fully in the drafting process as he had when he was a candidate.[34] According to Price, Nixon provided "pieces of texts, good ideas, and memos" for major speeches and sometimes marked up drafts for less important occasions. To keep lines of communication untangled, Nixon used only one writer per speech. That writer would often do many drafts since no important speech went through fewer than five drafts.

After the present author joined the Ford administration and established some degree of credibility, he suggested that two writers be assigned to each major speech and that they write independently of one another during the construction of the first draft. Hartmann with Ford would then decide which was the superior draft. The writer of that draft would then become the primary writer of the remaining drafts and incorporate what was valuable from the other writer's work. This process had at least two advantages: it produced a competitive environment that led to better speeches, and it assured continuity in Ford's style.

In both administrations, the vice presidents maintained their own speechwriting staffs. Spiro Agnew was allowed four writers of his own and a "research team," according to Herbert Thompson, one of his writers. Vic Gold, a pugnacious former journalist, emerged as the lead writer when he transformed Agnew into a household name with pithy lines that became instant sound bites.[35] Having much more time on his hands than Nixon, Agnew enjoyed reworking drafts that were submitted to him. Vice President Nelson Rockefeller retained the private speechwriters he had used for years and kept most of them off the government payroll.

Thus, the structure of speechwriting operations is often a matter of chance, depending on the whims of the president and strength of his staff. Regardless of the type of administrative structure, however, one thing remains constant: the need for a consistent writing style for a president's speeches. Writers who provide such continuity can become influential staff members in the White House. Continuity in style is important not only for the projection of a persona but to ease the delivery of the speaker by not forcing him to learn new or overly varied language and arguments for each speech.

Establishing a Reputation

How speechwriters gain credibility and influence with the president is a matter of luck, timing, effectiveness, and infighting. Kissinger, among others, notes that speechwriters can become important members of a president's staff. About the Nixon logographers he observes: "On a fast-moving foreign trip . . . there would be no time for extensive editing, and the speechwriters would come into their own. The choice of writers always determined the tone and not infrequently the substance of a Presidential speech."[36]

What makes a writer valuable to the president varies. Some chief executives like applause-getting lines; some like passages that prove memorable; some want an original approach to issues; others simply like the writer personally. At first, both Nixon and Ford took advice from their speechwriters because of their expertise. If certain strategies proved effective and impressed the president, the writer was able to suggest more alterations in invention, delivery, style, and arrangement. To explore the issue of influence in both the Nixon and Ford White Houses, three specific writers will be discussed: Patrick Buchanan, Robert Hartmann, and Craig R. Smith.

PATRICK BUCHANAN

Patrick Buchanan was working as a conservative editorialist for the *St. Louis Globe-Democrat* when he cornered Nixon at a cocktail party in Belleville, Illinois, in 1965 and asked to join his staff.[37] At first, he was turned down, but Nixon came to admire Buchanan's persistence, and after an interview in Nixon's office in New York, Buchanan became the first staff member for the 1968 campaign. He began as a researcher, but his ear for a good punch line soon advanced his career.[38] When Nixon became president, Buchanan took charge of compiling the daily news summary.[39] Because Buchanan knew the journalism business and compiled daily reports from every major news source, he soon found himself briefing the president for news conferences.[40] This proved to be a crucial placement of his skills because Nixon was obsessive about his press conferences. He wanted to present news more than he wanted to answer questions.[41] He wanted to appear spontaneous and direct, refusing to use notes, and thereby making Buchanan's briefings even more important. Nixon even went so far as to try to memorize the seating chart set up for the reporters.[42]

Buchanan's next step up the ladder of influence began with his suspicion that the press was trying to undercut the Nixon administration. When Buchanan heard the "instant analysis" of Nixon's address on Vietnam in May of 1969, he was convinced that the media was dominated by liberals out to destroy Nixon. Buchanan had not forgotten the damage done to Lyndon Johnson's war policy by opinion leaders such as David Brinkley and Walter Cronkite. So he devised a plan whereby Nixon would inoculate his audiences against hostile press reports. The president would deliver a speech specifically pointing out the tactics used by the news media and calling on the "silent majority" in America to exercise skepticism. Buchanan's plan sat on hold until November 3, 1969, when Nixon again spoke to the nation about the war in Vietnam. The vitriolic and cynical reaction of the media gave Buchanan the excuse he needed to present his "inoculation" speech to the president. Nixon, however, found the draft to be unpresidential and suggested that Buchanan show it to Vice President Agnew.[43]

Agnew was taken by Buchanan's plan and even more impressed by the address. He agreed to deliver it in Des Moines, Iowa, where it was broadcast live by the three major networks in late November of 1969. In the speech, Agnew characterized the broadcast media as a "small and unelected elite," "a small group of men," "a tiny, enclosed fraternity" who "decide what forty to fifty million Americans will learn of the day's events."[44] Agnew's and Buchanan's anti-intellectual, geographic, and gender biases were apparent in their use of localization for persuasive effect: "[T]hese commentators and producers live and work in the geographical and intellectual confines of Washington, D.C., or New York City, the latter of which James Reston termed the most unrepresentative community in the entire United States. Both communities bask in their own provincialism, their own parochialism."[45] Agnew said the cause of the so-called "credibility gap" in government was not the fault of officials in Washington, D.C., but "the networks in New York."[46] The response was sensational and Buchanan's credibility was firmly established.[47] Theodore White called it "one of the most masterful forensic efforts in recent public discourse."[48] By writing a speech that was delivered by a vice president, Buchanan had set the stylistic tone for Nixon and his presidential administration.

Perhaps because of that success, Nixon chose Buchanan to be the major writer of his address of April 30, 1970, concerning the "incursion" into Cambodia.[49] In preparation for the 1970 congressional elections, Buchanan sent Nixon an eleven-page analysis of Richard Scammon's and Ben Wattenberg's book, *The Real Majority.* Nixon embraced Buchanan's recommendations: "If this analysis was right, and I agreed with Buchanan that it was, then the Republican counterstrategy was clear: We should preempt the Social Issue in order to get Democrats on the defensive."[50] When the strategy paid off, Buchanan was elevated to the status of a presidential advisor and subsequently became a "Special Consultant to the President." In this new capacity, Buchanan wrote a book called *The New Majority* which extended some of the themes he had developed for Agnew.[51] He also advocated using the Federal Communications Commission's fairness doctrine to break up liberal control over the mass media. Writing in the twilight of the Nixon White House, John Osborne noted: "Buchanan . . . thrives as a special consultant to the President and as an assistant without portfolio. He still works on occasional speeches. His principle chore, however, is just to be there, at the President's beck when he is wanted."[52] Once the Watergate crisis began, he was often wanted.

Though Nixon recalled Ray Price to his speechwriting post when the Watergate crisis deepened, he did not include Price in his inner circle. Osborne reports that "only three assistants—General [Alexander] Haig, [Ronald] Ziegler and Patrick Buchanan—were consulted during the discussions of when and whether to follow up the August 22 [1973] press conference with another one in Washington."[53] An entry from Nixon's memoirs is emblematic of his reliance on Buchanan: "[Haldeman] had asked me to check with Pat Buchanan and find out how he felt. I had done so, and I wanted Ziegler to read to Haldeman what Buchanan had written to me." The issue was whether Haldeman and Ehrlichman should resign. A few pages later Nixon wrote, "I asked Buchanan if he would call Haldeman and tell him that I had come to this conclusion." Price was then asked to write the speech announcing the resignation of Haldeman and Ehrlichman for presentation on April 30, 1973.[54]

With Haldeman and Ehrlichman out of the picture, Buchanan's influence continued to grow. In September of 1973, he took an aggressive stance before the Senate Watergate Committee in contradistinction to the approaches taken by those going before him. His effectiveness before the Committee after the timid performance by Haldeman and the blustery appearance of Ehrlichman sealed Buchanan's bond with Nixon. He called Buchanan's testimony a "public death blow" to the televising of the hearings. The Watergate Committee was so cowed by Buchanan that it canceled the appearance of Kenneth Khachigian, fearing that another combative speechwriter would prove even more embarrassing.[55]

Nixon's respect for Buchanan's intellect is revealed in one of the stranger passages from his memoirs. Speaking of the brilliance of Syrian President Hafad Assad, Nixon writes: "What he reminded me of, curiously enough, was that he had a forehead like Pat Buchanan's, and my guess is he has the same kind of brain and drive and single-mindedness that Pat has."[56] Buchanan was now at the peak of his power. In matters such as managing the Watergate scandal, Nixon placed (or, rather, misplaced) considerable confidence in Buchanan's views. Nixon later recalled: "Pat Buchanan was assigned to go over these transcripts and compare them with John Dean's testimony. When I read Buchanan's report . . . I was reassured by the thought that anyone reviewing the tapes would agree with my view that Dean had lied. . . . Buchanan . . . was strongly in favor of releasing the transcripts. I shared his belief that if we could survive the first shock waves, the tapes would end up proving Dean a liar."[57] Obviously Buchanan's prediction was faulty, but despite his misperception of the rhetorical nature of the transcripts, he remained at the center of power. For example, Tricia Nixon Cox allied herself with Buchanan in opposing her father's resignation. Buchanan tried to work out a compromise wherein Nixon would be censured by the Senate but allowed to stay in office. In the end, however, even Buchanan saw that it was hopeless and finally came to the position that it was better to spare Nixon the humiliation of impeachment.[58] And so Buchanan's reign came to an end in that White House.

ROBERT HARTMANN

Few people were more influential with President Ford than Robert Hartmann. They enjoyed a long friendship that was still in existence when the ex-president was asked to address the Republican Convention in 1992. When Ford became president, he made Hartmann a "Counselor to the President," who in turn gave other speechwriters direct access to the president.

Hartmann's first chore was to craft a speech that Ford could deliver upon his ascendancy to the presidency. Hartmann's eloquent words resonated with the public and, consequently, Ford enjoyed a period of high ratings in the polls. But soon Hartmann and an ever-changing group of writers were faced with the daunting task of writing a speech that would grant Nixon a pardon. The situation was highly constrained, most significantly by the fact that Ford's pardon of Nixon would lead to speculation that a deal had been cut between them. Ford overrode the objections of his loyalists, particularly press secretary Gerald Terhorst, because he believed that pardoning Nixon would end the Watergate crisis and Nixon's suffering, would constitute an admission of guilt on Nixon's part, and would clear the way for Nixon to testify against others involved in the Watergate cover up.

However, both the speech that Hartmann wrote and the timing of the pardon announcement undercut Ford's objectives. By delivering it on Sunday morning, Ford opened himself to charges of trying to slip the pardon past the news media because the public paid less attention to news on the Sabbath. Ford presented the pardon as a fair and moral act, but he missed a major opportunity to justify his action when he failed to delineate the legal thinking behind the speech. There is some evidence that the speech was influenced by the circumstance that Ford needed some of Nixon's former staff members to help with the governing coalition.[59] In any case, the Gallup poll showed that Ford's popularity fell from 71 percent to 32 percent in the month following the pardon. Nonetheless, Hartmann's credibility with the president—based as it was on a long-standing friendship—endured. Although Hartmann survived the debacle of pardoning Nixon, Ford eventually would pay dearly for that executive action.

CRAIG R. SMITH

In the case of the present author, credibility with the president had to be earned. I was then a faculty member at the University of Virginia, and professors had not fared well as Ford speechwriters. During my first week on staff, I spent my time reading Ford's biography, his testimony when nominated for vice president, and all the speeches he had given as president. I noticed that Ford was giving too many different speeches and that their style was uneven. Despite these observations, I was precluded from making recommendations until I established my own credibility as a writer.

Almost as a challenge, the first speech I was commissioned to write was Ford's address to the Southern Baptist Convention in Norfolk, Virginia, in June of 1976. I was a Catholic composing a speech for an Episcopalian that would be delivered to Southern Baptists. I consulted with Baptist ministers, revised the draft after Ford refused to say the name Jesus Christ, and finally produced a speech he accepted. Once the speech was delivered, my influence grew because the address was interrupted by applause sixteen times and received a good review in the *Washington Star*—a rare event in Ford's rhetorical history.[60]

When Ford decided to deliver six major addresses during the celebration of the bicentennial of the Declaration of Independence, Hartmann recommended putting the speeches together into a booklet with a theme that tied them together.[61] He asked each of the speechwriters to submit a six-page outline for the speeches, one page for each speech. Hartmann added outlines that had been submitted from outsiders and friends of the president, such as Bryce Harlow and Phil Buchen. After first making sure that none of the authors were indicated, he presented the stack of outlines to Ford and asked him to choose the one he liked most. Ford picked two, one jointly written by David Borstin and Pat Butler, and mine. My influence thereby increased as the three of us coordinated the project.[62]

Because of the epideictic nature of the speeches, Hartmann allowed us considerable stylistic latitude, so long as there was no "whiff of pomposity or pretentious elegance."[63] Nonetheless, I argued for vivid imagery, periodic phrasing, and decorum. For example, at Valley Forge in a speech of which I was the primary author, Ford said:

> They came here in the snows of winter over a trail marked with the blood of their rag-bound feet. The iron forge that gave this place its name had been destroyed by the British when General Washington and his ragged Continental Army encamped here—exhausted, outnumbered, and short of everything except faith. . . . Yet, their courage and suffering—those who survived as well as those who fell—were no less meaningful than the sacrifices of those who manned the battlements of Boston and scaled the parapets of Yorktown.[64]

Hartmann also required that the speeches should reach "for the [future] while retaining a reverence for the past."[65] For example, at Independence Hall Ford said: "Each generation of Americans, indeed of all humanity, must strive to achieve these aspirations anew. Liberty is a flame to be fed, not ashes to be revered, even in a Bicentennial year."[66]

The speeches went well, helping to assure Ford's nomination at the 1976 Republican National Convention.[67] At that juncture, I wrote a memo calling for an integrated approach to issues during the ensuing presidential campaign. Hartmann took the memo to the president, who read it, signed it, and sent it to his campaign coordinators, who were more than a little annoyed at my interference.

Buchanan's and my experiences indicate that a speechwriter can gain influence by doing his or her job well and that the influence can carry over into campaign and even policy matters. Hartmann's case demonstrates that long friendships can create credibility for a writer, who can then be influential on matters beyond "wordsmithing." All three cases indicate that speechwriters can gain enough influence to have an effect on policy and political strategy.

Delivery as a Neglected Dimension of Speechwriting

The contributions of speechwriters would be more substantial (and therefore their influence greater) if instead of thinking of themselves as writers, they thought of themselves as rhetors. This is particularly true as it applies to the importance of delivery in presidential rhetoric. From the earliest treatises on rhetoric, delivery has been recognized as vital to success. The advent of electronic media has multiplied its importance. A presidential speech lives on not just as a written text, but in the form of video. Well-written and well-presented passages tend to be replayed on television news and public affairs program. Perhaps more to the point, the damage from gaffes in delivery are no longer limited to the immediate audience—they are broadcast and rebroadcast repeatedly to the detriment of a president's image. Most speechwriters—including presidential speechwriters—have watched their clients ruin a perfectly good speech with bad delivery; not enough speechwriters will admit that some of their clients have saved a mediocre speech with a stellar presentation.

Aristotle spends little time on delivery in the *Rhetoric*. In fact, he argues that delivery would be unnecessary to teach if audiences concentrated on the facts and arguments of a case. But people being what they are, Aristotle concedes that delivery is important. He discusses such matters as the volume of sound, modulation of pitch, "how the voice should be used in expressing each emotion . . . and what rhythms should be expressed in each case." Theophrastus, who succeeded Aristotle as head of the Peripatetic School, provides a fuller treatment of delivery in his lost book, *On Delivery*, by dividing his advice between voice and gesture.[68]

Cicero claims that delivery is "the dominant factor in oratory; without delivery, the best speaker cannot be of any account at all, and a moderate speaker with a trained delivery can often outdo the best of them."[69] Quintilian claims that "Demosthenes, when asked what was the most important thing in oratory, gave the palm to delivery and assigned it second and third place as well."[70] President Bill Clinton clearly understood this lesson. A close *reading* of his 1996 State of the Union address reveals its lack of evidence, its failure to develop arguments, and its swing to the right, especially on the issue of illegal immigration. Former Governor Jerry Brown called the speech a string of "vacuous bromides" when he appeared on the television program "Politically Incorrect" immediately following the address. But the address was widely praised by the media because it was so well delivered.[71] Senator Robert Dole delivered his response so poorly that the contrast with Clinton was glaring. Dole simply ignored the advice of Cicero, Quintilian, and Demosthenes. Poor or affected delivery is often subject to ridicule, especially in the postmodern world where a David Frye can make a fortune imitating Nixon's mannerisms and a Chevy Chase can launch a career by mimicking Ford's flubs.

In the end, the public will draw its own conclusions when political leaders reveal through their delivery that they are not in command of their own messages. Consider the case of Senator Edward Kennedy's televised apologia following the death of a female companion at Chappaquiddick. There were numerous substantive items with which to quarrel in Richard Goodwin's draft of that speech, but one feature of the speech that was most damaging to Kennedy's credibility was that Kennedy lost his place in the text—a glitch that revealed to the television audience that he was merely reading someone else's words rather than speaking his own convictions and concerns.[72]

In Gerald Ford's case, his verbal stumbling, combined with his pardon of Richard Nixon, nearly destroyed his presidency. The news media presented Ford's problems with delivery as a metaphor for lack of intelligence. Jules Witcover reports: "Ford's inability to pronounce difficult words, and some not so difficult was immediately seized upon as a measure of his brainpower. In a speech in Atlanta, in early February [1975], he stumbled an inordinate number of times in a speech on his energy proposals before getting out the word 'geothermal' correctly. A tape of the speech became an overnight box-office hit in the White House press room."[73] When Ford gave a campaign speech in Kansas making reference to the "Wizard of Oz," reporters composed the following ditty based on the song of the scare-crow:

> *I could while away the hours*
> *Reflecting on my powers,*
> *As we go down the drain.*
> *I could spend like Rockefeller,*
> *I could talk like Walter Heller,*
> *If I only had a brain.*[74]

In response, White House aides presented the speechwriters with lists of words that were not to appear in presidential speeches. Difficult locutions were to be avoided. But until the summer of 1976, no one discovered the two strategies that would salvage Ford's rhetorical record: the first was rehearsing speeches and the second was creating a sense of style. As this chapter has shown, Ford's bicentennial speeches and particularly his acceptance address achieved those ends. Ford recovered from a thirty-three point deficit in the polls to lose by only half a million votes in the 1976 presidential election.

In contrast, Richard Nixon had come to understand the importance of delivery well before the end of his presidency. He had correctly concluded that he had not presented himself and his ideas effectively on television during the 1960 presidential campaign against John F. Kennedy. When he ran again in 1968, Nixon was determined to master the art of speaking on television—to employ an effective oral style, as well as a more attractive visual image. He narrated many of his commercials in 1968, often repeatedly rehearsing his statements until he and his advisors were satisfied with both this language and delivery.[75] By 1972 his vocal delivery via electronic media had improved to the point that he realized that his voice without his face was a powerful persuasive tool. As a consequence, in 1972 Nixon commissioned Ray Price to write sixteen addresses for presentation only on radio.

If presidential speechwriters are to be as helpful as possible, they should do more than write in an oral style. They need to be delivery coaches. As a regular part of their jobs, speechwriters ought to perform diagnostic examinations of the delivery skills. Such an assessment should produce, at the very least, recommendations about the forum or venues in which the president is likely to perform best as a speaker. The failure to select the proper time and place for a particular speaker has created serious rhetorical missteps for presidents. For example, Ronald Reagan normally conducted his news conferences in the evening when most Americans could watch them. Unfortunately, this was one of Reagan's worst venues. At that time of day he tended to make verbal errors—not an unusual circumstance for a person whose tenure as president took him from age seventy to almost seventy-eight. His aides often spent that evening or the next day correcting "misstatements" by the president. As deputy director of the National Republican Senatorial Campaign Committee, the present author recommended to White House political advisor Ed Rollins in late 1981 that if Reagan continued to hold press conferences in the evening, he should do so sitting down with three or four reporters in conversation. When that advice was finally followed six years later, Reagan did extremely well in a joint interview with Tom Brokaw, Dan Rather, Bernard Shaw, and Peter Jennings—fairly tough interviewers in a competitive situation. Of course, by then Reagan had only about a year left in the White House. The change in venue came too late to have a significant impact.[76]

A contrasting example is ironic. As president, George Bush performed better in press conferences than in any other venue. And yet, so as not to be seen as imitating Reagan, he chose to conduct his press conferences during the day when few Americans could watch them. When he finally decided to hold an evening press conference in the summer of 1992, the television networks saw it as a political ploy and refused to carry it. In both cases, the presidents were ill-served by their advisors in terms of recommending proper venues.

Conclusion

This examination of the Nixon and Ford administrations has touched on the role a president's education plays in his sensitivity to speechwriting, analyzed how acceptance speeches reflect the speechwriting process, observed the paths to influence that are trod by speechwriters, and argued that presidential speechwriters should engage in coaching performance.

Several other salient points should be clear from this study. First, it is essential to have direct contact with the president. Access guarantees that writers will not lose their voices to other staff members less skilled rhetorically. Access prevents unschooled intermediaries from undoing the effective prose of writers. And access assures writers of an avenue of influence with their superiors. As an extension to this point, scholars should continue to study the ways in which speechwriters have risen to become policy makers. One way onto a president's brain trust is through effective speechwriting.

Second, polling data is essential to the speechwriting process. Rhetoric is a unique art form because it draws so many of its strategies from the audience. Understanding the American audience in terms of the issues it holds dear, the positions it takes on those issues, and the way it measures character is crucial to crafting speeches that resonate with the public. Furthermore, because of the modern media, the president often addresses more than one audience at a time. Having polling data that allow a comparison of the various audiences helps speechwriters to craft messages that build consensus and avoid alienation.

Third, having a sense of style is an important asset for a president and there are ways of providing one for most speakers. Often style evolves over time, as with Truman and Ford. It can become the hallmark of an administration, which may be remembered for its rhetorical trademarks whether they be a new frontier, a new deal, or a new beginning for America. Speechwriters can help the process by cooperating on drafts, by agreeing on a level of style that is consistent, and by competing with one another to produce the best of that style in important speeches.

Finally, speechwriters should coach the performance of presidential speeches. No effective speech has deficient delivery. Speechwriters may not want to take presentation seriously for fear that they will be identified with elocutionists, or even the ancient Sophists. But such speechwriters ought to remember that the Sophists dominated their culture, while Socrates was forced to take poison. They ought to recall that Plato's academy languished outside the walls of Athens, while the Sophists were receiving large tuition fees. Factors of performance are not beyond the realm of the speechwriters; they are integral to the messages that the writers draft. By ignoring presentation, speechwriters limit their influence as consultants and weaken their credibility with those who know the importance of delivery in the political world. The concept of presidential speechwriting needs to be expanded. In the age of electronic media, a presidential speech is not merely written; it is scripted, staged, and produced. Ultimately, a presidential speech is created at the moment of presentation, when a president gives voice to words.

Notes

1. Throughout the Nixon years, the present author was employed as a consultant to CBS News, a role affording the opportunity to interview members of the White House staff at conventions, at inaugurals, and on election nights. In 1968 and 1972, the author had direct access to the floor and dais of both political conventions. In 1972, he also covered election night and the inaugural, which included many interviews with members of speechwriting staffs and full access to CBS polling data, delegate surveys, and other demographics useful to this study. Information on the Nixon speechwriting operation also is based on observations and interviews with Patrick Buchanan, Kenneth Khachigian, Lee Huebner, and John Andrews at the 1972 convention and again in Washington, D.C., in November of 1973. The author met with Richard Nixon to discuss speechwriting in the fall of 1967 in his Broad Street office in New York City, and in July of 1975 at the San Clemente compound. The information gained from those sources was refreshed with recent interviews with Kenneth Khachigian, who began as a Nixon researcher in the 1968 presidential campaign, later joined the Nixon White House, and still later became a White House speechwriter under the supervision of Patrick Buchanan.

In 1976, the author was employed as one of President Gerald Ford's full-time speechwriters and had the opportunity to observe firsthand how the operation worked. He had daily contact with Robert Hartmann, counselor to the president; Bob Orben, our editor; and the other members of the writing team: George Dennis, Patrick Butler, Milt Friedman, and David Borstin. The author met with President Ford to discuss every major speech he wrote for him.

2. See, for example, James L. Golden, "John F. Kennedy and the 'Ghosts'," *Quarterly Journal of Speech* 52 (1966): 348–57.

3. See, for example, Russel Windes, Jr., "Adlai E. Stevenson's Speech Staff in the 1956 Campaign," *Quarterly Journal of Speech* 46 (1960): 32–43.

4. See, for example, Craig R. Smith, "Contemporary Political Speech Writing," *Southern Speech Communication Journal* 42 (1976): 52–67.

5. See, for example, L. Patrick Devlin, "The Influences of Ghostwriting on Rhetorical Criticism," *Today's Speech* 32 (Summer, 1974): 7–12; and Craig R. Smith, "Richard Nixon's 1968 Acceptance Speech as a Model of Dual Audience Adaptation," *Today's Speech* 29 (Fall, 1971): 15–22.

6. Theodore Sorensen, *Kennedy* (New York: Harper & Row, 1965), pp. 101–210.

7. Ironically, Nixon's success in his 1947 debate with a politically inexperienced John Kennedy in McKeesport, Pa., contributed to his willingness to accept the challenge from a more polished John Kennedy to debate in the 1960 presidential campaign. For Nixon's recollection of the 1947 debate, see Richard M. Nixon, *The Memoirs of Richard Nixon* (New York: Grosset & Dunlap, 1978), pp. 42–43. In an account of the McKeesport event written by one of Jimmy Carter's former presidential speechwriters, the debate is presented as a case of Nixon's superior argumentation versus Kennedy's attractive image; see Christopher Matthews, *Kennedy and Nixon: The Rivalry that Shaped Postwar America* (New York: Simon and Schuster, 1996), pp. 51–52.

8. Nixon's "Checkers" speech on September 23, 1952, was so well geared to the moment that Nixon would be haunted by it for the rest of his career, because only a
decade later it seemed out of time and out of place in a less gullible America. For
the text of that speech, see Richard M. Nixon, "My Side of the Story" in *Contemporary American Public Discourse,* 3d ed., ed. Halford Ross Ryan (Prospect
Heights, Ill. Waveland Press, 1992), pp. 123–32.

9. According to Joe McGinniss, excerpts from Marshall McLuhan's book, *Understanding Media: The Extensions of Man* (New York: McGraw Hill, 1964), were
distributed to Nixon's media advisors in the 1968 presidential campaign and their
campaign strategy was shaped, in part, by McLuhan's perspective on television.
See Joe McGinniss, *The Selling of the President, 1968* (New York: Trident Press,
1969), pp. 181–86, 187, 212.

10. For additional rhetorical studies of Richard M. Nixon, see (chronological):
Robert P. Newman, "Under the Veneer: Nixon's Vietnam Speech of November 3,
1969," *Quarterly Journal of Speech* 56 (1970): 169–78; Andrew A. King and Floyd
Douglas Anderson, "Nixon, Agnew and the 'Silent Majority': A Case Study in the
Rhetoric of Polarization," *Western Speech* 35 (1971): 243–55; Hermann G. Stelzner,
"The Quest Story and Nixon's November 3, 1969 Address," *Quarterly Journal of
Speech* 57 (1971): 163–72; Judith S. Trent, "Richard Nixon's Methods of
Identification in the Presidential Campaigns of 1960 and 1968: A Content Analy-
sis," *Today's Speech* 29 (Fall, 1971): 23–30; Forbes Hill, "Conventional Wisdom—
Traditional Form—The President's Message of November 3, 1969," *Quarterly
Journal of Speech* 58 (1972): 373–86; Richard A. Katula, "The Apology of Richard M.
Nixon," *Today's Speech* 23 (Fall, 1975): 1–5; Jackson Harrell, B. L. Ware, and Wil A.
Linkugel, "Failure of Apology in American Politics: Nixon on Watergate," *Speech
Monographs* 42 (1975): 245–61; Gage William Chapel, "Speechwriting in the Nixon
Administration [interview with Aram Bakshian, Jr.]," *Journal of Communication* 26
(1976): 65–72; Carol J. Jablonski, "Richard Nixon's Irish Wake: A Case of Generic
Transference," *Central States Speech Journal* 30 (1979): 164–73; William L. Benoit,
"Richard M. Nixon's Rhetorical Strategies in his Public Statements on Watergate,"
Southern Speech Communication Journal 47 (1982): 192–211; Roderick P. Hart, *Verbal
Style and the Presidency: A Computer-Based Analysis* (Orlando, Fla.: Academic Press,
1984), pp. 127–49; Celeste Michelle Condit, "Richard Milhous Nixon" in *American
Orators of the Twentieth Century: Critical Studies and Sources,* ed. Bernard K. Duffy
and Halford Ryan (Westport, Conn.: Greenwood Press, 1987), pp. 323–30; Halford
Ross Ryan, "Senator Richard M. Nixon's Apology for the 'Fund'," and Craig Allen
Smith, "President Richard M. Nixon and the Watergate Scandal" both in *Oratorical
Encounters: Selected Studies and Sources of Twentieth-Century Political Accusations and
Apologies,* ed. Halford Ross Ryan (New York: Greenwood Press, 1988), pp. 99–120,
201–26; Celeste Michelle Condit, "Nixon's 'Fund': Time as Ideological Resource in
the 'Checkers' Speech," and Thomas B. Farrell, "The Carnival as Confessional: Re-
Reading the Figurative Dimension in Nixon's 'Checkers' Speech," both in *Texts in
Context,* ed. Michael C. Leff and Fred J. Kauffeld (Davis, Calif.: Hermagoras Press,
1989), pp. 219–42, 243–52; Hal W. Bochin, *Richard M. Nixon: Rhetorical Strategist*
(Westport, Conn.: Greenwood Press, 1990); Thomas A. Hollihan, "President
Richard Nixon's Second Inaugural Address" in *Inaugural Addresses of Twentieth-*

Century American Presidents, ed. Halford Ryan (Westport, Conn.: Greenwood Press, 1993), pp. 223–32; Theodore Otto Windt, Jr., "The 1960 Kennedy-Nixon Presidential Debates" in *Rhetorical Studies of National Political Debates, 1962–1992,* 2d ed., ed. Robert V. Friedenberg (Westport, Conn.: Praeger, 1994), pp. 1–27; Carole Blair and Davis W. Houck, "Richard Nixon and the Personalization of Crisis" in *The Modern Presidency and Crisis Rhetoric,* ed. Amos Kiewe (Westport, Conn.: Praeger, 1994), pp. 91–118; Denise M. Bostdorff, *The Presidency and the Rhetoric of Foreign Crisis* (Columbia: University of South Carolina Press, 1994), pp. 92–122; Hal W. Bochin, "Richard Milhous Nixon" in *U.S. Presidents as Orators: A Bio-Critical Sourcebook,* ed. Halford Ryan (Westport, Conn.: Greenwood Press, 1995), pp. 249–73; Edwin Black, "The Invention of Nixon," in *Beyond the Rhetorical Presidency,* ed. Martin J. Medhurst (College Station: Texas A&M University Press, 1996), pp. 104–21; Carol Gelderman, *All the President's Words: The Bully Pulpit and the Creation of the Virtual Presidency* (New York: Walker, 1997), pp. 76–96; Edwin Black, "Richard Nixon and the Privacy of Public Discourse," *Rhetoric & Public Affairs* 2 (1999): 1–29; Robert Asen, "Nixon's Welfare Reform: Enacting Historical Contradictions of Poverty Discourses," *Rhetoric & Public Affairs* 4 (2001): 261–80.

11. Gerald R. Ford, "Remarks on Taking the Oath of Office, August 9, 1974," *Papers of the Presidents of the United States—Gerald R. Ford, 1974* (Washington, D.C.: Government Printing Office, 1975), pp. 1–2. Hereafter this publication series is cited as *Public Papers* (followed by the last name of president and the year).

12. For additional studies of Gerald Ford's presidential and vice presidential rhetoric, see (chronological): Hermann G. Stelzner, "Ford's War on Inflation: A Metaphor that Did Not Cross," *Communication Monographs* 44 (1977): 284–97; James F. Klumpp and Jeffrey K. Lukehart, "The Pardoning of Richard Nixon: A Failure in Motivational Strategy," *Western Journal of Speech Communication* 41 (1978): 116–23; Gage William Chapel, "Humor in the White House: Interview with Presidential Speechwriter Robert Orben," *Communication Quarterly* 26 (Winter, 1978): 44–49; Sidney Kraus, ed., *The Great Debates: Carter vs. Ford, 1976* (Bloomington: Indiana University Press, 1979); Lloyd Bitzer and Theodore Reuter, *Carter vs. Ford: The Counterfeit Debates of 1976* (Madison: University of Wisconsin Press, 1980); Dan F. Hahn, "Corrupt Rhetoric: President Ford and the Mayaguez Affair," *Communication Quarterly* 28 (Spring, 1980): 38–43; Hart, *Verbal Style and the Presidency,* pp. 150–75; Bernard L. Brock, "Gerald R. Ford Encounters Richard Nixon's Legacy: On Amnesty and the Pardon" in *Oratorical Encounters,* pp. 227–39; Bernard L. Brock, "President Gerald R. Ford's Inaugural Address, 1974" in *Inaugural Addresses of Twentieth-Century American Presidents,* pp. 233–43; Goodwin Berquist, "The 1976 Carter-Ford Presidential Debates" in *Rhetorical Studies of National Political Debates, 1960–1992,* pp. 29–44; Craig Allen Smith and Kathy B. Smith, "The Coalitional Crisis of the Ford Presidency: The Pardons Reconsidered" in *The Modern Presidency and Crisis Rhetoric,* pp. 119–36; Bostdorff, *The Presidency and the Rhetoric of Foreign Crisis,* pp. 123–43; Craig Allen Smith, "Gerald R. Ford" in *U.S. Presidents as Orators,* pp. 274–98; Gelderman, *All the Presidents' Words,* pp. 116–27; Timothy M. Resh, "The Evolution of a Vice Presidential Speechwriting Staff: Invention and Style in Gerald R. Ford's Ghostwritten Vice Presidential Speeches." (master's thesis, Texas A&M University, 1998); and Thomas W. Benson, "'To Lend a Hand': Gerald R.

Ford, Watergate, and the White House Speechwriters," *Rhetoric & Public Affairs* 1 (1998): 201–25.

13. See, for example, Henry Kissinger, *White House Years* (Boston: Little, Brown and Co., 1979), p. 503; and Theodore White, *The Making of the President—1972* (New York: Atheneum, 1973), p. 13. See also, Theodore White, *The Making of the President—1968* (New York: Atheneum, 1969), p. 254.

14. "Transcript of Acceptance Speeches by Nixon and Agnew to the G.O.P. Convention," *New York Times,* Aug. 9, 1968, p. 20. Cited hereafter as Nixon, "1968 Acceptance Address."

15. The chief author of this section of the speech was Nixon with some help in style from William Gavin who wrote the line, "He hears a train go by at night and he dreams of far away places where he'd like to go." Nixon, "1968 Acceptance Address."

16. Nixon led Humphrey 45 percent to 29 percent in the Gallup Poll following the 1968 Republican National Convention. In a poll undertaken in mid-September, 1968, Louis Harris found that Nixon's acceptance speech was the most memorable event of the Republican convention and the memory was favorable. Hubert Humphrey's acceptance speech, by comparison, was remembered much less favorably. Louis Harris, "Conventions: Nixon Gained, HHH Was Hurt," *Washington Post,* Oct. 3, 1968, pp. F1, F3.

17. Kevin Phillips, "How Nixon Will Win," *New York Times Magazine,* Aug. 6, 1972, p. 36.

18. William C. Sexton, "What Went Right—And Wrong," *Long Island* [Garden City, N.Y.] *Newsday* (Nassau edition), Aug. 23, 1976, p. 39.

19. Gerald R. Ford, "Remarks in Kansas City Upon Accepting the 1976 Republican Presidential Nomination, August 19, 1976," *Public Papers: Ford, 1976,* Book III, pp. 2159, 2161, 2163.

20. Interestingly, Nixon did not use the structure of the Eisenhower White House wherein writers reported to a "head" writer who in turn reported to Sherman Adams. Adams staffed the drafts to other senior advisors. One wonders if the difference in procedure would have been as pronounced had Nixon won the election of 1960 thereby following Eisenhower into the White House. Ford's sudden ascendance to the presidency certainly played a role in his emulation of the Nixon structure.

21. Kissinger, *White House Years,* p. 78.

22. In the summer of 1976, Ron Nessen (with the support of David Gergen) attempted to place the speechwriters under his control. Hartmann forced Nessen not only to retract the proposal but to apologize personally to the writers.

23. David R. Maxey, "How Nixon Decided to Invade Cambodia," *Look Magazine,* Aug. 11, 1970, pp. 22–25.

24. The influence gained through this process is noted by Theodore White, *The Making of the President—1972,* p. 251, 262–63.

25. Joe McGinniss claims that Nixon's aides even applied semantic differentials to the voters (see McGinniss, *The Selling of the President,* pp. 79–81). Kenneth Khachigian denies this.

26. Robert Teeter of Market Opinion Research in Detroit provided polling data to Ford's political operation.

27. Only the most prominent members of the speechwriting staff are discussed here, using Nixon's discussion of them in his memoirs as one measure of their importance.

28. Kissinger writes that "Buchanan was the resident conservative, deeply wary of those whom he suspected of deflecting Nixon from his natural right-wing orientation, convinced that a cabal of intellectuals was confusing the pristine quality of the President's philosophy, unwilling to accept that it was in the nature of our many-faceted principal to show a different face to different people." See Kissinger, *White House Years,* p. 78. Buchanan readily admitted the influence of his father who was an "authoritarian figure who revered Senator Joseph McCarthy and Spanish dictator Francisco Franco." See Richard S. Littleton, "The Making of Buchanan," *Time,* Feb. 26, 1996, p. 32.

29. Later Safire would denounce Nixon over Watergate and the discovery that Safire's telephone line had been tapped because he was suspected of leaking stories to the media. See William Safire, "Another Who Had A Party Phone Line," *Chicago Tribune,* Aug. 10, 1973, p. A23.

30. In his memoirs, Nixon refers to Price as his "principal idea man." See Nixon, *Memoirs,* p. 279. See also Kissinger, *White House Years,* pp. 77, 1093. In his book, Price, who had been a writer for the *New York Herald Tribune,* confesses to voting for Lyndon Johnson in 1964. See Raymond Price, *With Nixon* (New York: Viking Press, 1977), p. 3.

31. Like Theodore Sorensen, Price was fond of counterpoint and repetition: "And a party that can unite itself can unite America" (1968 Acceptance Speech); "By facing the realities of the world, . . . we can make peace a reality" (1972 Foreign Policy Radio Address); and repeated three times—"Nothing is served by silence" (1972 Vietnam Address). See Nixon, "1968 Acceptance Address"; Richard M. Nixon, "Radio Address About the Third Annual Foreign Policy Report to the Congress, February 9, 1972," *Public Papers: Nixon, 1972,* p. 193; and Richard M. Nixon, "Address to the Nation Making Public a Plan for Peace in Vietnam, January 25, 1972," *Public Papers: Nixon, 1972,* pp. 101–102. For Price's role in the resignation speech, see Theodore White, *Breach of Faith: The Fall of Richard Nixon* (New York: Atheneum, 1975), p. 30.

32. John Osborne, *The Fifth Year of the Nixon Watch* (New York: Liveright, 1974), p. 119.

33. Kissinger evaluates the Nixon speechwriters as "unusually talented and varied." Kissinger, *White House Years,* p. 77.

34. Part of the problem is that a president gives so many speeches. The burden was not limited to Nixon; for example, in his short tenure, Ford delivered 1,142 formal speeches and remarks.

35. Some attribute Agnew's clever lines to a campaign worker from Baltimore; others are attributed to Gold. However, the line "nattering nabobs of negativism" was Safire's.

36. Kissinger, *White House Years,* p. 77.

37. According to Buchanan, he sneaked into the party uninvited. Earlier he had once served as Vice President Nixon's caddie at the Burning Tree Country Club in Maryland near Washington, D.C. When Nixon needed to urinate, Buchanan showed him to the bushes and urinated beside Nixon in perhaps one of the oddest male-bonding rituals in presidential politics. See Littleton, "The Making of Buchanan," p. 33.

38. Buchanan's pugilistic rhetorical style reflected his combative personality. His father had encouraged his sons to box, and after entering Georgetown University, Patrick Buchanan got into an altercation with the local police, which resulted in a suspension from the university. He returned to school and graduated cum laude from Georgetown. He later earned a masters degree in journalism from Columbia University.

39. This function was retained in the Ford administration.

40. Buchanan often relied on the skills of Kenneth Khachigian, a former undergraduate debater at the University of California (Santa Barbara) in the 1960s, with a law degree from Columbia University, who would go on to write for Spiro Agnew, Earl Butz, Richard Nixon, and Ronald Reagan.

41. See William Safire, *Before the Fall: A Inside View of the Pre-Watergate White House* (Garden City, N.Y.: Doubleday, 1975), p. 351.

42. Joseph C. Spear, *Presidents and the Press: The Nixon Legacy* (Cambridge, Mass.: MIT Press, 1984), p. 81.

43. Nixon, *Memoirs,* p. 411.

44. Spiro T. Agnew, "Television News Coverage: Network Censorship," *Vital Speeches of the Day,* (Dec. 1, 1969), pp. 98–101.

45. Ibid., p. 99.

46. Ibid., p. 100.

47. Agnew became a mouthpiece for Buchanan's thoughts. In 1970, for example, Buchanan sent a memo to Agnew suggesting he craft a speech on integration: "In the South, the trend of integration of the schools will result in socioeconomic segregation, which is worse for education than racial segregation; it is unfair to the poor who integrate, while the middle class retain the freedom of choice to go to the schools they want." Agnew incorporated the philosophy into his addresses on school busing. "Buchanan Quote File," *Los Angeles Times,* Feb. 25, 1996, p. A21.

48. White, *Making of the President—1972,* p. 268.

49. This was the only foreign policy speech that Buchanan wrote; he relied on an outline provided by Kissinger's staff. Kissinger claims that the speech's "major thrust was Nixon's" (Kissinger, *White House Years,* p. 503).

50. Nixon, *Memoirs,* p. 491.

51. Political opponents criticized Buchanan because he used White House photographs in the book and was compensated by the publisher, but White House Counsel John Dean cleared him of wrong-doing.

52. Osborne, *Fifth Year,* pp. 63–64. See also White, *Making of the President—1972,* p. 13.

53. Osborne, *Fifth Year,* pp. 119, 147–48. White believed that Nixon's favorite writers were Safire, Price, and Buchanan, but even as a favored writer, Price lacked the

influence of Buchanan in the Nixon White House. See White, *Making of the President—1972,* pp. 221, 228, 364.

54. Nixon, *Memoirs,* pp. 836, 839, 849. Nevertheless, Nixon regarded Price as the "most honest, cool, objective man I know."

55. Nixon, *Memoirs,* p. 905; Osborne, *Fifth Year,* pp. 164, 194–97.

56. Nixon, *Memoirs,* p. 1014.

57. Ibid., p. 968.

58. As a consultant to CBS, the present author was in direct contact with Khachigian regarding Buchanan's machinations. See also Price, *With Nixon,* pp. 331–32.

59. See Craig Allen Smith and Kathy B. Smith, *The White House Speaks: Presidential Leadership as Persuasion* (Westport, Conn.: Praeger, 1994), pp. 55–77.

60. William Willoughby, "Righteous Ford Talks Like Carter, Wows Baptists," *Washington Star,* June 16, 1976, pp. A1, A15. For the text of the address, see Gerald R. Ford, "Remarks at the Southern Baptist Convention, Norfolk, Virginia, June 15, 1976," *Public Papers: Ford, 1976–77,* Book II, pp. 1877–80.

61. Hartmann informed the speechwriters that the theme would be "The American Adventure." He added: "All drafts should be short, taut, and straightforward. . . . [T]here should be no campaign code words or partisan insinuations whatsoever. . . . Noble and profound thoughts can be expressed in direct and simple words, as Jefferson and Lincoln did." Robert Hartmann to speechwriters, June 10, 1976, pp. 1, 3. Copy held by the present author.

62. Craig R. Smith was the primary writer for the Spirit of Washington address delivered at Valley Forge (July 4, 1976), the speech at the "Washington Gala" (July 3, 1976), and the speech at the opening of the centennial safe from the presidential administration of Ulysses S. Grant (July 1, 1976). His backup drafts for Independence Hall (July 4, 1976) and Monticello (July 5, 1976) were popular enough with the president that major portions were included in the final drafts. See *Public Papers: Ford, 1976–77,* Book II, pp. 1963–65, 1961–62, 1941–43, 1966–71, and 1973–77.

63. Hartmann to speechwriters, June 10, 1976, p. 2.

64. Gerald R. Ford, "Remarks in Valley Forge, Pennsylvania, July 4, 1976," *Public Papers: Ford, 1976–77,* Book II, p. 1963.

65. Hartmann to speechwriters, June 10, 1976, p. 3.

66. Gerald R. Ford, "Remarks in Philadelphia, July 4, 1976," *Public Papers: Ford, 1976–77,* Book II, p. 1969.

67. For example, the headline on the first page of the *New York Times* proclaimed: "Nation and Millions in City Joyously Hail Bicentennial." The subhead read: "President Talks: Philadelphia Throngs Told U.S. is Leader." A second story on the front page leads with a large picture of Ford traveling and quoted more material from his speeches. The newspaper also reported favorable comments on the speeches from persons in the crowd. See the *New York Times,* July 5, 1976, pp. 1, 18.

68. Aristotle, *On Rhetoric: A Theory of Civic Discourse,* trans. George Kennedy (New York: Oxford University Press, 1991), pp. 218–19 (III. 1. 3–7).

69. Cicero, *De Oratore,* trans. H. Rackham (Cambridge: Harvard University Press, 1942), p. 169 (3.56.213).

70. Quintilian, *Institutio Oratoria,* trans. H. E. Butler (Cambridge: Harvard University Press, 1922), Vol. 4, p. 245 (XI.iii.6). Also see Cicero, *De Oratore,* p. 169 (3.56.213).

71. For the text of the address, see Bill Clinton, "Address Before a Joint Session of the Congress on the State of the Union, January 23, 1996," *Weekly Compilation of Presidential Documents* 32, No. 4 (Jan. 29, 1996): 83–118.

72. Edward Kennedy's speech was broadcast nationally on July 25, 1969, from the home of his father, Joseph Kennedy. For a complete text, see Edward M. Kennedy, "Television Statement to the People of Massachusetts" in *Contemporary American Public Discourse,* pp. 249–52.

73. Jules Witcover, *Marathon: The Pursuit of the Presidency 1972–1976* (New York: Signet, 1977), p. 49.

74. Ibid., p. 50.

75. For an account of Nixon's rehearsals, see McGinniss, *Selling of the President, 1968,* pp. 10–23.

76. See Ronald Reagan, "Interview with Television Network Broadcasters, December 3, 1987," *Public Papers: Reagan, 1987,* Book II, pp. 1425–31. The interview was actually taped during the afternoon of December 3, 1987, and televised in the evening of the same day.

CHAPTER 7

Jimmy Carter

The Language of Politics
and the Practice of Integrity

JOHN H. PATTON

There are many pathways for exploring the nature and function of speechwriting in the presidential administration of Jimmy Carter, but this chapter begins the journey with two poems. The first, titled "On Using Words," complains that when the writer seeks "efficient words" to express a truth, he finds that "the vagueness is still there."[1] The second poem, "It Can Fool the Sun," laments the fate of America's homeless, while admiring the spirit of a destitute man who wryly observes that his cardboard shelter "can fool the sun, but not the rain!"[2]

The author of these lines is none other than Jimmy Carter in his 1995 volume of published poetry. The first tells us a great deal about Carter's gradually growing acceptance of the power of language, along with his continuing struggle to feel fully comfortable with the forms of discourse. His search, he explains, is for efficient language and while that search has led him to a much greater appreciation of language as an art, nonetheless, he concludes that the imprecision of meaning remains. The second poem reflects Carter's intrinsic altruism, fueled by his religious convictions, in a creative view of homelessness. The subtlety of phrasing and sharpness of imagery even in the phrase contrasting the sun and rain are precisely the kinds of rhetorical assets which his public discourse during his administration sorely needed and frequently lacked.

Carter's poems provide important starting points for two reasons, first because they show a sensitivity to language and imagery which seems to have been ironically reinforced if not newly discovered by the postpresidential Jimmy Carter; second, because they indicate both Carter's considerable skill at language usage when he truly wanted to express himself while at the same time showing his deep reluctance and even mistrust of language itself. The tension between creative and artful use of language and the idea that language is always artificial and consequently suspect was an enduring feature of the presidential discourses of Jimmy Carter. This chapter explores the major ways in which that tension worked itself out in the contexts of momentous events that summoned rhetorical responses. This essay argues that speechwriting in the Carter administration reflected, yet never fully resolved, this fundamental tension between descriptive, programmatic discourse and artful, creative rhetorical forms. In pursuit of that thesis, this chapter: examines the identities, roles, and functions of the major speechwriters in the Carter administration; analyzes a variety of speech texts and the speechwriting processes they involved; and considers the impact of speechwriting on the formation and development of major policies during the Carter administration.[3]

In the field of communication studies, Marie Hochmuth Nichols has raised especially important concerns about speechwriting. Nichols refers to Walter Bowman's term for the speechwriter as an "indispensable artisan." She notes that "there seem to be two varieties of the artisan: . . . the ghost writer who supplies the form, that is in so far as form can be separated from ideas and content . . . [and] the assistant who supplies both the form and the ideas, leaving nothing for the speaker but delivery." She then points out major problems with ghostwriting, especially the threat to individuality, or what we may now recognize as the "character issue." It could be that a ghostwritten speech "represents not the individual but the group. The reality of the character of the speaker passes into the pen of the ghostwriter."[4]

Carter's Speechwriters and the Speechwriting Process

Carter was never comfortable with the very idea of public speaking, much less speechwriting. In reflecting about his education at the U.S. Naval Academy, Carter underscored his dislike of speaking: "One of the most fearsome requirements was in after dinner speaking. It was necessary to prepare a speech, ostensibly humorous, or at least entertaining. Then, some fifteen or twenty of us would assemble in a group in formal attire and try to eat a banquet meal, presided over by a senior officer. About a third of us would be called on at each session to make our prepared speeches. No one knew who would be introduced next. Speaking and listening were equally painful, and cold sweat was everywhere."[5] His distaste for public speaking carried forward into his political career and was, in part, reflected by his reserving speechwriting to himself alone until he emerged on the national scene.

Carter came to use speechwriters quite reluctantly for the first time during his 1976 campaign for the presidency. Robert Shrum was given a brief, unsuccessful try, and there were even attempts by Theodore Sorensen to write for Carter. None of these writers fit and the task eventually fell to Patrick Anderson. To fully grasp the nature and quality of speechwriting during the administration itself, one must first understand the important role of Anderson as Carter's speechwriter during the 1976 campaign up to and including the inaugural address. Anderson represents a period when speechwriting was functioning in a relatively fluid, artful, and effective way for Jimmy Carter. As a writer of novels and political commentary, Anderson traveled to Georgia to do a piece on then-candidate Carter. It turned out to be a positive essay and was grounded in personal interviews, observations, and levels of conversation and interaction between writer and subject which would become conspicuously absent once Carter moved to the White House. As a self-described survivor of the 1972 campaign of Democratic presidential candidate George McGovern, Anderson indicates that "by chance I found myself working for Jimmy Carter, so I summoned my audacity and wrote my speeches about a better America, put all my anger and frustration and lingering idealism into them, and hoped they might do some good."[6] Indeed, he identifies audacity as the most important quality for a speechwriter. As this chapter reveals, the very different context of Carter's presidential administration greatly modified the ability of writers to be audacious and bold.

One of the campaign speeches that Anderson wrote for Carter was particularly revealing: Carter's address on June 1, 1976, dedicating a new wing at the Martin Luther King Hospital in Los Angeles. That speech both reveals the creative dimensions of the speechwriting process and provides a glimpse of rhetorical qualities that surfaced only rarely once Carter became president. Anderson saw the hospital dedication as a special opportunity to give voice to Carter's ideals and moral principles, and to use the phrase "I see an America" as a way of framing a theme which he had been designing for Carter's campaign addresses. He reports that he consulted "Dr. King's 'I Have a Dream speech'" and "Robert Kennedy's anguished remarks the night King was killed" as sources for ideas. After Anderson finished the text, Carter made only one change—"he deleted a critical reference to George Wallace."[7] The speech elaborated on the bond between

King and Carter, and included a section praising Carter's mother, Lillian, for her efforts to challenge segregation. The speech's language reflected directly on King and the dream for which he stood: "He was the man," it read, "more than any other of his generation, who gazed upon the great wall of segregation and saw that it could be destroyed by the power of love."[8] The speech paid tribute to Robert Kennedy and lamented the tragic events of 1968. About Richard Nixon's 1968 presidential campaign, the speech noted: "we lost the election that year to men who governed without love or laughter, to men who promised law and order and gave us crime and oppression. But the dream lived on."[9]

The Martin Luther King Hospital speech reveals much about Anderson's role as speechwriter and also a great deal about Carter's rhetorical strengths and potential. As Anderson saw it, "Carter's most attractive quality was his idealism, and the question was how it could best be presented."[10] In pursuing that task he seems to have had an innate sense of identification with Carter's view of the world. It is that kind of shared base which gives a writer the freedom and creativity to combine his voice with his subject to become functionally one. Anderson observes that "Carter may at first have viewed my rhetoric with mixed feelings, as when he warned the audience he was going to read something his staff had prepared, a tendency repeated during the administration in his announcement of paperwork reduction and the artificial stack of papers he refers to as a prop. He resented using someone else's words. Deep in his heart, he probably thought Kennedyesque rhetoric was frivolous and possibly sinful, but he could not ignore the success of the King speech."[11]

After the election of 1976, speechwriting for Carter became a much more complex and collaborative process. The Carter administration was served by a series of speechwriters whose functions seemed to emerge almost at random as events developed. Some of those events confronted the Carter presidency with a numbing set of challenges and risks ripe for rhetorical responses: the Arab oil embargo and the energy crisis; the rise of interest rates and double-digit inflation; the continuing implementation of civil rights laws; the Panama Canal treaties negotiations; the Middle East peace negotiations; the Russian invasion of Afghanistan; and, of course, the taking of American hostages by Iran. These were the kinds of issues that required presidential discourse both for public understanding and to develop sustainable policies.

All totaled, Carter had about a dozen presidential speechwriters over the course of his four-year term, with each writer joining and departing from the White House staff at various times between 1977 and 1981. These included James M. Fallows, Jerome H. Doolittle, Achsah P. Nesmith, Griffin Smith, Jr., Hendrik Hertzberg, Susan Battles, Caryl F. Conner, Gordon C. Stewart, Robert Lee Maddox, Christopher J. Matthews, and Robert B. Rackleff. Throughout the whole process, the primary speech editor was Carter himself. Fallows served as chief speechwriter from January, 1977, through November, 1978; Hertzberg became chief speechwriter in May, 1979, and held that position throughout the remainder of the administration; Gordon C. Stewart became deputy chief speechwriter in January, 1980.

Interestingly, the Carter speechwriting staff was smaller than many previous administrations and, more importantly, was given scant resources. Carter's speechwriters later recalled that "we had no researchers and just a couple of secretaries."[12] Added to this was a general sense of dislocation, a kind of nomadic aura, about where the speechwriting staff belonged and to whom it would report. At least three administrative plans were tried: an original one with speechwriting reporting to Press Secretary Jody Powell; a shift in 1978 putting speechwriting under media advisor Gerald Rafshoon; and finally placement in September, 1979, under presidential advisor Al McDonald. In all these arrangements, Hertzberg observed, the one constant was that "there was surprisingly little personal contact between us and the man we were writing for."[13]

During the first two years of the Carter presidency, chief speechwriter James Fallows was one of about twenty-four people who "had free access" to Carter "in memos, if not in the flesh."[14] Yet, when Fallows did confer with Carter in person about speeches, the instructions he received focused more on Carter's preference for an orderly system of speechwriting, than on substantive matters. Fallows recalled that "the worst tongue-lashings I received were not for bad speeches, of which there were too many, but for those that were disorderly in their preparation, or consumed too much of Carter's time. The virtues of an organization man . . . were those Carter prized; and if an attempt to produce more imaginative policies . . . , even better speech drafts, would violate these principles of order, it was not likely to prevail."[15] Such unpleasant exchanges between Carter and speechwriters were rare. In fact, Fallows observed that "[o]ther politicians are notorious for browbeating or humiliating their speechwriters; [but] Jimmy Carter was always decent to me."[16] In his exit interview upon departing the White House, Fallows succinctly summarized Carter's problems with speechwriting and speaking: "The relevant facts about Carter's mind as it relates to speeches are: First, that he lived most of his political life without speechwriters. . . . The second relevant fact is that whenever possible he feels much more comfortable extemporizing rather than reading from a text. . . . He just hates to use texts and he hates to practice to improve his delivery. The third relevant fact is if he had the time, he'd still write them all himself."[17] Fallows observations were largely confirmed by Gerald Rafshoon, who observed: "I think one of our problems, and I told him this, was that he spent more time on preparations of the speech and less time in preparing his delivery. He'd get into the text too much sometimes. We had a lot of problems later." The irony here is that Carter tried to do extensive editing on texts, yet texts were the very instruments he disdained most and trusted least. Despite the time he committed to editing, Carter did not like editing speech texts. Indeed, Rafshoon recalled that "he [Carter] could not stand to work with the text. He did not do well with the text." Rafshoon also affirmed that Carter's rhetorical strengths were energized in extemporaneous and relatively spontaneous settings. Rafshoon stressed that

> when he'd go off the cuff he was so good. When he ran for Governor and when he ran for President so many of those speeches were without a text. Impromptu speeches were usually good because he internalized the subject. Especially . . . human rights, civil rights. I've got so much film of Carter in black churches that would just bring tears to your eye, even when he was President, when a lot of the fire was out of him, when he talked to a group like that or he talked to a group of senior citizens or handicapped you could see that humanity come out. This was not the case if the speech had "the programs that I am going to deliver to you people."[18]

For Carter, the nature of standard presidential policy speeches presented an alienating context, a virtual rhetorical barrier. Speechwriters were constantly struggling with a speaker who rarely met with them, distrusted language, yet entered situations which called for written texts, and then felt that he had to modify final versions of those texts. Such policy speeches suppressed Carter's strong sense of humanity and spontaneity.

The result was a rhetoric of description and announcement of programs, not a rhetoric of appeal and influence about the reasons and justifications for policies. This manifested itself frequently in a "listing" procedure that became the mainstay of many speeches, although many in the speechwriting staff knew the ineffectiveness of this approach. After writing speeches for

Carter for almost two years, Fallows concluded: "Carter thinks in lists, not arguments; as long as the items are there, their order does not matter, nor does the hierarchy among them." When Carter provided the speechwriters with a speech outline, "it would consist of six or seven subjects . . . rather than a theme or tone. . . . Whenever he edited a speech, he did so to cut out the explanatory portions and add 'meat' in the form of a list of topics."[19]

Carter's speeches continued to be composed of lists of policy proposals not only because of Carter but also because major policy speeches were viewed as stages on which every department and advisor wanted to play a visible part. Rafshoon noted that there was "a never ending fight of keeping other people out of the speechwriting arena. Everybody wanted a piece of the speech. . . . And by the time everybody got in with what they wanted you would wind up having a laundry list of things." In particular, he cited the annual State of the Union address as "just horrendous because everybody had to have in something and they all wanted a laundry list."[20]

Achsah Nesmith, one of two females on the speechwriting staff and one of the few southerners in that group, had covered Carter as a reporter for the *Atlanta Constitution* from her days in the legislature of Georgia. During the 1966 campaign in Georgia she was frequently the only reporter assigned to travel with Carter. She recalled: "I was underfoot all the time . . . every day, every minute. If he was on the beach I was on the beach. . . . If he was having breakfast at the Lion's Club, I was having breakfast with the Lion's Club. We got to know each other pretty well during that [period]." In response to a question about why she was selected for speechwriting, Nesmith replied, "Well, I hope because he liked the way I wrote or maybe he liked the way I thought. I don't know. He never exactly said. Maybe that tells something, I don't know. I always expected that at some point he would say, the reason I brought you here was this and either you're doing it or you're not doing it."[21] But she waited in vain for that kind of presidential guidance.

Gordon Stewart brought to the speechwriting staff the unique, and much needed, perspective of drama. He has described his background as fraught with the dilemma of having to decide whether to enter law school or drama school, and choosing drama. When he received a call from Hertzberg to join the speechwriting staff, he was directing *The Elephant Man* in New York City. He also had a previous record as a speechwriter, especially for liberal Republican John Lindsay during his term as Mayor of New York. In the White House, Stewart became primarily interested in writing speeches on energy and foreign policy. With regard to the importance of his training in theater, Stewart offered a telling observation: "What drama training produces in the way of bias in speechwriting is a great concern for what the soul of this material is, which is both the content and its emotion. You begin by addressing the question, 'Why are we doing this?' It's very similar to directing a play."[22] He went on to observe that "the most important decision you make is why do you direct this, why have you chosen this play, what is it about this material that you think is going to interest anybody at this time? Why do this play now? . . . I always find that would color the discussions on speechwriting—why are we having the President speak about this subject now? What can we possibly gain by doing this?"[23]

Like other speechwriters, Stewart found that Carter was quite resistant to working to improve his speaking: "When we tried to get him to change his voice or change anything, the resistance to that was so strong, central, and fundamental."[24] In addition to the speechwriting staff per se, there were a number of other key participants in the speechwriting process who surfaced periodically to greatly influence, and sometimes disturb, the shape and direction of policy addresses. Carter's policy advisor Stuart Eizenstat and media advisor Gerald Rafshoon were clearly in this category, especially on domestic issues. Patrick Caddell, the president's pollster, was the energizing force for the psychological aspect of the famous Crisis of Confidence energy speech. Carter's national security advisor Zbigniew Brzezinski and Secretary of State Cyrus Vance competed both openly and secretly for rival versions of foreign policy messages. The president's wife, Rosalyn Carter, and Jody Powell reviewed Carter's farewell address. Speechwriting in the Carter White House was almost never a simple or direct process. Speechwriters were not only distanced from Carter, they were frequently left in a subsidiary position to the potential and actual eruptions of a wide range of influential persons who could have great sway over issue-specific speeches.

There was no single, clear voice serving Carter as the functional equivalent of an autobiographer. In short, no one functioned for Carter as Theodore Sorensen had for John F. Kennedy. The exception, significantly, was Carter himself. He had been his own speechwriter during his campaigns for the governorship of Georgia and during most of his time in that office. In the White House, Carter continued to put the finishing form on major addresses. Yet, he lacked talent as a speechwriter—especially with policy speeches. Moreover, that situation was coupled with an enduring problem for speechwriters throughout his administration: lack of direct and consistent access to and interaction with the president. Hertzberg noted: "Throughout our four years the administrative pattern of speechwriting was the separation of function and responsibility from authority. The President never worked in any consistent way or directly with the people who wrote his speeches. . . . There was this constant and futile search for an intermediary between Carter and his speechwriters who would magically produce the desired results. Of course, it was a doomed search."[25] One reason that Carter needed an intermediary was that his staff of speechwriters came to the White House with backgrounds quite dissimilar from Carter's background. Carter's religious convictions were central both to his character and his public persona. Hertzberg refers to that dimension of Carter as a "religious style of leadership." But Hertzberg also notes that "our speechwriting office . . . was populated mostly by diehard secular humanists." Reflecting their own distance from Carter's deep Christian faith, the speechwriters "used to joke that it was no accident that the man's initials were J. C."[26]

The problem with the speechwriting process was a crucial factor in the quality of Carter's speeches. Speechwriting in the Carter White House frequently was done, if not in a vacuum, at least at an appreciable distance from the president until the final editorial stages. Only with the final draft did Carter turn his attention to a speech. Nesmith reported that "very often the very last draft we didn't see or had very little contact with except on the really major speeches."[27] Interestingly, the Carter White House had no formal system for the speechwriters to meet with senior aides to analyze speeches Carter had presented them. Such reviews might have helped the writers with subsequent addresses, but they rarely took place. Hertzberg noted: "there were no formal postmortems, but there were informal ones with Jody [Powell] especially. A lot of second guessing occurred." To overcome the strictures of distance, physical and psychic, the speechwriters typically went through a process Hertzberg described as "Carterization." According to Hertzberg: "One technique I think we all used was reading *Why Not the Best?* Carter is one of the few politicians who had a literary style, undistinguished though it may have been. He actually wrote *Why Not the Best?* It was plain the way that book showed how he used language. Strunk and White *(The Elements of Style)* was another pretty good guide because that was Carter's style. It was very simple, declarative, verging on flat. That was one way, and the other ways were simply listening to everything he said."[28]

While the speechwriters seem to have been drawn into a fragmented process, they labored mightily to reshape and overcome the constraints they encountered. For example, Achsah Nesmith stressed: "we did explore the books, religious sources, poetry, and music that he drew from, as well as constantly trying to get people to share anecdotes from his life that illuminated his thoughts and feelings."[29] In particular, she noted, "I read Niebuhr and Dylan Thomas and Admiral Rickover and the Bible and Agee as part of that effort to understand his ideas and what shaped them. I also read his accounts of his childhood and what he admired about his mother, played back in my mind conversations we had had about incidents when he was in Mexico or people in the county next to Sumter [County in Georgia] who knew how to make split oak baskets or how praying for his enemies changed his feelings toward them."[30]

From a slightly different perspective Christopher Matthews added that he wrote for Carter largely by listening to him: "We listened to tapes. As I said, the Army Signal Corps taped everything he said and most of his speaking occasions were off-the-cuff and therefore you got pretty much pure Carter."[31] In addition, starting in the second year of the administration at least one speechwriter accompanied Carter on all of his trips. Significantly, in response to the question of why they had not gone on presidential trips from the beginning, Hertzberg replied: "because we were not important in the eyes of the people running the trip."[32] Within that difficult context, Carter's speechwriters marshaled inventional resources to shape responses for the rhetorical situations that confronted the Carter administration.

Speechwriting and the Articulation of Policy: Frustrations

Carter's speechwriters lamented that their speechwriting was detached from policy decisions. After serving as the chief speechwriter, James Fallows concluded that speechmaking and policy rarely merged, that Carter tended to view speechmaking as a non-policy activity, and that certainly his best speeches were usually those which allowed him to be extemporaneous— usually not a feature of policy addresses. Fallows had entered the White House with high hopes that he could contribute to policy making. He sent memos to Carter and his top aides on a wide range of subjects not directly related to any upcoming speech. He reports that after several months, "I learned to stop. It was not that my superiors disagreed with me . . . , but rather that I was out of my place. My job was to write speeches and edit memos, and to that job I quietly returned."[33] Fallows' successor, Hendrik Hertzberg, also concluded that Carter saw decision making and speech making as two different and separate realms.[34]

Nonetheless, all presidents face rhetorical situations that inevitably re-quire the use of discourse to define, explain, and defend policy. In the case of Jimmy Carter, the tendency to separate policy making from speechwriting meant that opportunities for rhetorical argument and appeal were neglected and underutilized. A representative example of this problem occurred in the National Energy Plan address of April 20, 1977. Delivered to a joint session of Congress, Carter began the speech effectively by attempting to link this speech to his last appearance on inauguration day. But in his third paragraph of text he declared: "This cannot be an inspirational speech tonight. I don't expect much applause. It's a sober and difficult presenta-tion." He noted that work on energy was "a thankless job, but it is our job."[35]

The speech discussed energy in terms of percentages of consumption and growth of trade deficits, and then offered a seven-point list of "specific goals." Those included statements such as: "to reduce gasoline consump-tion by 10 percent"; "to insulate 90 percent of American homes and all new buildings; [and] to use solar energy in more than 2½ million Ameri-can homes."[36] There was a striking reliance on rates, percentages, quantifi-cation about an issue that the public was experiencing in distinctly per-sonal terms. Given Carter's own personal qualities and his ability to connect with audiences on a very human level, as was the case with the King Hos-pital, it is ironic that he abandoned personal and "inspirational" language in discussing energy policy.

The last part of the speech concentrated on energy conservation, which Carter defined in terms of "waste"—a decidedly negative concept. In an effort to punish the production and use of "wasteful automobiles," Carter proposed his unpopular gas-guzzler tax: "a graduated excise tax on new gas guzzlers that do not meet Federal standards."[37] That was followed by the proposal for a gasoline tax—"an additional 5 cents a gallon that will auto-matically take effect each year that we fail to meet our annual targets in the previous year." Those punitive measures were certainly perceived in per-sonal terms by public audiences—a sharp contrast to Carter's effort to de-scribe them in impersonal ways. His lone attempt to reach out to the affected audiences came in a generalized "if . . . then" sentence: "Now, if the Ameri-can people respond to this challenge, we can meet these targets."[38] The imagery of "targets" and management goals clearly represented Carter's engineering, structured, and decision-making orientation to policy.

In this speech Carter was true to his word: he said it would not be inspirational and he did not expect applause. That forecast was confirmed in this and a considerable number of Carter's other policy addresses because of the sharp separation between the description of policy decisions and the communication of those decisions to diverse and frequently fragmented audiences. For example, communication scholar Craig Allen Smith and political scientist Kathy B. Smith give a vivid account of the same sort of problem in Carter's Panama Canal treaty address. They note that on September 14, 1977, "shortly after the treaty signing, speechwriter James Fallows urged the President to go on television for a 'Fireside Chat' about the treaties. Fallows feared that the public would conclude that 'we've abandoned the fight. We're leaving all the public argumentation to the other side, . . . and by letting their [Carter's opponents'] crazy charges go unanswered for the moment we suggest that we don't have any answers'."[39] This problem continued into 1978.

The 1977 energy plan speech, the Panama Canal address, and other major policy speeches by Carter clearly illustrate one of his speechwriters' main concerns throughout the four years of his administration: Carter's resistance to symbolic themes. Looking back on his experience in the White House, Fallows concluded in 1979 that Carter had "not given us an idea to follow." In Fallows' view, "the central idea of the Carter Administration" was "Jimmy Carter himself." Commenting on Carter while he was still president, his former speechwriter explained: "I came to think that Carter believes fifty things, but no one thing. He holds explicit, thorough positions on every issue under the sun, but he has no large view of the relations between them."[40]

On numerous occasions Hertzberg tried mightily to have Carter adopt a clear symbolic theme to give direction to the administration. His first choice was "the Beloved Community," which would have cast Carter as the continuing voice of the moral principles that guided the civil rights movement. That phrase had been used repeatedly by Martin Luther King, Jr., and after his assassination the phrase was carried on by younger civil rights leaders, such as Carter's fellow Georgian John R. Lewis. Had Carter used the theme of "the Beloved Community," it might have advanced his presidential initiatives on race relations, human rights, and the international peace—efforts for which Carter became widely known once he left the White House.[41] The theme never made it to the surface, in part, because the Carter White House considered speechwriting to be extremely low in order of importance—especially early in the administration. Hertzberg then engaged in a relatively sustained effort to launch "the New Foundation" as the basic theme for Carter. He argued for this theme based on the Roosevelt and Kennedy administrations' adoption of such symbolic terms as the New Deal and the New Frontier. He managed to insert "the New Foundation" language into the 1979 State of the Union address and was temporarily hopeful that Carter would embrace the theme and turn a fresh rhetorical corner.

Carter began his 1979 State of the Union address with the words: "Tonight I want to examine in a broad sense the state of our American Union—how we are building a new foundation for a peaceful and prosperous world." The "new foundation" theme was skillfully woven into the text, providing a structure and rationale for key ideas in the speech. It was used to cast a vision: "The challenge to us is to build a new and firmer foundation for the future—for a sound economy, for a more effective government, for more political trust, and for a stable peace." It was also used in an almost sermonic section to debunk existing "myths" and unite seeming contraries: "In our economy, it is a myth that we must choose endlessly between inflation and recession. Together, we build the foundation for a strong economy"; "In our government it is a myth that we must choose between compassion and competence. Together we build the foundation for a government that works—and works for people"; "In our relations with our potential adversaries, it is a myth that we must choose between confrontation and capitulation. Together we build the foundation for a stable world of both diversity and peace."[42]

The theme evolved throughout the speech and was clearly evoked in the conclusion, where Carter asked Congress "to join me in building that new foundation—a better foundation—for our beloved country and our world."[43] This was an opportunity for a rhetorical turning point. Carter, however, simply saw this as one among many ways of wording and did not seize "the New Foundation" as his symbolic sword. If anything, he tended to turn that sword against himself. At a news conference held three days after the 1979 State of the Union address, a journalist asked Carter: "[W]ho thought up the slogan 'New Foundation'? [*laughter*]." In Hertzberg's recollection of that press conference, Carter responded that it was just something his speechwriters had put in the address and gave it no special significance.[44]

Hertzberg's memory had apparently been colored by his disappointment with Carter's rhetorical failures, for Carter had initially ignored the laughter from the press and had tried to explain that "the New Foundation" was a good theme for his address, because it expressed his view that his policies—while not paying "immediate political benefits"—were nevertheless essential as "investment at the present time for future dividends for

America." He continued: "Some of the decisions that I am making right now, in having a tough and stringent budget for 1980, may not be politically popular, but I think in the long run the control of inflation will pay rich dividends for our country. And the fact that we are building a foundation for future progress was the reason we chose that as a theme for the speech." Yet, Carter could not conceive of an overarching rhetorical theme that would span many addresses and serve as an organizing principle for public perception of his administration. The journalist who initially raised the issue suggested that Carter's theme was a gimmick like the "New Frontier or Great Society or whatever." He then asked Carter why he suddenly felt the need for a "motto" after three years as president, and concluded with the query: "[D]o you think this slogan will survive . . . ?" The speechwriters' hearts must have sunk as Carter replied: "I doubt if it will survive. [*laughter*] We are not trying to establish this as a permanent slogan."[45]

The episode at the press conference revealed another frustration in the speechwriting process: Carter's tendency to close the windows of rhetorical opportunity when they appeared. An equally vivid example of the opening and closing of a rhetorical window occurred in the much discussed Crisis of Confidence speech of July 15, 1979. That speech was important in its own right, but in the present analysis it is appropriate to note that the speech was initially hailed as a success—so much so that many in the administration believed that it had allowed Carter to "reinvent" his presidency and restore what was by then a serious loss of public confidence. According to Hertzberg, that opportunity was lost within days of the speech, when Carter did the one thing that had the potential to turn the initial success into an enlarged negative perception: he asked for resignations of his cabinet and then fired some key cabinet officers, including Joseph Califano—secretary of health, education, and welfare.[46]

Perhaps no speech better captured the complications, frustrations, and successes of speechwriting for Carter than his Crisis of Confidence energy address. Carter was extremely reluctant to give that speech and was very tired from foreign travel at the time it was scheduled. According to Hertzberg, "everyone was exhausted to the marrow of their bones." By 1979, gas lines had formed and the country was extremely concerned about energy prices. Carter's previous speeches on energy had been largely ineffective and that was one of the reasons he did not want to make just another energy speech. The actual scheduling of the Crisis speech revealed an important dimension of the speechwriting process. Hertzberg has re-called that the decision to make this major address was done "in a pretty haphazard fashion. There was a meeting of a few people in the Oval Office, saying, 'You better have a speech,'. . . Then, practically in the anteroom in a kind of flash of bravado, Jerry Rafshoon picked up the phone and called the network pool and said, 'The President will address the nation next Wednesday at 9:30 [P.M.].' This was a little premature actually."[47]

A draft was prepared under what the writers called "horrendous condi-tions" and was sent to Carter at Camp David. That draft, according to Stewart, was "highly programmatic. . . . not unlike the previous couple of energy speeches."[48] Stewart focused on the weaknesses of the program-matic approach, and tried to provide a clear audience orientation by deal-ing with why the public would be listening: "'We're listening because we don't want to wait in gas lines.' The public has no tolerance, no sympathy; they're like baseball fans and they want to win and that's it and they'll boo the quarterback. Even if they understand that he's got a shoulder separa-tion."[49] He and Hertzberg argued that unless the speech was reframed there was no reason to give it. Stewart announced: "I don't see where it is here, folks. What's going to convince people that things are going to get better in, if not their lifetime, at least the lifetime we have left in this office?"[50] They were both relieved when Carter decided he simply did not want to do another energy speech and canceled it.

The speech was eventually rescheduled and its orientation redirected toward a larger problem identified by the speechwriters: "the idea was that there was something bigger happening here than gas lines."[51] That prob-lem was cast in terms of a spiritual and cultural malaise, an idea that Carter had been reading and reflecting about well before the preparation of this particular speech. Robert Maddox, "a Baptist preacher from Calhoun, Georgia who had been brought in for a while as a speechwriter," along with advisor/pollster Patrick Caddell, had a great deal to do with the mal-aise concept.[52] Hertzberg reported that Maddox "had been working on it for months and had written an immense memo to Carter about the crisis of confidence."[53] After the original cancellation of this energy speech, Maddox's and Caddell's ideas surfaced to shape part of the speechwriting agenda. Hertzberg noted: "what happened here was that with the cancella-tion of the energy speech, with Carter up in Camp David, with everybody else in Washington, and nobody, including the people closest to him, re-ally having a clear idea of just what was going on, just why he canceled the speech and just what he wanted, into this void came Pat's [Caddell] idea."[54]

In contrast to Caddell's argument for a speech depicting the national malaise, presidential advisor Stuart Eizenstat and Vice President Walter Mondale led a faction that argued for a speech with energy policy as its main component. This was part of a recurring pattern in many of Carter's policy address: the problem of reconciling or blending the spiritual and the programmatic. In this case, however, programmatic is not quite the right word. Eizenstat and Mondale (who made one of the pilgrimages to Camp David during the speech preparation process) began to develop a pragmatic rationale to match Caddell's spiritual orientation. According to Hertzberg, the issue of "how to make the energy segment of the speech come across boldly was inadvertently solved by Stu Eizenstat, who was so angry at the whole idea of the malaise part of the speech that he said, 'God damn it, this is an energy speech and here's what we ought to say, point one, point two, point three—and he virtually dictated it on the spot."[55] Stewart recalled this as Eizenstat's "finest moment rhetorically" because of the intensity and passion which produced a clear and dramatic theme.[56] The definiteness and clarity of this section of the speech draft was striking to the speechwriters, who were accustomed to seeing speeches modified and dulled by so much input from so many White House staff members along the way. Recalling the speech's declaration that "we will never again import more oil than we did in 1979. Never,"[57] Stewart remarked: "That is the stuff which was totally uncharacteristic of us. . . . It had no qualifiers, no semi-colons, or none of that."[58] Stewart viewed this address as one of the few speeches in which a successful synthesis of moral principles and policy pragmatics was accomplished.

The consequences of this speech were remarkable. The immediate public opinion polls showed a very favorable rating increase, with the CBS-*New York Times* poll showing a sixteen-point gain within a few days of the speech.[59] Moreover, there was the strong sense that the speaker was truthful. Stewart put it in terms of Carter's argument making sense to the public because "the President was speaking the truth, which was not just about crisis of confidence but also about a sense of selfishness, a lack of community which I think was really the stronger message of that opening part."[60]

Yet, after the initial burst of favorable response, the tide turned completely. Hertzberg expressed frustration over seeing a potentially positive address become viewed as a failure: "You could say that the speech was only a disaster in the following sense. It held out a promise that the administration and the President were unable or unwilling to keep. That was the promise that the administration itself and the Carter presidency itself would

be reborn and would change its ways."[61] Carter did not explicitly connect
the subsequent cabinet firings with the speech itself, but the public clearly
made that connection. The message of the speech was translated into a
weak and inadequate version of administrative rebirth and redirection. One
of the primary persons fired was Secretary Califano, who had no direct
link to the energy issue. He was, however, perceived to be disloyal to the
administration. At the same time, some Carter "insiders" with records of
indifferent performance remained in place.[62] The expectations raised by
the truth-telling, "confessional" portion of the speech were simply not
matched by actions that seemed to be rooted primarily in political loyalty.
Thus, at many levels this speech reveals how complicated a speech text
becomes as it develops and is translated through the lenses of diverse public experiences.

Why did this kind of thing occur? The lack of a single, clear voice—
either from the speechwriters or from the White House staff—was a major
part of the problem. According to Stewart, "Had there been any individual in the administration other than the President who was in a position to synthesize, this might not have happened. There was no synthesizer in the White House other than the President, who was the one and
only person to preside over these various disagreements."[63] In the case of
the Crisis of Confidence speech, Carter failed to synthesize his subsequent
actions of reorganizing his cabinet with his nationally televised address.
While the Crisis of Confidence speech was a striking example of this void
in the Carter White House, that speech was merely a symptom of the need
for a person—whether a president or an advisor—who could have woven
the many strands of information and opinion into a single, unified fabric.

Speechwriting and the Articulation of Values
and Moral Principles: Fulfillment

Clearly, there were exceptions to the detached pattern that had the effect of
both separating the writers from the president and in corollary fashion
creating distance between their messages and the public audiences that
consumed them. While speechwriting and policy making seldom merged
in the normal course of policy addresses, such a relationship did occur in
many ceremonial and civic contexts. On such occasions Carter was able to
speak of the values and feelings that were central to his beliefs. Speechwriters
such as Hertzberg, Nesmith, Stewart, and Matthews point in particular to
several speeches which were among Carter's best and which seemed to

overcome or reduce the distancing problem. Foremost among these was Carter's address at the dedication of the John F. Kennedy Library on October 20, 1979. On that occasion Carter was not simply making a ceremonial address. Rather, as the rhetorical theorist Chaim Perelman maintains, the speaker was involved in a singular rhetorical moment—he was developing and arguing about values and the reasons for adherence to basic beliefs.[64] Other speeches in this category included Carter's address to the Parliament of India and his 1981 farewell address. Ironically, these speeches failed to receive extensive media coverage or public exposure, in part because they were not explicitly about policy proposals. Yet, it is precisely on these kinds of topics and occasions that Carter's speechwriters found themselves in closest harmony with the inner qualities of Carter's heart and mind. These were the kinds of speeches in which Carter articulated the values and premises that guided and directed his major policy decisions. For that reason, it is important to examine some of these addresses in detail.

Carter began his dedication speech at the Kennedy Library in October, 1979, by comparing the building to "a great cathedral," an interesting choice of terms.[65] He went on to paint an intimate and telling portrait of John F. Kennedy, noting that while he never met JFK, they shared a common love of politics and laughter—especially when the two were merged. From that opening Carter told the story of President Kennedy's response to a question about Ted Kennedy's potential interest in the presidency: "I wonder if you could tell us first if you had it to do over again, would you work for the Presidency and, second, whether you can recommend this job to others?" JFK had replied: "Well, the answer to the first question is yes, and the second is no. I do not recommend it to others—at least for a while." Carter finished by adroitly commenting: "As you can all see, President Kennedy's wit and also his wisdom—[*laughter*]—is certainly as relevant today as it was then [*laughter*]."[66] Carter's comment, of course, was a facile and engaging use of language to deal with the impending challenge that the same Ted Kennedy would soon launch against the Carter presidency.

Carter mentioned what it was like to be a southerner who responded to the moral thrust of JFK's civil rights messages: "As a southerner, as a Georgian, I saw at first hand how the moral leadership of the Kennedy administration helped to undo the wrongs that grew out of our nation's history." Carter then disclosed his own reactions to the Kennedy assassination in sharply personal terms: "On that November day almost 16 years ago, a terrible moment was frozen in the lives of many of us here. I remember that I climbed down from the seat of a tractor, unhooked a farm trailer, and walked into my warehouse to weigh a load of grain. I was told by a group of farmers that the President had been shot. I went outside, knelt on the steps, and began to pray. In a few minutes I learned that he had not lived. It was a grievous personal loss—my President. I wept openly for the first time in more than ten years—for the first time since my own father died."[67] That language was inserted by Carter himself and is a clear example that his personal and private realm was a deep repository for public discourse. At the same time, it shows that personal and private realm as fortified and resistant to the inventional resources of external speechwriters. Carter ended the speech by pointing to the proliferation of new problems which the country was facing a decade and a half after Kennedy's death. In doing this, he used the inclusive language of "we" far more than in many of his speeches: "And we face these times when centrifugal forces in our society and in our political system as well—forces of regionalism, forces of ethnicity, of narrow economic interests, of single-issue politics—are testing the resiliency of American pluralism and of our ability to govern. But we can and we will prevail."[68]

Carter returned to what he regarded as JFK's enduring message: "the appeal for unselfish dedication to the common good." Although a person of Carter's mindset would be terribly suspicious of artful language, Carter used that most significant rhetorical form—the symbolic theme—in order to summarize the meaning of the Kennedy Library itself. "The overarching purpose of this Nation remains the same," he declared: "to build a just society in a secure America living at peace with the other nations of the world. The library that we dedicate today is a symbol, above all, of that unchanging purpose. Through our study here of his words and his deeds, the service of President Kennedy will keep its high place in the hearts of many generations of Americans to come after us."[69]

Carter's address to the Parliament of India on January 2, 1978, (written largely by Hertzberg) reflected even more of the symbolic, connotative themes that enabled Carter to find his truest and fullest voice. He began by calling attention to democracy: "There are those who say that democracy is a kind of rich man's plaything, and that the poor are too preoccupied with survival to care about the luxury of freedom and the right to choose their own government . . . . The evidence, both in India and America, is plain. It is that there is more than one form of hunger, and neither the rich nor the poor will feel satisfied without being fed in body and in spirit." That led to a clear central theme stated as two connected questions: "Is democracy important? Is human freedom valued by all people?"[70]

When Carter told the Indian Parliament that "in the field of politics, freedom is the engine of progress," he was using but one of several metaphors that expressed a series of shared concerns between the two countries.[71] That was all the more noteworthy in light of Rafshoon's comment that Carter hated metaphors. The final section of the speech was particularly striking in the language Carter used to establish the bond between the United States and India. He sought to develop a sense of mutuality through a distinctive use of personal, private-writ-public experience: "I come to you as a national leader," but "I come also as a pilgrim." The next two paragraphs were Carter at his personal/religious/rhetorical best: "When I was growing up on a farm in the State of Georgia, in the heart of the Southern United States, an invisible wall of separation stood between me and my black classmates, schoolmates, playmates, when we were old enough to know what segregation was. But it seemed then as if that wall between us would exist forever. But it did not stand forever. It crumbled and fell. And though the rubble has not yet been completely removed, it no longer separates us from one another, blighting the lives of those on both sides of it."[72]

Carter skillfully affirmed that the reason for this transformation was the witness of Martin Luther King, Jr., whose method of nonviolent resistance was rooted in the teachings of Mahatma Ghandi. Of King, Carter said: "He was a son of Georgia and a spiritual son of Mahatma Ghandi."[73] Of both Ghandi and King he observed: "These men set a standard of courage and idealism that few of us can meet, but from which all of us can draw inspiration and sustenance."[74] Near the end of the speech Carter used language to unite the political and moral concerns of the two countries. In doing so, he provided a clear view of the basic moral premises that oriented his own approach to government. Carter expressed it in terms of people responding to "our most pressing common challenge: how our political and spiritual values can provide the basis for dealing with the social and economic strains to which they will unquestionably be subjected."[75]

Speechwriters Hertzberg, Nesmith, and Stewart have all cited Carter's farewell address as a speech that came out very much as they hoped it would. The speech was an alternative to giving a final State of the Union message to Congress. Hertzberg explained that "the speech was conceived as being both his last speech as a President and . . . more important . . . his first speech as a former President. It was to set his agenda for his ex-Presidency. And indeed, since he's left office, those three or four points are the ones he's tended to speak on."[76] The three focal points of the speech were stewardship of the environment, nuclear stability, and human rights.

The speech also dealt with special interests and the current state of American politics. Interestingly, the reason that Hertzberg regarded it as "a very good speech" was partly because "it was not a political speech in the sense that it did not have to be brokered. It did not have to go through the internal White House mill. There was no longer anything to fight over."[77] The usual process of circulating drafts was eliminated. Besides Hertzberg and Stewart, only Jody Powell and Rosalyn Carter saw the final versions.[78] Ironically, only after losing his bid for re-election was Carter able to express his fullest sense of self and purpose in a speech. Hertzberg observed: "suddenly it seemed as if the administration had had a theme and had had a vision, and it was one that was only apparent in retrospect, in that moment of defeat."[79] Stewart concurred, noting that "people said, 'why didn't you do this all along?'"[80]

The speech began with Carter establishing a clear identity—the kind of personal and thematic focus that many of his aides and speechwriters had sought during his four years as president. "In a few days," Carter stated, "I will lay down my official responsibilities in this office, to take up once more the only title in our democracy superior to that of President, the title of citizen."[81] The questions of what it means to be a citizen and the responsibilities involved in citizenship became the vehicles for Carter to discuss not only what his administration had attempted, but also the role that he expected to play in the future. Carter contrasted the current demands of government with the original system designed by the founders, expressing particular concern for the "disturbing trend" of special interest politics. He warned: "It [special interests politics] tends to distort our purposes, because the national interest is not always the sum of all our single or special interests. We are all Americans together, and we must not forget that the common good is our common interest and our individual responsibility."[82] Here was both a moral claim and a rationale to explain it. That was the kind of reasoning and explanation that Carter had frequently omitted from his crucial policy addresses.

From that point the speech took up Carter's three main topics. He provided a brief history of the evolving threat of nuclear destruction since the dropping of the atomic bomb on Hiroshima. He argued for maintaining military strength ("We must and we will remain strong"), while at the same time stressing the need for managing and reducing nuclear threat: "But with equal determination, the United States and all countries must find ways to control and reduce that horrifying danger that is posed by the enormous stockpiles of nuclear arms."[83] The inclusive pattern of reasoning emerged more cogently here because Carter had dramatically established the need for nuclear control.

In one of the best transitions found in any of his speeches—a feature frequently lacking in his presidential addresses—Carter moved to the theme of protecting "the quality of this world within which we live." He continued: "nuclear weapons are an expression of one side of our human character. But there's another side. The same rocket technology that delivers nuclear warheads has also taken us peacefully into space. From that perspective, we see our earth as it really is—a small and fragile and beautiful blue globe, the only home we have."[84] Here the speech deftly united the nuclear threat with the concern for the planet under the governing idea of human character. Carter had often failed to inspire the nation through exhortation, for he had sounded like a harsh preacher. But in his farewell address, Carter succeeded as an interpreter and exhorter because he focused on the character of human life, which allowed his orientation to moral principles to emerge and flow easily.

In developing his third topic, Carter added an increasingly personal tone by discussing human rights as one of the "beneficial forces that we have evolved over the ages." He argued: "The struggle for human rights overrides all differences of color or nation or language. Those who hunger for freedom, who thirst for human dignity, and who suffer for the sake of justice, they are the patriots of this cause."[85] He added emphatically, "I believe with all my heart that America must always stand for these basic human rights at home and abroad. That is both our history and our destiny."[86]

In the final section of the speech, Carter presented an autobiographical repositioning: "As I return home to the South, where I was born and raised, I look forward to the opportunity to reflect and further to assess I hope with accuracy, the circumstances of our times."[87] He pledged support to the new president and then affirmed: "I intend to work as a citizen, as I've worked here in this office as President, for the values this nation was founded to secure."[88] In the final analysis, for Carter the language of politics was the expression of values. His farewell address revealed what his presidency was really about: the practice of citizenship, with his role as president emblematic of the composite values of American citizenship. Carter's life has given new importance to his final presidential speech. After leaving the White House, he was true to his words in carrying out the practice of citizenship—precisely what he urged Americans to do in his farewell address.

Conclusions and Continuances

After examining speeches, speechwriters, and speechwriting it is appropriate to return again to Carter as poet. In fact, the notion of Carter-as-poet is a useful complement to Hertzberg's account of Carter-as-saint. Both Hertzberg and Fallows argue that in contrast to presidents like Reagan, Carter never had a political ideology. Instead, Carter had a set of religious and moral principles.[89] Those principles manifested themselves as beliefs—beliefs about God, about human nature, about the world. Beliefs are intricate mixtures of cognition and feelings that together give them strength or conviction. In Carter's case, the usual language of political policy seemed an inappropriate or ill-fitting mechanism for the incorporation and expression of his moral beliefs. Notable exceptions were in the development of human rights policy and in more ceremonial contexts where Carter was his rhetorical best.

Poets are often uncomfortable in formalized settings, frequently dubious of any language except their own, and often fueled by a depth of feeling which may not always find avenues for expression. In his poem "A Committee of Scholars Describe the Future Without Me" Carter offers academic readers the opportunity to laugh a bit at themselves by continuing to contrast plain language, the language of "just saying," with the language of "euphemistic words."[90] Poetry comes hardest to those like Carter who, as Rafshoon has noted, thought "that the time for rhetoric is over" and, even more, "did not like metaphors." About Carter's aversion to figurative language, Rafshoon said: "Maybe he thought it was dishonest."[91] If by plain speaking one means a Trumanesque directness and vivacity that connects with the everyday lives of most people, then it is a powerful rhetorical instrument. But if it means primarily the *absence* of metaphor, symbolic themes, and the language of feeling, then a very different type of rhetoric emerges—a rhetoric in which the human connective tissue is left frequently undeveloped. It was the latter form of plainness that dominated many of Carter's major addresses.

Yet, Carter's moving poem about his mother, "Miss Lillian," reveals that his shortcomings as a presidential rhetor were not the whole story of his capacity to communicate. That poem is one of the best and most profound summaries of Carter's ethical-moral-religious principles. It was an appropriate place for a statement of his principles, for his mother was clearly his prime mentor. The next to last stanza of the short poem is especially important. It tells of Miss Lillian's weeping out of a selfless moral concern for others, but notes that she would not weep long. Why? Because "she never had learned how."[92] One should not *learn* how to weep. Indeed, the presence of too many tears may be a sign of contrived crying; it may be morally dishonest. Similarly, too many words, especially too many polished words, especially too many strategically practiced words and well-placed verbal and visual images, especially too resonant and too skillful delivery of the words and images, may signal dishonesty and a lack of principle.

Perhaps the presidential candidate who told the American people "I'll never lie to you"[93] simply could not consistently make the connection between his own moral convictions and the language of public policy. The tension between Carter's creative impulses with language and his notion of language as artificial remained largely unresolved during his presidency. But it did not hamper Carter in his post-presidential years, when he was no longer responsible for national policy making. In his post-presidency Carter remained remarkably consistent. No singular political ideology appeared, but his reliance on deeds—the performance of moral actions more than language about them—was even stronger than during his presidential administration. And what was the core of that consistency? It was the practice of integrity, which has been usefully defined by ethicist Stephen L. Carter as something far more demanding than even honesty. He argues that integrity "requires three steps: discerning what is right and what is wrong; acting on what you have discerned, even at personal cost; and saying openly that you are acting on your understanding of right and wrong."[94] Carter ranks very high by these criteria. Yet, his presidential speeches that articulated the framework for the practice of integrity tended to be localized and rarely the center of mass media attention. In other cases, those speeches were given on occasions not primarily associated with policy making.

In the moments when those obstacles were overcome, Carter was able to reach public audiences and evoke deep feelings about personal and civic values. The full range of Carter's speeches reveals both the problems entailed by a programmatic language of description and the powerful and personal rhetoric of moral conviction. Perhaps if Stewart's recognition of the need for a synthesizer close to Carter's heart and soul had been understood early in the administration, the struggle and often the duality between words and deeds would have been minimized. But it was not. Carter remained a president possessive of rhetorical skills, distrustful of language, suspicious of the very process of speechwriting, and often his own worst enemy because of the constraints he imposed on his own creativity. Yet, Carter was a president who cared deeply. When he was able to define political issues in terms of human character, Carter was an effective voice for the values of citizenship. Hertzberg's assessment of Carter as "saint" and this chapter's portrayal of Carter as "poet" present a dual identity—a duality that helps to account for Carter's difficulties in the realm of pragmatic politics and for his successes in the realm of civic virtue.

Notes

1. Jimmy Carter, "On Using Words" in his *Always a Reckoning and Other Poems* (New York: Random House, 1995), p. 123.
2. Carter, "It Can Fool the Sun," *Always a Reckoning,* p. 75.
3. For studies of Jimmy Carter's rhetoric, see (chronological): John H. Patton, "A Government as Good as Its People: Jimmy Carter and the Restoration of Transcendence to Politics," *Quarterly Journal of Speech* 63 (1977): 249–57; Christopher Lyle Johnstone, "Electing Ourselves in 1976: Jimmy Carter and the American Faith," *Western Journal of Speech Communication* 42 (1978): 241–49; J. Louis Campbell III, "Jimmy Carter and the Rhetoric of Charisma," *Central States Speech Journal* 30 (1979): 174–86; Sidney Kraus, ed., *The Great Debates: Carter vs. Ford, 1976* (Bloomington: Indiana University Press, 1979); Ronald A. Sudol, "The Rhetoric of Strategic Retreat: Carter and the Panama Canal Debate," *Quarterly Journal of Speech* 65 (1979): 379–91; Lloyd Bitzer and Theodore Reuter, *Carter vs. Ford: The Counterfeit Debates of 1976* (Madison: University of Wisconsin Press, 1980); Dan F. Hahn, "Flailing the Profligate: Carter's Energy Sermon of 1979," *Presidential Studies Quarterly* 10 (1980): 583–87; Les Altenberg and Robert Cathcart, "Jimmy Carter on Human Rights: A Thematic Analysis," *Central States Speech Journal* 33 (1982): 446–57; Dan F. Hahn, "The Rhetoric of Jimmy Carter, 1976–1980," *Presidential Studies Quarterly* 14 (1984): 265–88; Dan F. Hahn and J. Justin Gustainis, "Anatomy of an Enigma: Jimmy Carter's 1980 State of the Union Address," *Communication Quarterly* 33 (1985): 43–49; Roderick P. Hart, *Verbal Style and the Presidency: A Computer-Based Analysis* (Orlando, Fla.: Academic Press, 1984), pp. 176–211; Craig Allen Smith, "Leadership, Orientation, and Rhetorical Vision: Jimmy Carter, the 'New Right,' and the Panama Canal," *Presidential Studies Quarterly* 16 (1986): 317–28; Robert A. Strong, "Recapturing Leadership: The Carter Administration and the Crisis of Confidence," *Presidential Studies Quarterly* 16 (1986): 636–50; J. Michael Hogan, *The Panama Canal in American Politics: Domestic Advocacy and the Evolution of Policy* (Carbondale: Southern Illinois University Press, 1986); Robert Underhill, *The Bully Pulpit: From Franklin Roosevelt to Ronald Reagan* (New York: Vantage Press, 1988), pp. 327–83; Craig Allen Smith, "President Jimmy Carter's Inaugural Address, 1977" in *Inaugural Addresses of Twentieth-Century American Presidents,* ed. Halford Ryan (Westport, Conn.: Greenwood Press, 1993), pp. 245–58; Denise M. Bostdorff, *The Presidency and the Rhetoric of Foreign Crisis* (Columbia: University of South Carolina Press,

1994), pp. 144–74; Goodwin Berquist, "The 1976 Carter-Ford Presidential Debates," and Kurt Ritter and David Henry, "The 1980 Reagan-Carter Presidential Debate," both in *Rhetorical Studies of National Political Debates, 1962–1992,* 2d ed., ed. Robert V. Friedenberg (Westport, Conn.: Praeger, 1994), pp. 29–44, 69–93; Craig Allen Smith and Kathy B. Smith, *The White House Speaks: Presidential Leadership as Persuasion* (Westport, Conn.: Praeger, 1994), pp. 101–32; Charles J. G. Griffin, "Narrative Character in Presidential Crisis Rhetoric: Jimmy Carter and the Iranian Hostage Crisis" in *The Modern Presidency and Crisis Rhetoric,* ed. Amos Kiewe (Westport, Conn.: Praeger, 1994), pp. 137–53; Dan F. Hahn and Halford Ryan, "Jimmy Carter" in *U.S. Presidents as Orators: A Bio-Critical Sourcebook,* ed. Halford Ryan (Westport, Conn.: Greenwood Press, 1995), pp. 299–315; and Carol Gelderman, *All the President's Words: The Bully Pulpit and the Creation of the Virtual Presidency* (New York: Walker, 1997), pp. 128–43.

4. Marie Hochmuth Nichols, *Rhetoric and Criticism* (Baton Rouge: Louisiana State University Press, 1963), pp. 40–41, 44–45.

5. Jimmy Carter, *Why Not the Best?* (New York: Bantam Books, 1976), p. 45.

6. Patrick Anderson, *Electing Jimmy Carter: The Campaign of 1976* (Baton Rouge: Louisiana State University Press, 1994), p. 27.

7. Ibid., p. 32.

8. Ibid.

9. Ibid.

10. Ibid.

11. Ibid.

12. Hendrik Hertzberg interview, including Christopher Matthews, Achsah P. Nesmith, and Gordon C. Stewart, Miller Center Interviews (Dec. 3–4, 1981), *Carter Presidency Project,* Vol. XXI, p. 1, Jimmy Carter Library, Atlanta, Ga. Cited hereafter as Hertzberg, Matthews, Nesmith, and Stewart interview.

13. Ibid., p. 2.

14. James Fallows, "The Passionless Presidency: [Part I] The Trouble with Jimmy Carter's Administration," *Atlantic Monthly,* May, 1979, p. 38. Cited hereafter as Fallows, "Passionless Presidency I."

15. James Fallows, "The Passionless Presidency [Part] II: More From Inside Jimmy Carter's White House," *Atlantic Monthly,* June, 1979, p. 78. Cited hereafter as Fallows, "Passionless Presidency II."

16. Fallows, "Passionless Presidency I," p. 35.

17. James Fallows, White House Exit Interview, Jimmy Carter Library.

18. Gerald Rafshoon interview, Miller Center Interviews, *Carter Presidency Project* (April 8, 1983), Vol. XXI, pp. 20–22, Carter Library.

19. Fallows, "Passionless Presidency I," p. 42.

20. Rafshoon interview, pp. 20–21.

21. Hertzberg, Matthews, Nesmith, and Stewart interview, pp. 7–8.

22. Ibid., p. 4.

23. Ibid., p. 5.

24. Ibid., p. 15.

25. Ibid.

26. Hendrik Hertzberg, "Jimmy Carter, 1977–1981" in *Character Above All: Ten Presidents from FDR to George Bush,* ed. Robert A. Wilson (New York: Simon & Schuster, 1995), p. 184.

27. Ibid., p. 9.

28. Ibid., pp. 9, 111.

29. Achsah P. Nesmith, correspondence with author, Washington, D.C., March 1, 1996, p. 3.

30. Ibid.

31. Hertzberg, Matthews, Nesmith, and Stewart interview, p. 111.

32. Ibid.

33. Fallows, "Passionless Presidency II," p. 79.

34. Hertzberg, "Jimmy Carter, 1977–1981," p. 184.

35. Jimmy Carter, "National Energy Plan: Address Delivered Before a Joint Session of Congress, April 20, 1977," *Public Papers of the Presidents of the United States: Jimmy Carter, 1977* (Washington, D.C.: Government Printing Office, 1977), Book I, p. 663. Hereafter, this publication series is cited as *Public Papers: Carter* (year). Unless otherwise indicated, all speeches cited from this publication series were presented in Washington, D.C.

36. Ibid., p. 664.

37. Ibid., p. 665.

38. Ibid., p. 666.

39. Smith and Smith, *The White House Speaks,* p. 119.

40. Fallows, "Passionless Presidency I," p. 42.

41. Hendrik Hertzberg, "Hendrik Hertzberg on Jimmy Carter" in *Character Above All,* ed. Robert A. Wilson (New York: Audioworks—Division of Simon & Schuster, 1996), sound recording, tape 5. Cited hereafter as Hertzberg lecture. Hertzberg's essay "Jimmy Carter, 1977–1981" (cited above) is based on this lecture presented at the Lyndon B. Johnson School of Public Affairs, University of Texas–Austin, Feb. 17, 1995. A number of statements from the lecture were removed when it was rewritten for publication. In those instances, Hertzberg's statements are cited from this sound recording of his lecture.

42. Jimmy Carter, "State of the Union: Address Delivered Before a Joint Session of Congress, January 23, 1979," *Public Papers: Carter, 1979,* Book I, pp. 103–104.

43. Ibid., p. 109.

44. "The President's News Conference of January 26, 1979," *Public Papers: Carter, 1979,* Book I, p. 172; and Hertzberg lecture.

45. "The President's News Conference of January 26, 1979," p. 172.

46. Hertzberg, "Jimmy Carter, 1977–1981," pp. 192–93.

47. Hertzberg, Matthews, Nesmith, and Stewart interview, pp. 59, 61.

48. Ibid.

49. Ibid., p. 62.

50. Ibid. Although Stewart jumbled his statement, his meaning as well as his emotional reaction are clear.

51. Ibid., p. 63.

52. Ibid., p. 64.

53. Ibid., p. 63.

54. Ibid., p. 64.

55. Ibid., p. 67.

56. Ibid.

57. Ibid., p. 67. Stewart's recollection of the speech text was good, but not perfect. What Carter actually said was: "Beginning this moment, this Nation will never use more foreign oil than we did in 1977—never." See Jimmy Carter, "Energy and National Goals: Address to the Nation, July 15, 1979," *Public Papers: Carter, 1979, Book II*, p. 1239. Carter's White House called this address "the Crisis of Confidence speech," but the press and Carter's political opponents in the 1980 presidential campaign (Edward M. Kennedy, Ronald Reagan, and others) called it "the Malaise speech." For a journalistic analysis of the entire episode of this speech and its impact on the 1980 presidential election, see Jack W. Germond and Jules Witcover, *Blue Smoke and Mirrors: How Reagan Won and Carter Lost the Election of 1980* (New York: Viking Press, 1981, pp. 23–47.

58. Hertzberg, Matthews, Nesmith, and Stewart interview, p. 67–68.

59. Ibid., p. 66.

60. Ibid., p. 71.

61. Ibid.

62. Hertzberg lecture. For reports of Califano's alleged disloyalty to Carter, which were published two months prior to the Crisis of Confidence speech, see Fallows, "Passionless Presidency I," pp. 39–40.

63. Hertzberg, Matthews, Nesmith, and Stewart interview, p. 78.

64. For example, see the discussion of "The Epideictic Genre" in Ch. Perelman and L. Olbrechts-Tyteca, *The New Rhetoric: A Treatise on Argumentation,* trans. John Wilkinson and Purcell Weaver (Notre Dame, Ind.: University of Notre Dame Press, 1969), pp. 47–51.

65. Jimmy Carter, "Remarks at Dedication Ceremonies for the John F. Kennedy Library, [Boston,] October 20, 1979," *Public Papers: Carter, 1979,* Book II, p. 1979.

66. Ibid., p. 1979.

67. Ibid., pp. 1980–81.

68. Ibid., p. 1982.

69. Ibid.

70. Jimmy Carter, "Remarks Before the Indian Parliament, [New Delhi, India,] January 2, 1978," *Public Papers: Carter, 1978,* Book I, p. 5.

71. Ibid., p. 6.

72. Ibid., p. 10.

73. Ibid.

74. Ibid., p. 11.

75. Ibid.

76. Hertzberg, Matthews, Nesmith, and Stewart interview, p. 96.

77. Ibid., p. 101.

78. Ibid., p. 109.

79. Ibid., p. 96.

80. Ibid.

81. Jimmy Carter, "Farewell Address to the Nation: Remarks of the President, January 14, 1981," *Public Papers: Carter, 1980–81,* Book III, p. 2889.

82. Ibid., p. 2890.

83. Ibid., p. 2891.

84. Ibid.

85. Ibid., p. 2892.

86. Ibid.

87. Ibid., p. 2893.

88. Ibid.

89. Hertzberg, "Jimmy Carter, 1977–1981," pp. 185–86; Fallows, "The Passionless Presidency I," pp. 42–43.

90. Jimmy Carter, "A Committee of Scholars Describe the Future Without Me," *Always a Reckoning,* p. 25.

91. Rafshoon interview, pp. 22–23.

92. Jimmy Carter, "Miss Lillian," *Always a Reckoning,* p. 19.

93. See Robert W. Turner, *"I'll Never Lie to You": Jimmy Carter in His Own Words* (New York: Ballantine Books, 1976).

94. Stephen L. Carter, "The Insufficiency of Honesty," *Atlantic Monthly,* Feb., 1996, p. 74.

CHAPTER 8

Ronald Reagan's Bully Pulpit

Creating a Rhetoric of Values

WILLIAM K. MUIR, JR.

More than any other modern president, Ronald Reagan sought to exploit the moral possibilities of the rhetorical presidency. He used his "bully pulpit" to try to convince the public that his values and ideas about personal responsibility and the good society were right. In other words, he sought to change the *mores* of Americans.

All presidents pay attention to the hearts and minds of the American people, but in most cases they see rhetoric as a means to passing their legislative agenda. For Ronald Reagan, policy was incidental to rhetoric. Policy was important because it reinforced the moral changes Reagan pursued through power of speech. Believing that the secret to improving America was elevating the character of Americans, Reagan preached untiringly and eloquently.[1] His ability to pursue this agenda was enhanced significantly by his speechwriters and by the speechwriting process in the Reagan White House.

An effective presidential administration selects a focus, which gives meaning and coherence to all its actions. Bill Clinton's was the economy, for example; Lyndon Johnson's poverty; Harry Truman's the Cold War. Ronald Reagan's focus was morals—the personal philosophies by which Americans planned their lives and the values by which they measured their behavior and made their choices. The central idea in Reagan's moral vision was that humans were masters of their own destiny. They were free, a notion he caught with this memorable image of a ship's navigator: "History is a river that may take us as it will. But we have the power to navigate, to choose direction . . . ."[2]

The central value was that individuals must be honored, not for "succeeding," but choosing to try. If circumstances conspire to foil immediate success, the effort made is no less praiseworthy than if the attempt had achieved its objective. The president's most eloquent statement of the value of effort came when he quoted a Jewish Holocaust survivor, who wrote: "We who lived in concentration camps can remember the men who walked through the huts comforting others, giving away their last piece of bread. They may have been few in number, but they offer sufficient proof that everything can be taken from a man but one thing: The last of the human freedoms—to choose one's attitude in any given set of circumstances, to choose one's own way."[3] Not achievement in the material world, but triumph in the spiritual realm was the measure of the good life.

For Reagan, individual freedom and personal responsibility were the foundations of hope, and hope was the key to America's vitality and courage. A century and a half ago Alexis de Tocqueville introduced his study of *Democracy in America* with the identical sentiment: "The first of the duties that are at this time imposed upon those who direct our affairs is to educate democracy; to reawaken, if possible, its religious beliefs; to purify its morals."[4] To imagine the Reagan presidency as the contemporary installation of Tocqueville in the White House is to have correctly identified its special character. Like Tocqueville, Reagan set out to combat the moral nihilism of his time, especially the belief that individuals (in Tocqueville's words) "are never their own masters here below, and that they necessarily obey some insurmountable and unintelligent power, arising from anterior events, from their race, or from the soil and climate of their country."[5] For Reagan, his central task as president was to refute the hopelessness and irresponsibility implied by such a secular and nihilistic outlook.

Ronald Reagan was a president with a mission, determined to penetrate the confusion and pessimism prevailing among Americans after the turbulent 1960s and 1970s. He once wrote to his chief of staff James A. Baker: "a sense of optimism is the most important thing we have tried to restore to America during the past four years."[6] That is, Reagan sought (as the poet Robert Frost put it) to "give his people character."[7]

Reagan's presidency was not devoid of policy accomplishment. In eight years in the White House, he oversaw the reduction of tax rates and red tape, the diminution of the role of the federal government, and the toppling of Marxist-Leninism. While the pursuit of these objectives was vitally important to him, he delegated the job of developing policies to achieve them to specialists, providing them executive support and protection against political attack. In contrast, he reserved for himself the moral task of infusing hope.

For two decades prior to becoming president, he had been expressing ideas about humankind's capacity for freedom, its power to persist and overcome, and the efficacy of trying. When he attained the presidency, he used its bully pulpit to amplify his answer to the question, why try? Why should Americans use their personal freedom to serve a purpose larger than themselves? The "bully pulpit" was the center of Ronald Reagan's presidency. He sought to prepare Americans for the burden of living free.

The Reagan Speechwriters

In his eight years as president, Reagan spoke nearly 4 million words of prepared text. Those words, crafted into nearly 2,500 sets of remarks, were provided by the Speechwriting Department in the Executive Office of the President. In a typical month Reagan delivered twenty formal speeches, gave five weekly radio talks, and appeared at three press conferences (each of which began with a prepared set of remarks).

How did Reagan's White House Speechwriting Department organize itself to carry out this task? In answering this question, this chapter describes the speechwriting operation in 1984–85, the years when the author observed the department directly.[8] The years of 1984 and 1985 happened to be a particularly stable and productive time for the department. There was little turnover of personnel, and it was fun. The speechwriters relished the challenges of the reelection campaign and inauguration of a second term.

The president employed six full-time writers in the department. Bentley Elliott was its chief and bore the additional responsibilities of editing and making assignments. In the early 1970s he had been a television writer and producer for CBS. There he came face-to-face with what he felt was a pervasive media bias that seemed "to regard business as predators."[9] Believing the opposite, convinced that "capitalism has made . . . America better," and inspired by the rhetoric of then-presidential candidate Ronald Reagan, he quit CBS in 1975, hiring on as a professional writer for Gerald Ford's treasury secretary William Simon and later for U.S. Chamber of Commerce President Dick Lesher. In 1981, he came to the Reagan White House Speechwriting Department, where he earned a reputation for writing about complicated economic matters with simplicity and eloquence. In 1983, Elliott assumed the responsibilities of chief of the department.

Tony Dolan was one of his colleagues. Widely respected for his political astuteness, literary power, and sense for an opponent's jugular, Dolan worked as speechwriter from the first to the last day of the Reagan presidency. An intense competitor and a passionate man of letters, he was a protégé of William F. Buckley, Jr., who had recommended his appointment to Reagan. Dana Rohrabacher also served as speechwriter from the outset of the Reagan presidency. He was a former newspaper reporter whose patron was one of Reagan's earliest political advisors, Lyn Nofziger. Rohrabacher was well connected to the conservative Californians who had supported Reagan from the first.

Elliott had personally hired the other three speechwriters. Peggy Noonan was a former colleague of Elliott's at CBS. A generation younger than Elliott, she wrote prose that sparkled with wit and anecdote. She was a brilliant political writer, especially of what she called "tonal" speech. Allan A. (Al) Myer had been a career military officer who had come to the White House on assignment to the National Security Council and the Joint Chiefs of Staff. His writing skills and knowledge of international security impressed Elliott, who hired him. Peter Robinson, the most junior of the speechwriters, worked in the White House as a speechwriter for Vice President George Bush, when Elliott noticed him. Catholic, literate, quick-witted, and Oxford-trained, Robinson had a wry, kindly, and self-effacing sense of humor, in perfect sync with the president's.

The six speechwriters were not close friends. They worked in separate offices, and they had different literary heroes. But the striking thing about them was that they were men and women of letters, Rohrabacher and Myer excepted. In a capital city where most speechwriters were former journalists, only Rohrabacher thought of himself as a newspaperman, and even he had written several film scripts.

What distinguished them was their love of language. Their shoptalk was of writers; they could speak easily of the prose styles of F. Scott Fitzgerald and Evelyn Waugh and other lesser and greater masters of the English language. They believed that language made a difference in the way mankind thought about itself and, therefore, how men and women treated one another. With its fun, beauty, and solace, rhetoric (whether in oratory or in literature) made people live better lives.

Typically, Peter Robinson talked of the writing craft he loved and the craftsman he loved most—Chaucer:

> Chaucer taught me that his end in writing was profoundly Christian. What he wants to do is help the reader save his soul. It struck me, that's not Hemingway's aim. His was a purely secular one, to tell a good story. Reading

Chaucer was the first time I understood that all endeavors could be bent to a moral—and, for me, a Christian—end. An artist, reflecting beauty, could help his viewer participate in the joy of creation.

At the same time, Chaucer is a great corrective against Puritanical impulses. There is no straitlaced stuffiness about him. The Miller's Tale—such bawdiness. I went to my Oxford don, and I challenged him, "Is there any point to this beside the fun of it?" "The point of it," he said, "is the fun of it." That was pretty good news. And while he's tough on all the people in his tales, all the portraits are drawn with such compassion that you forgive them and feel sorry for them—in the end. I took Chaucer's standard as my standard. Here he was writing about the thirteenth century. That was a pretty miserable century—illness, wars, plagues—but his spirit was soaring.

The six speechwriters felt a mutual respect for the others' craftsmanship and dedication. They were good, but there was no star system. It was a group that functioned ensemble. Peggy Noonan spoke for them all with her comment: "This is a first-rate speechwriting staff. It just is. It's a good staff. It's populated by people who have lots of things to do. The high points of their lives will not be their years in the White House."

The Speechwriting Process

The routine by which speeches were written and edited was straightforward. The chief speechwriter assigned an event to himself or to one of his colleagues, who prepared a first draft and handed it over to the chief for editing. Thereafter, the speech was circulated for comments—both from within the White House and from all relevant executive agencies. Responding to their suggestions, the speechwriter wrote a second draft, which was then forwarded to the president for his changes and approval. The routine was as uncomplicated as that. Each speech proceeded through these six steps: assignment, drafting, editing, circulation, revision within the Speechwriting Department, and revision by the president himself. Still, these procedures had several distinctive features.

First, the speechwriters in the Reagan White House never specialized in particular subjects. True, each of them had personal preferences, each had areas of special knowledge, and each was reputed to be handier with some kinds of events than with others. But none of these factors determined who won a particular assignment. For example, Al Myer, the former military officer, always hankered to write on matters of war and peace, and he was good at it. But Elliott was just as likely to assign a national security speech to someone else and put Myer to work on a domestic topic of which he had little immediate knowledge. Much like the judiciary's tradition against specialization, the procedure of rotating topics met three primary needs: to keep all the writers enthusiastic and informed, to free the process of over dependence on any one individual, and to keep the speeches rhetorically fresh.

Second, the circulation of draft speeches outside the department frequently produced contention among the various bureaucracies. White House and agency officials were interested in what the president was going to say because his speeches had the force of policy within the executive branch. Presidential speeches gave the government direction, and the energies they set in motion could accelerate or stymie the objectives (and careers) of officials who really cared about their responsibilities. The circulation of a draft speech aroused strong-willed individuals. Those who knew what mattered in the Reagan administration converged on speeches.

Third, the range of disagreement over a speech could be surprisingly wide. Where you stand depends on where you sit, the saying goes, and specialized responsibilities caused individuals to see things differently, assessing events in shorter or longer time perspectives and in terms of diverse objectives.

Fourth, amidst whatever contention the drafts provoked, the speechwriters dominated. After all, they had written the words that precipitated the turmoil in the first place. They had framed the issues and structured the content. Those to whom the drafts were circulated were asked for their reactions, and in responding they tended to focus their criticisms at the margins. Usually, they urged only those changes touching their particular responsibilities, concentrating on altering only what was critical to their jobs. As Rohrabacher observed, "80 percent of what we write is spoken by the president, without change."

Fifth, the speechwriter dominated because in the typical controversy, the numerous officials to whom the draft was circulated would clash with one another. It was the speechwriter who adjudicated their disagreements, who was the referee among warring factions. Of course, when those opposed to the draft were united in their views, the speechwriter had to be more accommodating. But usually there was conflicting advice, leaving the writer in the catbird seat. While speechwriters had to defend the choices they made, around the negotiating table they were always the ones who made the initial judgment.

Sixth, the president mattered. The president had the last word: no one disputed his right to make a revision or resolve a disagreement his way. The speechwriters anticipated his likes and dislikes and wrote to accommodate them.

Seventh, the speechwriters tended to focus on the immediate audience for an address, rather than primarily writing for news media consumption. The minimal influence of the media in the Reagan speechwriting process was striking. True, the speechwriters gave attention to the crafting of the one sentence that television might be expected to put on the evening news or that newspapers might pick up for a lead to their stories. Equally true, the threat of exposure of gaffes and misrepresentations led to accuracy. But the majority of speeches were never covered, and even with those that were, limits of space and time permitted the media to report little more than a fraction of a speech. What the reporters would not report, they could not influence. Rohrabacher pointed out: "Reagan's average major speech is around fifteen up to twenty-five minutes, depending on the audience's laughter and applause. That's somewhere between ten and twelve pages. One segment of the speech is newsworthy, because in it you're talking about policy. The rest is rhetorical and of not much use, except to the audience itself. That part contains his philosophy, his fundamental ideas." The immediate audience, with its anticipated reactions, became the principal consideration in the writer's mind. Who the audience would be was determined by factors internal to the administration and outside the control of the media.

Speechwriting, Public Values, and Public Policy: The 1984 Address to the National League of Cities

Reagan's greatest speeches were ceremonial in nature, philosophical in purpose, and addressed to the common sense of the American people. Pointe du Hoc in 1984 (celebrating the fortieth anniversary of D day in the Second World War), the "evil empire" speech to the National Association of Evangelicals in 1983, the British Parliament speech in 1982, the Japanese Diet speech in 1983, the 1988 United Nations speech, the inaugural addresses, the *Challenger* accident in 1986—all spoke to the ideals and values of Americans or their allies in the Cold War. They announced no new policies.

The speechwriting process, however, can be best illustrated with a case study of a typical policy speech—Reagan's 1984 address to the National

League of Cities, where the audience consisted of local political officials and the topic was prospective presidential actions. Although the League had invited the president to address it, the audience of several thousand mayors and city officials was expected to be at best skeptical (and, at worst, hostile). In general, the audience did not believe that the Reagan administration wanted to keep in place previous policies of fiscal support. Moreover, most of the city officials in attendance would come, expecting a speech in which the president would inform them of his specific agenda. Had Reagan presented a ceremonial speech, he would have surprised and disappointed them.

The president's senior staff anticipated the League's expectations. As a matter of fact, they had coveted the League's invitation precisely because it was an opportunity to define the administration's urban policy as it was supposedly being developed in the agencies (notably the Department of Transportation, the Department of Treasury, and the Department of Housing and Urban Development). They instructed the Speechwriting Department to list "our" urban policy proposals.

The chief assigned the speech to Al Myer, the former military officer, who had never written a speech on urban matters. His knowledge of American cities was minimal, and he knew virtually nothing about past or current federal policy toward them. He started from scratch. Myer phoned up the agencies that had responsibility for the programs that touched the cities. "I'm not an urban specialist," said Myer with a touch of understatement. He later recalled: "So I went out and asked the urban specialists, 'What is our urban policy?' Well, it almost seemed that none of them had ever been asked that before, but their answers consisted of little chips of various pieces. And there were lots of pieces: New Federalism, block grants for sewers, mass transit, hospitals, and so on." The more Myer listened to what they told him, the less satisfactory he found their point of view. In fact, he was deeply troubled by what he heard; the pieces of the "policy" did not cohere, and, worse, they all boiled down to the federal government bankrolling city programs, and little else. Myer remarked: "If that were our policy, to give out money to the cities, then the Democrats would always outbid us. That could not be our urban policy, and especially in an election year when the Democrats could out-promise us without qualms."

Myer soon became aware that the urban experts he consulted were not looking at things from the same vantage point as the president. So when he sat down to put words on paper, he found himself acting independently of the instructions given him by the senior staff. "Well, the more I thought about it," he explained, "the more convinced I was that we needed a better, more comprehensive definition. Sooner or later, I came up with an outline, and since no one had ever defined it that way, it stood as the Reagan 'urban policy.' But it was a definition under which the Republicans could do better than the Democrats."

As Myer saw it, his speechwriting role drove him to address the big questions. He had to speak about the meaning of things:

> What is it that will bring people to want to live in cities? What is it that will incline corporations to want to build in cities, particularly in northern cities? Well, in part, it's mass transit, and in part, it's New Federalism, which places decision-making authority at lower levels of government and lots of people there have responsibility. But, in part, it's safe streets, less crime, less drugs, better schools, and improvement of all of education. It's a feeling of neighborhood, with all the traditional values of neighbor helping neighbor, of a feeling of togetherness and belonging, values we Republicans are always talking about.

Knowing that the specific audience was the National League of Cities obliged Myer to understand the feelings of the mayors and responsible local officials—their pride, their honor, the apprehensions they felt in their work. To overcome their suspicions, he knew he first had to give expression to their feelings. Then, to convince them to consider new governmental purposes, he had to offer a different way of looking at things—a new scale of meaning, a new definition of "progress," a new public philosophy.

Thus, despite initial ignorance of urban policy and despite instructions from above to write of concrete proposals, Myer drafted a philosophical speech. When it was eventually circulated to the agencies and his ideas were exposed to the review process, each specialized department made objections to this sentence or that paragraph, but none rejected the outline that Myer had originated. A number of little changes were made, but the philosophy stayed—and, thus, it became the Reagan "urban policy" because Myer, having written the initial draft, maintained the dominant position in the process.

What was the nature of the outline that stayed intact? Myer structured the speech around four principles. In doing so, he used specific policies to illustrate those principles. Here was the core of his handiwork, the heart of the president's remarks to the National League of Cities:[10]

Rebuilding cities begins with economic growth, and I believe our economic recovery is the most important urban renewal program in America today. . . .

The second key to success is a renewed emphasis on federalism. We believe that when it comes to running cities local officials can do a better job from city hall than bureaucrats can from Washington. . . .

Public-private partnerships are the third important key for sparking economic opportunity and development of urban areas. . . .

The fourth and final key to a stronger, more prosperous, and stable urban America is a strengthening of basic values through renewal of community life. People coming together in a spirit of neighborhood is what makes cities worth living in. It's what keeps businesses and attracts new ones. And . . . if our cities can create thriving neighborhoods that offer excellence in education, efficiency and affordability, safety on—but drugs and crime off—our streets, then they can become great centers of growth, diversity, and excitement, filled with sound, colors, warmth, and delight. . . .

"Economic growth" (which meant lower income tax rates), reduced federal government responsibility, "public-private partnerships" (which meant increased private charity), and increased volunteer neighborhood organization—those were not the concrete proposals of federal agencies. Those were the philosophical principles of Ronald Reagan, as formulated in what Myer liked to call "the conscience of the presidency"—the Speechwriting Department.

With obvious relish, Myer smiled as he observed of his success: "It illustrates that the bottom line is the spoken word. The president forces the government to treat with broad issues in a comprehensive way—if he does it right. From his position as president, whether it's urban policy or relations with West European allies, he forces the whole government to focus on that issue."

Reagan and Speechwriting

The speechwriters were proud of the special bond between them and Reagan. Their sense of mission was almost palpable. In their minds the Speechwriting Department was the soul of the administration, appointed to provide the government and the American people with a direction for their energies. Reagan's writers were not embarrassed about asserting the importance of their place in the White House. They were convinced that "speeches [were] where it's at in this administration."

What was the special importance of Reagan to presidential speechwriting? For one thing, Reagan was the master stylist. In his role as spokesman for General Electric, he wrote his own material for nearly a quarter of a century before he reached the White House in 1981.[11] As a result, there already existed a body of articulate, personal, political philosophy, and the speechwriters could read it and imitate it. Then, too, having been a writer himself, the president was neither timid nor tactless in his editing of fellow writers.

Consider Elliott's description of how he learned the president's style: "What I personally did to sound like Reagan was to spend the three weeks before I went to work for him, reading all his speeches and making these sheaves of notes—on war, on blacks, on rhetoric, on the economy—and I just absorbed his way of expressing things." Reagan's style was so distinctive that, as speechwriter replaced speechwriter, the difference was hardly detectable.

But Reagan was more than a stylist. He inspired his speechwriters to do their best. His philosophy was so clear and his argument so articulate that his speechwriters were challenged to be clear and articulate in how they justified things. Too, his public presentation of himself was so artful that they knew their handiwork would not be wasted. His calm delighted them, his jokes amused them, and his personal anecdotes gladdened them. They were disciplined by his understatement, intrigued by his improvisations, and pleased by his pleasure in their work. They knew he liked general ideas and the building of an argument. In short, they loved the reasonableness of this nice man and the niceness of this man of reason. They appreciated that he was responsible for connecting them to America's purpose.

A Passion for Ideas

Tony Dolan—a formidable, cigar-chomping Boston-Irish alumnus of Yale—spoke of politics this way:

> Some think that speechwriting is an adjunct to what the candidate [or official] does, and for that reason campaigns and government budgeting always starve it. They think that what governing is about are meetings, conferences, phone calls, rules, and decisions. That's wrong. I would argue that ideas are the stuff of politics. Ideas are the great moving forces of history.

If you acknowledge that, then not only do you make speechwriting important, you make it the most important management tool you have. Ronald Reagan knows how important his speeches are. Not only do they provide a statement of purpose for the government; it is through his speeches that managers understand where they're going. And especially is that important in our form of government, where we do not have a parliamentary majority. Here you have to mobilize public opinion to make the government work in the direction the president wants. And Ronald Reagan—or any president, for that matter—does that through his speeches.

Dolan paid attention to the ideas of others. He was suspicious of people, whether they were members of the public or managers of government, until he had discerned their fundamental assumptions about human nature, society, and personal values. He phoned people who had written things he liked and encouraged them to write more. He wrote articles himself. He planted philosophy in a presidential speech, fumed if it were ever weeded out for some technical reason, and replanted it repeatedly in future speeches, so that he wore resistance down or got the support of the president himself to insert it. It was legend in the department how, once, Dolan was so determined to prevent last-minute changes in a speech written for a presidential visit to Europe that he had paid his own way to France just so he could personally fend off changes suggested by the president's inner circle.

Dolan stood sentry against others' efforts to load the president's speeches with the stuff of "meetings, conferences, phone calls, rules, and decisions"—the stuff that Dolan felt was the detritus of politics. By example and precept, he inspired his colleagues to fight for what they knew was right for the president. A passion for ideas pervaded the speechwriting process of the Reagan White House. It abided there because Dolan and each of his speechwriting colleagues knew they were writing for a president with whom they were in tune and because Reagan was as convinced as they were that "ideas were the stuff of politics."

The Role of Presidential Rhetoric

Ronald Reagan understood that Americans perceived themselves as free and self-reliant. But he and his speechwriters knew that freedom is an iffy thing. We Americans have the freedom to associate with whomever we choose—if anyone chooses to associate with us. We can marry whom we want, if another will accept us. We can work where we want, if other people are willing to pay for our services. We can travel where we want, if someone will take us in once we get there. We are at liberty to discuss everything on earth, if somebody will bother to converse with us. We are even free to take comfort from whatever religion pleases us, if our God is sufficiently pleased by our faith or good works to give us solace. We Americans live free, but we are free on one condition—that we please others. In order to get help, we have to help others. These reciprocating habits are epitomized by the marketplace, but they pervade every aspect of American life. We Americans are obliged to give fair weight, to return something of value tomorrow if we want something of value today.

The contingency of personal freedom shapes our character. It prompts us to care about one another and to cultivate our capacity to walk in others' shoes, for if freedom depends on pleasing others, it is necessary to learn to discern what it is that pleases them. The practice of voluntary give-and-take entangles us in the affairs and hopes of our neighbors, making America a tolerant and considerate society. That moral effect is the upside of personal freedom.

But its contingent nature has a second consequence—a downside. Freedom is mentally and emotionally exhausting. Occasional feelings of shortcoming, disappointment, and loneliness are inescapable aspects of the free life. Personal freedom exacts high emotional costs. President Reagan used to say to groups of newly made citizens, "You've joined a country that has been called 'the least exclusive club in the world—with the highest dues'."[12]

We Americans have trouble appreciating—or admitting—just how tough life is in our self-reliant society. Because of the general diffusion of wealth and comfort, we tend to belittle our own hardihood out of the belief that, in the ironic verse of Ira Gershwin in "Summertime," "the livin' is easy." But "the livin'" is not easy. A multitude of responsibilities impinges on each of us—to balance the obligations of work and family; to help a neighbor; to enlist in the effort to build a church or a YMCA or a hospital; to take care of a mentally ill family member; to keep a business going, with its employees who depend on it. Moreover, because of the conditional character of freedom, our lives are filled with opportunities to fail—to be divorced, to go broke, to be lonely or degraded or over committed. When disappointment strikes—when a relationship goes awry, when severe economic fluctuations occur, when the decisions of others turn sour—the principle of self-reliance inclines us to shoulder the blame personally.

Attention has to be paid to the wear and tear of freedom. If the threads of hope are not continually being repaired, they soon unravel, "delivered up to the ruin of time," in Hannah Arendt's fine phrase.[13] If we leave undispelled the confusions we face, the lonelinesses we feel, the despairs we fear—if we cannot, on an ongoing basis, lighten the "fardels" we bear, then the duty to keep trying becomes unbearably difficult. And if we cease to try, our country falls apart. For a free society "relies" (to borrow Tocqueville's words once again) "upon personal interest to accomplish [its] ends and gives free scope to the unguided strength and common sense of the people."[14]

To individual leaders at each level of a free society falls the job of motivating the people to use their strength and common sense to their own betterment. People need leaders to suggest reasons why they should try in the face of disappointment and failure, to explain how it is that personal effort often makes a difference, and to remind each of us we are not alone. When leadership does not stand by us, when it fails to encourage us to keep fighting, when it omits to motivate us "to take up arms against [our] sea of troubles," then we start whimpering helplessly, "What is going to happen to me?"—instead of thinking purposefully, "What action am I going to take?"

Leaders in a self-governing society—coaches, company heads, military commanders, mayors—shape a public philosophy and influence the personal philosophies of those they lead. By public philosophy I mean nothing more than the general ideas by which people direct their lives, their answers to the big questions—and, in particular, three specific questions:

What is human nature?
What is human society?
What are the right human values?

In this light the president of the United States has a crucial responsibility. If he wants to and knows how, he becomes the exemplary leader—the role model for lesser leaders, a demonstration of what leading a free people entails. The president occupies a uniquely prominent point in our bustling, cacophonous society. He can be heard by virtually every segment of our people. He is free to use the rhetorical prominence of the presidency to clarify the ideas that animate his people and give purpose to their actions.

Now, there are wise general ideas, and there are bad general ideas. There are ideas, like Shakespeare's, that rejuvenate and invigorate, inspire and bond humankind—and have done so across cultures and centuries. And there are ideas that dull and discourage, demoralize and poison the soul—

and have done so since Genesis. Ideally, the American president will constantly teach the best ideas with a command over metaphor that will enable his notions to triumph in their contest with bad ideas.

What counts as a "bad idea?" Consider the following example, which has the additional virtue of illustrating why it is vital that presidents have a metaphorical skill. Now, a metaphor is a way of conveying a realistic picture of what's going on and calling for the need to face up to it. Metaphor supplies what sociologists like to call "a controlling definition of the situation." In supplying an answer to the question, "What's going on here?," metaphors enable individuals to anticipate the ways of strangers and to know how they ought to behave toward them. Bad metaphors create faulty expectations and lead us to act inappropriately. Rooting out bad dominant metaphors and supplying good ones is the president's first duty.

During much of the second half of this century the dominating metaphor depicting American society was that life was like running in a perpetual footrace. Recall its most powerful expression in President Lyndon Johnson's 1965 commencement address at Howard University in Washington, D.C.: "You do not take a person who for years had been hobbled by chains and liberate him, bring him to the starting line of a race, and then say, 'You are free to compete with all the others,' and still justly believe that you have been completely fair."[15] That passage appeared in a speech justifying the newly prominent role of the federal government in undoing America's legacy of racial segregation.

The footrace image became the controlling definition of American society for the era. It turned out to be a bad metaphor with at least three invidious implications. First, it depicted a society in which there were countless losers and where the many were defeated by the hard work, skill, and bravery of a few of their own countrymen. If life was like a footrace, it was a zero-sum game.

Second, in a footrace, logically no competitors should stop to help the slow and the fallen. Moreover, in a footrace it is only the officials—the governors of the race—who have the responsibility to assist the slow, handicap the fast, dole out food to the hungry, and give rest to the tired. If citizens were to lend a helping hand to a fallen runner, either they were fools or charlatans. The metaphor, in other words, promoted both envy and narrow selfishness—unintentionally, of course, but actually. It also devalued—even rendered invisible—the countless acts of cooperation the market enables and the vast extent of voluntarism that exists in the nation. The footrace metaphor promoted dependency on the state.

Third, it portrayed the essence of American life as class warfare. LBJ's phrase resonated with a metaphor in *The Communist Manifesto:* "The proletarians have nothing to lose but their chains. They have a world to win." Like Marx's image of oppression and resistance, Johnson's footrace metaphor depicted a society in which a privileged group was waging a "more or less veiled civil war" against a shackled and helpless class. To win the group struggle, the shackled underdogs were encouraged to turn their envy into hatred against their oppressors and destroy them. Interpreted that way, the footrace metaphor was a call for violence. As Garry Wills, the classicist-turned-commentator, observed, "the metaphor is a mess."[16]

A president, if he is to lead well, must understand the minds and hearts of Americans and the ongoing philosophical battles for dominion over them. He must be morally attuned, able to identify the pervasive presence of bad ideas—not only Marxian notions of society as civil war but also Freudian notions of human nature as passive, and impossibly optimistic notions inherent in American pragmatic thought which result in denying dignity to persons who make a "good" try but fall short of actual success. Marxism, Freudianism, material pragmatism: these are all bad ideas because they deaden hope.

Ronald Reagan, throughout his presidency, confronted these three notions through argument and instructed his countrymen in three opposing and vitally important, self-evident truths:

1. The central feature of a free society is not competition between individuals, but a voluntary and reciprocating association among them. Human beings are one another's partners, capable of combining their strengths and talents and obliged to do so if they are to solve their problems and promote undertakings of significance. The secret of human prosperity in a free society is the art of teaming up.
2. Human nature is not perfectible. It consists of a divided self, with hate and love inextricably mixed. Every individual has both the capacity for cruelty and the free will to overcome the countless temptations to hate and to hurt. No one is an angel, but no one has to be an evil beast.
3. The measure of human worth is not the consequences of our actions but the magnitude of our efforts to transcend our worse selves and uphold our better selves. In other words, what matters

about individuals is whether they try to do their best with what they have. Not their material, but their spiritual achievements count: effort is what merits honor.

None of these "truths"—concerning social partnership, human imperfectability, and personal responsibility—was new or radical. Each had deep roots in Western civilized thought, but each had to be fitted into the personal philosophies of Americans so as to make sense of the contemporary world, inspire American pride in their contribution to that world, and offer consolation for the inevitable disappointments of life. Orchestrating these truths was the paramount task Reagan assigned himself. Unless he did so, he believed, things would fall apart; the center would not hold.

It is not easy for a president to lead, and it requires a little luck. To lead effectively, a president must be respected. Sometimes events conspire to strip him of his respectability. Placed under attack, he then has to devote his energies entirely to self-defense. A hounded and wounded presidency—whether the wounds are self-inflicted or not—is a mute presidency, and the national community suffers as a result. For nearly two years the Reagan presidency was silenced by the scandal of Iran-Contra, which consisted of two related, allegedly illegal acts: selling arms to Iran and covertly transferring financial support to the anti-Communist resistance in Nicaragua. Fortunately, the scandal subsided, and the energies of his presidency regained their focus.

Real problems, like racial bigotry and severe inequality, do not suddenly disappear simply because a president substitutes an affirming public philosophy for a philosophy of despair. Rhetoric cannot go it alone, but must be joined with government policies to make others' lives better. But one thing is certain: No democratic society can long remain tolerant and generous if the bulk of its members are personally ignorant and selfish. Bigotry, inequality, and conditions like them, with roots three hundred years deep in American society, will only worsen if government ineptly crafts programs that demoralize the people, stifle their personal generosity, and inhibit their spirit of voluntary teamwork.

Ronald Reagan proved once again that the president's job as moral leader, while difficult, is doable. Some presidents have done it well in the past; Washington, Lincoln, the two Roosevelts, Eisenhower, and Kennedy come to mind. Human nature does not change. Citizens today have much the same spiritual needs as their forebears. They need understanding, hope, and a feeling of partnership with their countrymen. What worked in the past, what worked in Washington's or Lincoln's or the Roosevelts's time is likely to be just as effective today. If a modern president emulates the best of our moral leaders of yesterday, he or she may succeed as they succeeded. That is the point President Reagan made in his final remarks to the National Governors' Association in 1988: "I suppose, it's the destiny of every second generation or so to think for awhile that maybe they're wiser than our Founding Fathers. And it's the destiny of the generation that follows to realize that this almost certainly is not true and to try to bring the Nation back to its first principles."[17]

Conclusion

Did Reagan's public speechmaking make a difference? Did his 4 million words, with their notions of partnership, human imperfection, and spiritual values, change the personal philosophies and behavior of Americans?

Where might we look for answers to such an important question? Anecdotes? During the 1980s the media related countless stories about individual Americans. Some were upbeat, particularly during calamities (such as earthquakes) and epidemics (such as AIDS), when the newspapers and television carried tales of sacrifice and hope. Some were downers. Reporters were able to round up the usual scandalous suspects in politics and business—and even in goodly institutions like the church—proving once again (as James Madison reminded us in 1788) that we Americans were no angels. Vice remained abundantly visible.

A vice-free world, however, was not the proper standard by which to gauge the effectiveness of Reagan's bully pulpit, if for no other reason than that was not his or his speechwriters' purpose in speaking. Effectiveness ought to be measured by the objective the Reagan presidency set out to achieve—the revival of hope. Did Reagan achieve his goal?

Consider that just before Reagan entered the White House, Americans were deeply apprehensive about their futures. Recall that in 1979 President Carter used nationwide television to announce that "a majority of our people believe that the next five years will be worse than the past five years."[18] From such pessimism in 1979, Americans turned hopeful in the 1980s. Surveys of one thousand Americans in 1974, 1979, and 1988 asked each respondent the same three questions concerning the quality of their lives as represented by the rungs of a ladder, with the tenth rung symbolizing the "best possible life" and the first the "worst possible life":

1. On which step of the ladder do you personally stand *at the present time?*
2. On which step would you say you stood *five years ago?*
3. And, just as your best guess, on which step will you stand in the future, say about *five years from now?*

The three surveys revealed striking differences across time.[19] In 1979, the year President Carter spoke, Americans responding to this survey thought they stood below the halfway step on their "ladder of life" (4.7 on a scale of 10). These same people, in 1979, looked back with nostalgia to the previous five years when they perceived themselves to have been standing near the sixth step (5.7). As they looked ahead to the future, they saw themselves slipping still further down the ladder (4.6). That was pessimism.

In 1974 Americans surveyed at the end of the Nixon presidency thought they were worse off than they had been five years earlier, but they were optimistic about rebounding in the future. In 1974 they saw themselves between the fourth and fifth steps on the ladder (4.5); they recalled being near the sixth step (5.9) five years earlier; they believed they could get back close to the sixth step (5.7) again in the next five years. That was resilience.

In 1988 when Americans were surveyed once again at the end of the Reagan presidency, their outlook was distinctly more positive. They saw themselves on the sixth step of the ladder and moving toward the seventh step (6.6)—more than a step higher than they recalled being five years earlier (5.5). They expected to rise to the eighth step of the ladder (8.1) within the next five years. That was optimism.

Did Reagan's words have anything to do with lifting hopes? Or was the upbeat outlook determined by economic and material factors? After all, the 1980s provided Americans ample reason to be hopeful: inflation and interest rates were down; new jobs were being created at a rate of 250,000 *per month;* the nation was enjoying the longest sustained peacetime prosperity ever; the unemployment rate was falling virtually everywhere; high school achievement scores were up; drug use and violent crime were on the decline; there was an unexpected increase in the numbers of Americans going to college; church attendance rose; technology continued to produce miracles; more minorities were participating in politics; morale in the armed services was boosted by fair pay increases; Americans were not engaged in any wars abroad (the first such decade since the 1920s); democracy was spreading throughout South America and East Asia; communism seemed to be collapsing; the Soviet Union had agreed to reduce its nuclear weaponry; the Persian Gulf was secured; international trade was expanding among the nations of the noncommunist world; and America's position in the United Nations was on the ascendant.

There was sufficient bad news, however, to support an inclination to pessimism: a seeming growth in homelessness among the poor; the twin epidemics of AIDS and "crack" cocaine (a strongly addictive narcotic); a startling stock market crash in October, 1987; the worrisome bankruptcy of several major financial institutions; an unexpectedly large federal budget deficit; a continuing international trade deficit; the intractability of war in the Middle East; worldwide terrorism; and the puzzling Iran-Contra affair.

Given all these events, what if the Reagan presidency had said nothing, or had said something other than what it did? Would Americans have been just as optimistic? At best, any answer must be speculative.[20] The evidence one way or another is insufficient to convince anyone with a skeptical turn of mind, but at the same time the conjunction of heightened optimism and the president's purpose in creating it give cause to consider the moral value of coherent presidential rhetoric.

Notes

1. For scholarly studies of Reagan's presidential rhetoric, see (chronological): Robert L. Ivie, "Speaking 'Common Sense' About the Soviet Threat: Reagan's Rhetorical Stance," *Western Journal of Communication* 48 (1984): 39–50; Martin J. Medhurst, "Postponing the Social Agenda: Reagan's Strategy and Tactics," *Western Journal of Communication* 48 (1984): 262–76; Paul D. Erickson, *Reagan Speaks: The Making of an American Myth* (New York: New York University Press, 1985); Bruce E. Gronbeck, "Ronald Reagan's Enactment of this Presidency in his 1981 Inaugural Address," and Roderick P. Hart, "Of Genre, Computers, and the Reagan Inaugural," both in *Form, Genre, and the Study of Political Discourse,* ed. Herbert W. Simons and Aram A. Aghazarian (Columbia: University of South Carolina Press, 1986), pp. 226–45, 278–98; Richard L. Johannesen, "Ronald Reagan's Economic Jeremiad," *Central States Speech Journal* 37 (1986): 79–89; Robert C. Rowland, "The Substance of the 1980 Carter-Reagan Debate," *Southern Speech Communication Journal* 51 (1986): 142–65; Ronald H. Carpenter, "Ronald Reagan," *American Orators of the Twentieth Century: Critical Studies and Sources,* ed. Bernard K. Duffy and Halford R. Ryan (New York: Greenwood Press, 1987), pp. 331–36; William F. Lewis, "Telling America's Story: Narrative Form and the Reagan Presidency," *Quarterly Journal of Speech* 73 (1987): 280–301; Craig Allen Smith, "MisteReagan's Neighborhood: Rhetoric and National Unity," *Southern Speech Communication Journal* 52 (1987): 219–39; Ellen Reid Gold, "Ronald Reagan and the Oral

Tradition," *Central States Speech Journal* 39 (1988): 159–76; John Kenneth White, *The New Politics of Old Values* (Hanover, N.H.: University Press of New England, 1988); Roger C. Aden, "Entrapment and Escape: Inventional Metaphors in Ronald Reagan's Economic Rhetoric," *Southern Communication Journal* 54 (1989): 384–400; Kenneth S. Zagacki and Andrew King, "Reagan, Romance and Technology: A Critique of 'Star Wars,'" *Communication Studies* 40 (1989): 1–12; Mary E. Stuckey, *Playing the Game: The Presidential Rhetoric of Ronald Reagan* (New York: Praeger, 1990); David Henry, "Ronald Reagan and Aid to the Contras: An Analysis of the Rhetorical Presidency," *Rhetorical Dimensions in Media: A Critical Casebook,* 2d ed., ed. Martin J. Medhurst and Thomas W. Benson (Dubuque, Iowa: Kendall/Hunt, 1991), pp. 73–88; Amos Kiewe and Davis W. Houck, *A Shining City on a Hill: Ronald Reagan's Economic Rhetoric, 1951–1989* (New York: Praeger, 1991); David E. Procter, *Enacting Political Culture: Rhetorical Transformations of Liberty Weekend 1986* (New York: Praeger, 1991); Rebecca S. Bjork, *The Strategic Defense Initiative: Symbolic Containment of the Nuclear Threat* (Albany: State University of New York Press, 1992); William Ker Muir, Jr., *The Bully Pulpit: The Presidential Leadership of Ronald Reagan* (San Francisco: Institute of Contemporary Studies, 1992); Kurt Ritter and David Henry, *Ronald Reagan: The Great Communicator* (New York: Greenwood Press, 1992); Michael Weiler and W. Barnett Pearce, eds., *Ronald Reagan and Public Discourse in America* (Tuscaloosa: University of Alabama Press, 1992); David Henry, "President Ronald Reagan's First Inaugural Address, 1981," and Kurt Ritter, "President Ronald Reagan's Second Inaugural Address, 1985," both in *Inaugural Addresses of Twentieth-Century American Presidents,* ed. Halford Ryan (Westport, Conn.: Praeger, 1993), pp. 259–70, 271–81; Kurt Ritter and David Henry, "The 1980 Reagan-Carter Presidential Debate," in *Rhetorical Studies of National Political Debates, 1990–1992,* 2d ed., ed. Robert V. Friedenberg (Westport, Conn.: Praeger, 1994), pp. 69–93; Kurt Ritter, "Ronald Reagan," in *U.S. Presidents as Orators,* ed. Halford Ryan (Westport, Conn.: Greenwood Press, 1995), pp. 316–43; G. Thomas Goodnight, "Reagan, Vietnam, and Central America: Public Memory and the Politics of Fragmentation," in *Beyond the Rhetorical Presidency,* ed. Martin J. Medhurst (College Station: Texas A&M University Press, 1996), pp. 122–52; Carol Gelderman, *All the Presidents' Words: The Bully Pulpit and the Creation of the Virtual Presidency* (New York: Walker, 1997), pp. 96–115; Martin J. Medhurst, "Writing Speeches for Ronald Reagan: An Interview with Tony Dolan," *Rhetoric & Public Affairs* 1 (1998): 245–56; and Rachel L. Holloway, "The Strategic Defense Initiative and the Technological Sublime," in *Critical Reflections on the Cold War: Linking Rhetoric and History,* ed. Martin J. Medhurst and H. W. Brands (College Station: Texas A&M University Press, 2000), pp. 209–32.

2. "Remarks at Fudan University in Shanghai, China," April 30, 1984, *Public Papers of the Presidents of the United States: Ronald Reagan, 1984* (Washington, D.C.: Government Printing Office, 1986), Book I, p. 607. Hereafter documents from this publication series are cited as *Public Papers* followed by the year, book, and pages.

3. "Remarks at a White House Ceremony Commemorating the Day of Remembrance of Victims of the Holocaust," April 20, 1982, *Public Papers: Reagan, 1982,* Book I, p. 496.

4. Alexis de Tocqueville, *Democracy in America,* trans. Henry Reeve, ed. Philipps Bradley, rev. Francis Bowen (New York: Vintage, 1990), Vol. I, p. 7.

5. Tocqueville, *Democracy in America,* Vol. II, p. 334.

6. "Letter Accepting the Resignation of James A. Baker III as Assistant to the President and Chief of Staff," Feb. 1, 1985, *Public Papers: Reagan, 1985,* Book I, p. 105.

7. Robert Frost, "How Hard It Is to Keep from Being King When It's In You and in the Situation," *In the Clearing* (New York: Holt, Rinehart and Winston, 1962), p. 79.

8. While on leave from his position as a professor of political science at the University of California, Berkeley, the author worked in the Reagan White House for nineteen months during the period of 1983–85 as a member of the staff of then-vice president George Bush. His job as a vice presidential speechwriter permitted him to observe directly the daily routines of presidential speechwriting. He conducted formal interviews with all of the presidential speechwriters working in the White House during this period, as well as with most of the principal speechwriters for the members of Reagan's cabinet.

9. All direct quotes from speechwriters Bentley Elliott, Tony Dolan, Dana Rohrabacher, Peggy Noonan, Al Myer, and Peter Robinson derive from interviews with the author in 1984 and 1985 in Washington, D.C.

10. "Remarks at the Annual Conference of the National League of Cities," March 5, 1984, *Public Papers: Reagan, 1984,* Book I, pp. 300–302.

11. See Ritter and Henry, *Ronald Reagan,* pp. 11–60.

12. "Remarks at Naturalization Ceremonies for New United States Citizens in Detroit, Michigan," Oct. 1, 1984, *Public Papers: Reagan, 1984,* Book II, p. 1395.

13. Hannah Arendt, "The Crisis of Education," in *Between Past and Future* (New York: Viking Press, 1961), p. 192. Arendt continues: "Because the world is made by mortals it wears out; and because it constantly changes its inhabitants it runs the risk of becoming as mortal as they. To preserve the world against the mortality of its creators and inhabitants it must be constantly set right anew."

14. Tocqueville, *Democracy in America,* Vol. I, p. 434.

15. "Commencement at Howard University: 'To Fulfill These Rights'," June 4, 1965, *Public Papers of the Presidents of the United States: Lyndon B. Johnson, 1965* (Washington, D.C.: Government Printing Office, 1966), p. 636.

16. Garry Wills, *Nixon Agonistes: The Crisis of the Self-Made Man* (Boston: Houghton Mifflin, 1970), p. 238. Wills asks: "For where, when one gets down to it, is the starting line? Does a man begin the race at birth? Or when he enters school? When he enters the work force? When he attempts to open a business of his own? Or is the starting line at each of these points? And if so, then why not at the intermediate points as well? And how does one correlate this man's starting line (or lines) with the staggered endlessly multiplied starting lines of every other individual? How do we manage the endless stopping of the race involved in starting it so often? One second after the gun has sounded, new athletes pop up all over the

field, the field itself changes shape, and we must call everybody in, to line them up once more. We never even get to surmise where, in this science-fiction world of starting and racing, the finish line might be. Or, rather, the staggered, infinite finishing lines for each runner. The metaphor is a mess."

17. "Remarks to Members of the National Governors' Association," Feb. 22, 1988, *Public Papers: Reagan, 1988,* Book I, p. 237.

18. "Energy and National Goals: Address to the Nation," [the "malaise speech"], July 15, 1979. *Public Papers of the Presidents of the United States: Jimmy Carter, 1979* (Washington, D.C.: Government Printing Office, 1980), Book II, p. 1237.

19. Survey results presented to the Republican National Committee by the Wirthlin Group, Richard B. Wirthlin (principal investigator), 1363 Beverly Road, McLean, Va., 22101.

20. For a skeptical view of the potential for presidential speeches (in particular, Reagan's speeches) to influence the public and a response to that view, see: George C. Edwards III, "Presidential Rhetoric: What Difference Does It Make?" and Martin J. Medhurst, "Afterward: The Ways of Rhetoric," both in *Beyond the Rhetorical Presidency,* pp. 199–217, 218–26.

Enduring Issues in Presidential Speechwriting

MARTIN J. MEDHURST

If persistent myths have hampered the scholarly study of presidential speechwriting, then just as surely enduring issues have characterized both the practice itself and analysis of that practice. Several of these enduring issues are highlighted in this volume. Four seem paramount.

One such issue revolves around the idea of access—who has it, how it is used, and what consequences, positive or negative, come about as a result of having access or being denied access to the president. One generalization seems indisputable: those speechwriters who have had relatively easy access to the principal have been, on the whole, better able to engage their craft and, I will argue, to produce prose that better serves the interests and goals of the administration. The relationship need not be as close as that of the Kennedy-Sorensen "collaboration." The speechwriter need not become the "alter ego" of the president, as Sorensen was alleged to have become. Even so, the most successful relationships between writers and principals have been characterized by more or less direct access at three crucial moments: the moment of ideational conception when the principal decides what he wants to say, the moment of compositional closure when the speechwriter is close to producing what she or he considers to be a "final" draft, and the moment of administrative imprimatur when the other involved parties—cabinet secretaries, agencies, bureaus, and the president's inner circle—"vet" the speech as drafted. Speechwriters who are directly involved at these three crucial moments tend both to be more satisfied with their work and also, I believe, to produce better work.

The first issue is often related to the second—the relationship of speechwriting to policy making. As this volume has shown, the evolution of White House speechwriters has been, until quite recently, in the direction of becoming more and more estranged from the policy-making process. There is no doubt that writers such as Raymond Moley, Clark Clifford, C. D. Jackson, and Theodore Sorensen had direct, and in some cases decisive, influence on specific policy decisions. Over the course of the last three decades, however, that ability to influence policy has steadily eroded in part because of access issues but also because of the growth of specialization among policy advisors.

Advisors who consider themselves to be the specialists on a particular topic are not anxious to have non-specialists—which speechwriters tend to be—mucking around with their carefully crafted policy positions. And speechwriters are in a unique position structurally within the White House apparatus to do just that. One consequence of this growth in specialization has been the tendency of some policy advisors to see speechwriters as enemies who must be overcome rather than as allies to be embraced. While it is often true that the speechwriters are not experts in a particular policy area, it is equally true that they are oftentimes much more alert to issues such as image construction, meaning, significance, audience analysis, and how certain ideas are likely to play in Peoria—the strategic dimensions of language use. To divorce speechwriting completely from the policy process—even from the discussion of policy—is to institute a set of relationships that is ultimately counterproductive to both writers and policy makers.

One aspect of the modern presidency that has contributed to the bifurcation between policy making and speechwriting is the restructuring of the White House apparatus. The most significant such restructuring with respect to speechwriting happened in 1978 when the Carter speechwriters were brought into the White House Office of Communications, under the direction of Gerald Rafshoon. The Office of Communications had been created in 1969, but speechwriting had not been part of the office under Nixon or Ford. With the subsuming of the speechwriting function, a new structure quickly emerged whereby the director of the speechwriting unit reported to the head of the White House Office of Communications who, in turn, reported to the president. In the case of Rafshoon, who had the title assistant to the president for communications, there was direct access to the Oval Office. But in subsequent administrations the person who headed the White House Office of Communications did not always have such an elevated title nor such direct access. Indeed, the trend has been for more and more distance to be created between the people who actually write the president's speeches and the president himself. Layer upon bureaucratic layer has often resulted in presidential speechwriters operating in both a policy and a personal vacuum—cut off from policy-making sessions and estranged from the Oval Office. Most people are surprised to learn that after writing speeches in the Reagan White House for five years, Peggy Noonan had actually met Ronald Reagan only three times.

A third issue is that of constraints that attend the speechwriting process. Some constraints are internal—the structure of the particular White House, the role played by the chief of staff, the vetting or speech "clearance" process, and the president's attitude toward speeches and speechwriting chief among them. Presidents who disdain the rhetorical aspects of the presidency—Carter and Bush the elder come to mind—create their own unique set of constraints that are virtually impossible to overcome through good staff work. A president who adamantly refuses to practice his speeches or to take coaching on matters of delivery, for example, can be a real constraint on even the best-prepared speech text. These are all internal constraints, but there are external constraints as well.

Speechwriting always exists in close relationship to situations and audiences, and when those situations and audiences change—often on a moment's notice—so, too, must the speech that is designed to address those circumstances. Some speeches can be prepared well in advance of delivery; others, however, must be produced under great pressures, both chronological and psychological. In moments of crisis speechwriters must adapt to situational constraints that could in no way have been anticipated. One thinks, for example, of the *Challenger* disaster, the bombing at Oklahoma City, and, most recently, the tragedy of September 11, 2001. In such instances the situation imposes constraints that cannot be ignored—the president must speak, and quickly. On such occasions, speechwriters more than earn their keep; they help the president express the emotions of an entire nation. Such situational constraints come with the job, and on a fairly regular basis: people die, accidents happen, natural disasters befall, wars flare, terrorists strike, economies collapse, coups ensue. For presidential speechwriters the old motto to "expect the unexpected" must surely resonate.

Perhaps the most enduring issue of all is that of presidential leadership and the relationship of speech making to that leadership. Presidents speak a lot—too much according to some scholars.[1] Yet the use of the bully pulpit and the rise of the rhetorical presidency are hallmarks of the office as it has emerged from the twentieth century.[2] It is highly unlikely that we will ever go back to the managerial or administrative presidencies of the nineteenth century. Ours is a mediated age where communication is a god term. Presidents must communicate with their constituencies, domestic and foreign, friend and foe. The spoken word is—and likely will remain—their primary means of communication. Consequently the preparation and delivery of those words remains an important topic for scholarly investigation. For better or worse, presidents are judged largely on their ability to "connect" with their publics—diplomatic, congressional, domestic, or foreign. Some presidents—FDR, JFK, Reagan, Clinton—seem to do so with relative ease while others—Ford, Carter, Bush the senior—struggle with the symbolic and rhetorical dimensions of the presidency. By studying how speeches are produced and edited by speechwriters prior to their delivery by the president, scholars can better understand how those rhetorical dimensions of the office function—and how they might be made to function even better.

Notes

1. Roderick P. Hart, *The Sound of Leadership: Presidential Communication in the Modern Age* (Chicago: University of Chicago Press, 1987), esp. chap. 6.
2. See Jeffrey K. Tulis, *The Rhetorical Presidency* (Princeton: Princeton University Press, 1987); Martin J. Medhurst, ed., *Beyond the Rhetorical Presidency* (College Station: Texas A&M University Press, 1996); Samuel Kernell, *Going Public: New Strategies of Presidential Leadership*, 3d ed. (Washington, D.C.: CQ Press, 1997); Richard J. Ellis, ed., *Speaking to the People: The Rhetorical Presidency in Historical Perspective* (Amherst: University of Massachusetts Press, 1998).

Contributors

MOYA ANN BALL, associate vice president for academic affairs and associate professor of speech communication at Trinity University in San Antonio, Texas, is the author of *Vietnam-on-the-Potomac* and numerous articles and chapters on the decision making of presidents and their advisors. Her dissertation from the University of Minnesota won the National Communication Association's Dissertation Award.

DIANA B. CARLIN, dean of the graduate school and international programs and professor of communication studies at the University of Kansas, is coauthor of *The 1992 Presidential Debates in Focus*. Her work on political debates and speechwriting has appeared in *Political Communication, Argumentation and Advocacy,* and *Rhetoric & Public Affairs.*

CHARLES J. G. GRIFFIN, associate professor of rhetoric and communication at Kansas State University, is the author of works on presidential discourse, narrative in social movements, and the rhetoric of autobiography. His essays have appeared in *Presidential Studies Quarterly, Quarterly Journal of Speech,* and *Western Journal of Communication.*

MARTIN J. MEDHURST, professor of speech communication and coordinator of the Program in Presidential Rhetoric in the George Bush School of Government and Public Service at Texas A&M University, is the author of *Dwight D. Eisenhower: Strategic Communicator* and editor of *Eisenhower's War of Words: Rhetoric and Leadership* and *Beyond the Rhetorical Presidency.* He recently coedited *Critical Reflections on the Cold War: Linking Rhetoric and History* with H. W. Brands.

WILLIAM K. MUIR, JR., professor of political science at the University of California, Berkeley, is the author of *The Bully Pulpit: The Presidential Leadership of Ronald Reagan, Legislature: California's School for Politics,* and *Prayer in the Public Schools: Law and Attitude Change.* Professor Muir worked in the Reagan White House as a speechwriter for Vice President Bush.

JOHN H. PATTON, associate professor of communication and a Fellow of Newcomb College at Tulane University, is the author of numerous articles and chapters focusing on political communication, rhetorical theory and criticism, and visual communication. His essays have appeared in the *Quarterly Journal of Speech, Communication Monographs, Rhetoric Society Quarterly,* and the *Southern Communication Journal.*

KURT RITTER, professor of speech communication at Texas A&M University, is coauthor of *Ronald Reagan: The Great Communicator* and *The American Ideology.* He is the author of numerous articles and chapters appearing in such books as *The Inaugural Addresses of Twentieth-Century American Presidents, The Modern Presidency and Crisis Rhetoric,* and *U.S. Presidents as Orators.* He is the recipient of both the Winans-Wichelns Award and the Karl R. Wallace Memorial Award from the National Communication Association.

HALFORD RYAN, professor of public speaking at Washington and Lee University in Lexington, Virginia, is the author or editor of numerous books, including *Franklin D. Roosevelt's Rhetorical Presidency, The Inaugural Addresses of Twentieth-Century American Presidents, U.S. Presidents as Orators, American Rhetoric from Roosevelt to Reagan, Oratorical Encounters,* and *Harry S. Truman: Presidential Rhetoric.* He is also the coeditor of *American Orators of the Twentieth Century.*

CRAIG R. SMITH, professor of communication studies and director of the Center for First Amendment Studies at California State University, Long Beach, is the author or editor of twelve books, including *Freedom of Expression and Partisan Politics, To Form a More Perfect Union, Silencing the Opposition: Government Strategies of Suppression,* and *Rhetoric and Human Consciousness.* Professor Smith served as a speechwriter for Gerald R. Ford.

THEODORE O. WINDT, JR., professor emeritus of communication at the University of Pittsburgh and currently a scholar-in-residence at the Chautauqua Institution, is the author or editor of five books, including *Presidents and Protesters, The Cold War as Rhetoric,* and *Essays in Presidential Rhetoric.* His articles and chapters on political communication have appeared in the *Quarterly Journal of Speech* and *Communication Quarterly.*

INDEX

ISBN 1-58544-225-9

90000